# STUDIES IN
# ENTERTAINMENT

**Studies in Entertainment** Critical Approaches to
Mass Culture is Volume 7 in the series
THEORIES OF CONTEMPORARY CULTURE
Center for Twentieth Century Studies
University of Wisconsin-Milwaukee

General Editor, KATHLEEN WOODWARD

# STUDIES IN
# ENTERTAINMENT

*Critical Approaches to
Mass Culture*

Edited by
# Tania Modleski

*Indiana University Press
Bloomington and Indianapolis*

Manufactured in the United States of America

**Library of Congress Cataloging-in-Publication Data**

Studies in entertainment.

(Theories of contemporary culture; v. 7)
1. Mass media criticism. 2. Popular culture.
3. Mass media and women. I. Modleski, Tania,
1949–    . II. Series.
P96.C76S78        1986              302.2'34          85–45980
ISBN 0–253–35566–4
ISBN 0–253–20395–3 (pbk.)

1  2  3  4  5  90  89  88  87  86

# CONTENTS

# FOREWORD

The Center for Twentieth Century Studies at the University of Wisconsin-Milwaukee is a multidisciplinary research institute devoted to the study of contemporary culture from the point of view of the humanities and with an emphasis on critical theory. *Theories of Contemporary Culture*, the Center's book series with Indiana University Press, represents the Center's commitment to crossdisciplinary and collective research in contemporary cultural studies. Subjects of Center books already published include performance in postmodern culture, technology and culture, aging and psychoanalysis, and displacement and deconstruction, among others. The eighth volume in the series will be on feminist theory, and research is planned in television/video studies and social theory. In the future *Theories of Contemporary Culture* will also include single-authored collections of essays.

*Studies in Entertainment: Critical Approaches to Mass Culture*, the seventh volume in *Theories of Contemporary Culture*, had its beginnings in 1984-85, a year devoted to research on the subject of mass culture. Work by the Center's resident fellows and invited scholars and critics from the United States and abroad culminated in a conference on Mass Culture in April 1985 which was organized with the superb advice of Tania Modleski and Andreas Huyssen, to whom I extend my warmest thanks.

The work of the Center has continued to thrive under the administration of many people at the University of Wisconsin-Milwaukee. I would like to thank especially Dean William F. Halloran of the College of Letters and Science and Dean George Keulks of The Graduate School for their ongoing support. Most importantly, Tania Modleski, who edited *Studies in Entertainment*, and I would like to thank all those at the Center who helped us make this book a palpable reality—Jean Lile, Carol Tennessen, Shirley Reinhold, Jon Erickson, Laura Roskos, Ed Schelb, and Debra Vest.

KATHLEEN WOODWARD
Director, Center for Twentieth Century Studies
General Editor, *Theories of Contemporary Culture*

# INTRODUCTION

As the title of this book is meant to indicate, to study popular or mass entertainment is to engage in a paradoxical enterprise—one which ensures that the analyst will be unable to capture the "essence" of the object under investigation or accurately to understand the experience of those for whom entertainment is, simply, entertaining. Given the paradoxical nature of critical analyses of mass culture, it is hardly surprising to find that they have generally erred in one of two directions. Some critics hold mass culture to be a very serious business indeed—so serious that they hold little hope that the masses will ever be able to extricate themselves from their benighted condition and (in the humanist version of this pessimistic account) engage in serious artistic contemplation, or (in the Marxist version) take to the streets to liberate themselves. Actually, in the history of mass culture criticism these two versions have not been as different as they might seem on the face of it. Although humanist and Marxist intellectuals have had very different motives for concerning themselves with the issue of mass culture, both have shared a faith in the importance of great art, which they value for being all that mass art is not. Thus the Marxist theorists of the Frankfurt School—Adorno, Horkheimer, and Marcuse—held that high art could keep alive the utopian promise once offered by religion.[1] Mass culture, on the other hand, was thought to reconcile its consumers to the status quo, thus serving the interests of capitalism. According to the Frankfurt School, with the advent of the mass media, culture itself had become an industry.

If it can be argued that theorists like Adorno and Horkheimer took mass culture too seriously—that is, assumed its power to be monolithic and so pervasive that it virtually eradicated any revolutionary potential in the masses—there are those for whom entertainment is a far less critical problem—in fact, is only a problem insofar as other people *think* it is one. Thus, every so often a critic will decry the "elitism" of those who refuse to acknowledge the liberating nature of mass culture. Leslie Fiedler's work provides the most recent example of a criticism that indulges in a celebration of "the antinomian or dionysiac impulses" of mass culture.[2] Castigating the "middle-class citizens" who campaign against violence on television shows as well as those "Bible Belt fundamentalists" and "radical feminists" who protest pornography's abuse of women, Fiedler accuses them of remaining "ignorant that beneath their overt rationalization lurks an underlying fear of

freedom as well as a contempt for the popular arts."[3]   It is interesting
that Fiedler can so confidently locate mass culture in the realm of
freedom while Adorno maintains that mass culture has colonized the
minds of the people. The difference between the positions of these
two men is at least in part due to a difference in political orientation:
despite a certain amount of rhetoric that might appear to suggest the
contrary, Fiedler is uninterested in the kinds of problems that preoc-
cupy Marxists. For example, his failure to distinguish between "popular art," which arises "from the people," and "mass art," which is
imposed from above, indicates his lack of concern about issues of
power and profit.

Today a new generation of mass culture analysts who place themselves politically on the left are trying to find a balance between the
two extreme positions outlined above. Unlike the members of the
Frankfurt School, who came from another country with its very different traditions and found themselves relocated in an alien culture,
the new generation is composed of people who grew up on mass
culture—literally danced to the kind of "standardized" music which
so alarmed Theodor Adorno that he pondered how to turn jitter-
bugging "insects" back into men and women.[4] While wishing to retain
the critical edge of the Frankfurt School's Critical Theory, these analysts reject what they regard as the oversimplifications of the Frankfurt
School, especially the emphasis on the way mass culture "manipulates"
its consumers, imposing on them "false needs" and "false desires" and
preventing them from coming to understand their own best interests.
One of the first essays to take issue with the Frankfurt School on this
point was written by Hans Magnus Enzensberger in 1970. In "Constituents of a Theory of the Media," Enzensberger argued that the
left was misguided in its claim that mass culture imposes false consciousness and false needs on the masses. Rather, he maintained, the
strategies of mass culture could only be as successful as they were
because they appealed to *real* needs and desires on the part of the
people, although these needs and desires were inevitably distorted by
the "consciousness industry."[5] Following Enzensberger's cue, theorists
such as Fredric Jameson and Richard Dyer have since elaborated on
his basic insight, and have attempted to show that mass entertainment
invariably contains a utopian component.[6] This view obviously represents a significant departure from the thought of the Frankfurt
School, which insisted on high art as the last preserve of the utopian
spirit that mass culture was threatening to extinguish.

The effort on the part of the newer generation of mass culture
critics to rescue the masses from the critical opprobrium heaped on
them from right and left has caused some analysts to turn directly to
a study of *audiences* rather than texts. For if it can be shown that the

consumers of mass culture are not wholly taken in by the promises of the "consciousness industry," but are actively and creatively appropriating its slogans, images, and artifacts, then there is reason to suppose that all revolutionary hope is not dead—the masses have not been utterly brainwashed. The Birmingham School of Culture Theory in England is probably best known for its studies in forms of audience resistance to the homogenizing forces of mass culture. Desirous of showing that people are not "cultural dopes," the Birmingham critics and their followers have attempted to demonstrate the complexity of the audience's potential response to mass culture. For example, Stuart Hall has discussed three forms this response can take: dominant, negotiated, and oppositional.[7] According to Hall, the dominant reading of a mass cultural text accepts the text's messages at face value; the negotiated response might dispute a particular claim while accepting the overall system; and an oppositional response rejects the capitalist system in the interests of the subordinate class. The way a particular message is received, then, obviously depends not only on the text or the medium in question, but on the audience's political beliefs and general social experience. It follows from such a premise that critics should study this social experience rather than examine texts in isolation from the people who consume them. And indeed, the Birmingham School has produced some brilliant and edifying studies that reveal the ways in which particular subcultures "negotiate" the dominant culture, appropriating its objects and symbols to produce group unity and solidarity. Probably the most widely read study of this sort is Dick Hebdige's remarkable study of youth subcultures, *Subculture: The Meaning of Style.*[8]

But for all the salutary effects this approach has had on the study of mass culture, the new emphasis is not without its problems and dangers. In certain cases the insight that audiences are not completely manipulated, but may appropriate mass cultural artifacts for their own purposes, has been carried so far that it would seem mass culture is no longer a problem for some "Marxist" critics. A recent article on rock 'n' roll, for example, argues that since we do not want to think of its fans as "cultural dopes," we must assume that rock music is "empowering." The article proceeds to search for the ways and means of this empowerment.[9] Obviously, this is an extreme case, but for that reason it serves to illustrate the danger I wish to point out. If the problem with some of the work of the Frankfurt School was that its members were too far outside the culture they examined, critics today seem to have the opposite problem: immersed in their culture, half in love with their subject, they sometimes seem unable to achieve the proper critical distance from it. As a result, they may unwittingly wind up writing apologias for mass culture and embracing its ideology.

Thus, the examples of "resistance" that these critics cite are in fact often anticipated and even prescribed by the culture industry. To claim, for instance, that the sexism of rock 'n' roll can be countered by the strategy of scratching out particularly offensive songs on one's copy of a record[10] is simply to endorse the pluralism of consumer society, whereby if you do not care for a certain product or brand of product you are "free" to reject it and choose another. Or, to take another example (from a study of the "semiotics of television"), to detail the way in which a certain television program makes women into sexual objects and then show how it is possible "to arrive at a personal decoding that is *aberrant*" so that "Mum and Dad will each find different . . . parts of the [program] to enjoy"[11] is to underwrite television's view of itself as "family entertainment," providing something for everyone. In the face of so much affirmation of the individual consumer's right to *choose*, it is easy to lose sight of the point of mass cultural analysis. As Terry Eagleton put it in a parody aimed at reader-response critics: "A socialist criticism is not primarily concerned with the consumers' revolution. Its task is to take over the means of production."[12]

A related danger of the new emphasis on audiences is that critics may be reproducing in their methodologies the very strategies by which consumer society measures and constructs its audiences. Thus the empiricist who relies on surveys, questionnaires, and interviews is often duplicating the methods developed under contemporary capitalism for testing products, new television programs, etc. Again, the critical distance insisted on by the Frankfurt School would seem to be imperiled, so that in surveying certain sectors of the masses, conducting "ethnographic studies" of subcultural groups, mass culture analysts may be collaborating with the industry in forming the kind of "serial" units that keep people in a state of what used to be called "false consciousness."

The collusion between mass culture critic and consumer society may be further cemented by the practice—unfortunately rather common today—of invoking analogies based on older cultural forms in order to explain the functioning of mass cultural artifacts. Thus one "ethnographic" critic compares women's reading of romances to "folk performances" which "contest the hegemonic imposition of bourgeois culture on . . . subordinate groups."[13] And other critics have praised television's "bardic function" in contemporary society. Television, it is argued, takes the place of "lost storytellers, priests, wise men or elders." Its "bardic function . . . restores much of the personal autonomy to the viewer in the sense that he supplies the conditions, both semiotic and social, under which any specific message becomes meaningful."[14] It is surely in the interests of the captains and sponsors of the television industry that we think of television as standing in for a culture's "elders" and its serialized viewers as an organic community of listeners who render the television message meaningful. Not only does this view rule out a truly critical approach to television studies, it also hampers our ability to discern what Margaret Morse here calls "new cultural forms and redrawn boundaries of a complex nature."

There seemed, then, a need for a book which would adopt a more critical view of mass cultural production and mass cultural artifacts, one in particular that would concentrate on texts without, however, disregarding contexts. As Raymond Williams observes in the interview here, the study of texts is the most neglected aspect of mass culture: "People study audiences; they study the history of the institutions; and they study the technologies. . . . People have always studied effects." What is most urgently required, according to Williams, is an approach "which tries to understand precisely the production of certain conventions and modes of communication right inside the form." But as the example of his own work suggests, and as Williams reminds us later in the interview, there is also the danger of narrowing our notion of text *too much*, of analyzing "the discrete single work," and by doing so of missing the normal or characteristic experience of mass culture, which in the case of television, for example, is one of "flow." Each of the textual analyses in this collection focuses on a unit larger than the discrete single work: rock 'n' roll music, television sound, television news, advertisements, popular novels for women, fashion, contemporary horror films, and so on. One of the strengths of the volume, I believe, is that it exhibits "the mass cultural sensibility" of the writers—a sensibility that Stuart Hall has argued is crucial for understanding our world—at the same time that it maintains a critical view of the objects of investigation.

To argue for a more critical approach than has often been adopted in recent years is emphatically not to advocate a return to a position that glorifies high art and opposes it to the debased artifacts of mass culture. As I attempt to show in my essay included here, such an opposition is especially untenable today when postmodern art has more and more frequently tended to incorporate forms of popular or mass culture and when mass art has increasingly usurped modernism's "adversarial" role. For me, as well as for many of the other contributors to this book, the critical view that can provide genuinely new insights into mass culture is a feminist one. In the interview with Raymond Williams, Gillian Skirrow insists on the significance of the "one voice" that "has been consistently opposed to the technological euphoria and also the joy of destruction which seems to have invaded all kinds of technology, including video games . . . and that voice has been the women's movement." Skirrow intimates that *all* people and

not just women must engage the question of the relationship of popular culture to gender. Just such an engagement is at the heart of many
of the essays in this collection.

A section of the book is devoted to feminist studies in entertainment
and contains articles on advertisements, popular novels, and fashion.
However, the "voice of the women's movement" is not confined to
this single section but reverberates throughout the book, forcing us
to consider women's relation to mass culture as well as bringing an
important new perspective to bear on the theories that have traditionally been used to explain the workings of mass culture. Thus, for
example, Patricia Mellencamp's article on women in early situation
comedy asks what it means when women are both subjects and objects
of laughter rather than the mere objects they are in the Freudian
paradigm of jokes. By foregrounding the issue of gender, Mellencamp
calls into question the general validity of a theory that is often invoked
in studies of comedy. Similarly, Kaja Silverman's essay on fashion
challenges the sufficiency of explanations frequently given for the
"Great Masculine Renunciation" of elaborate dress that occurred in
the eighteenth century. Historians have generally accounted for this
development solely in terms of class and "have failed to address the
psychic implications of this change for sexual difference." In the process of rectifying this omission, Silverman manages to relativize psychoanalysis by showing how certain vicissitudes of the male psyche
are historically produced. Finally, Andreas Huyssen's essay shows that
it is not only in the analysis of specific mass cultural texts that feminist
insights can be revealing. In "Mass Culture as Woman: Modernism's
Other," Huyssen shows modernism itself to have been engaged in a
kind of "Great Masculine Renunciation"—a reaction formation in the
face of the threat of mass culture, which has typically been concep-
tualized as feminine. Once it is recognized that a misogynistic attitude
lies at the very core of the high culture/mass culture opposition, the
need for new ways of thinking and new theoretical paradigms becomes
obvious.

Indeed, most of the essays included here make significant contributions to mass culture theory in the process of analyzing given texts.
Moreover, as we have seen is the case with many of the feminist essays,
theory is not simply *applied* in a mechanical way, but is frequently
*implicated* in the analyses and qualified or invalidated by the texts
themselves.[15] For instance, my article on the contemporary horror
film points out that this form of mass art is as "adversarial" as the
various modern and postmodern theories that continually attack the
"monstrous" entertainment industry. And Judith Williamson's essay
on women and advertising suggests that current radical feminist theo-

ry may be duplicating the strategy of advertisers in stressing sexual difference to the exclusion of all other differences, such as those having to do with race and class. Some of the other theories invoked in the course of the analyses include: Frankfurt School Critical Theory (Gendron), linguistic theory (Morse), psychoanalytic theory (Mellencamp, Silverman), and theories of modernism and modernization (Huyssen).

The book opens with an interview of Raymond Williams. Williams's work over the last few decades has significantly expanded the field of cultural studies—to the point, indeed, where we are now able to perceive mass culture *as* culture. Although Williams has recently had occasion to assess his work in a book of interviews, *Politics and Letters*, issues of mass culture were slighted there and, as Stephen Heath points out, Williams's book, *Television: Technology and Cultural Form*, was mentioned only once. The interview here is meant to correct that omission. In this far-ranging discussion, Williams looks at some major terms in the history of mass culture criticism—including "mass culture" itself—and points out some of the unnoticed—and often undesirable—associations they carry with them. He also reflects on television's creation of a popular memory and on the way it serves important human interests no longer engaged by most serious art; and he elaborates further his notion of "flow," which was first advanced in the book on *Television* and has since become a "key word" in most discussions of the television experience. The interview was conducted by Stephen Heath and Gillian Skirrow, who were co-authors of one of the first in-depth, theoretically sophisticated studies of television, "Television, a World in Action," published in *Screen* in 1977. In the course of the interview it becomes clear that a creative tension exists among the three participants, whose positions on mass culture differ considerably from one another, especially in the degree of optimism each feels in the face of mass culture's homogenizing tendencies.

The next essay in the section deals with the work of another major theorist of mass culture. In "Theodor Adorno Meets the Cadillacs," Bernard Gendron argues that Adorno's work on standardization in popular music has been unfairly dismissed by students of rock 'n' roll, although it is as applicable to popular music today as it was to the Tin Pan Alley music that reigned in Adorno's time. Building on a conceit that compares the industrially produced Cadillac automobiles to the musical texts of "doo-wop" groups like the Cadillacs, Gendron shows in what ways Adorno's work succeeds as well as how it ultimately fails. Despite crucial problems in Adorno's formulations, Gendron argues, a reappraisal of his work can help us avoid the pitfalls of approaches which, like those I have critiqued here, exaggerate the freedom of the consumer in creating his or her own meanings. He concludes by counseling students of mass culture to "engage Adorno's productivist approach in a constructive dialogue with the more recent and fashionable reception approaches."

The next section of the book consists of three studies of television, clearly the most important form of mass culture today. The first two essays analyze the way television promotes itself as a form of what linguistic theorist Emile Benveniste calls "discourse." Rick Altman begins his essay on television sound by situating himself in relation to the work of Raymond Williams and proposes that Williams's notion of "flow" must be understood in connection with a parallel notion of "household flow." After discussing the function of television sound in mediating between these two kinds of flow, Altman concludes that, unlike Hollywood film, television appears to be openly discursive, "involving spectators in dialogue, enjoining them to look, to see, to partake of that which is offered up for vision." Margaret Morse's essay on "The Television News Personality and Credibility" focuses and refines this insight by showing how the network news anchor appears to engage spectators in dialogue, so that television news may now be considered a subjective form that exists in contrast to the older ideal of objective journalism. Morse proceeds to speculate on the effects of this subjective journalism on our modes of knowing and believing.

Patricia Mellencamp's essay forms a bridge between this section and the next one, "Feminist Studies in Entertainment." Mellencamp analyzes two early situation comedies, *The George Burns and Gracie Allen Show* and *"I Love Lucy,"* arguing that they functioned to encourage women to stay within the confines of domesticity. Like the other two essays in the section on television, this one endeavors to distinguish television from previous media in order to determine precisely how it functions as an ideological apparatus. Mellencamp argues that narrative in television is not as important a means of "containing" women as it is in film; rather, she sees in a program like *"I Love Lucy"* a significant contradiction between narrative and performance, with the latter empowering women and the former working to ensure their defeat. Rejecting theories of narrative as inadequate tools for understanding the contradictory position of women in television comedy, Mellencamp turns to a consideration of Freud's theories of jokes, comedy, and humor in order to explain the power of these programs and their appeal to both male and female spectators.

That woman exists in a contradictory relation to mass culture—as well as to its theories—suggests the importance of foregrounding the issue of sexual difference in our analyses. The next section is meant to illustrate the benefits of such an approach. It begins with two essays that attempt to explain the connections between sexual difference and other forms of difference in mass culture. In "Woman Is an Island: Femininity and Colonization," Judith Williamson weaves her essay together with commentaries on the accompanying illustrations of recent ads to show that "femininity" in advertising becomes an expression of many different forms of otherness, otherness that capitalism works to destroy even though "it needs *constructs* of difference in order to signify itself at all." And Jean Franco analyzes Harlequin Romances and Mexican comic strip novels (situating the latter within a history of the Mexican culture industry) to demonstrate that mass culture "plots" or incorporates women into the social order in different ways according to their position in the international division of labor. "There is not a single model for the sex/gender system under capitalism," Franco concludes, "but multiple options."

The third essay in the section, Kaja Silverman's "Fragments of a Fashionable Discourse," is also concerned with relating issues of class and gender, but it is more psychoanalytic than the others and addresses itself primarily to the "psychic consequences" of a major development in the history of fashion, a development that resulted from a shift in class structures. Using examples from literature and film, and grounding her speculations in the psychoanalytic theories of Jacques Lacan and his followers, Silverman explores the psychic effects of the "Great Masculine Renunciation" in clothing and the consequent repression of male exhibitionism. She ends by advising feminists not to mimic masculine renunciation in fashion and endorsing the mode of dress known as "retro," a potentially subversive feminist subcultural style.

The final section of the book rethinks the dichotomy between art and entertainment that has sustained many contemporary theories of art and culture. My essay, "The Terror of Pleasure: The Contemporary Horror Film and Postmodern Theory," uses the example of the currently popular "slasher" films to question some basic assumptions of postmodern theory—in particular its belief that mass culture is the realm of pleasure and serves as the support of bourgeois ideology, reinforcing and sustaining the bourgeois ego. I argue that the contemporary horror film is as hostile to meaning, form, pleasure, and what Lionel Trilling called the "specious good" as any of the forms of high art that are set up in opposition to mass culture. Since contemporary theory has lost its adversary, or, rather, has been outdone by it, it is time to question the efficacy and the value of an adversarial position. Feminists in particular have good reason to resist adversary aesthetics since women have often been identified with the specious good, with pleasure, and with mass culture itself.

In "Brief Encounters: Mass Culture and the Evacuation of Sense," Dana Polan continues the questioning of the high/mass art polarity by examining a series of contemporary mass cultural artifacts in the light of current theories of narrative. Polan demonstrates that certain forms of mass art "employ much of the nonrealist, nonnarrative rhetoric that a discourse of formal deconstruction" celebrates in the most avant-garde kinds of art and theory: thus, for example, he wittily applies the kind of analysis Roland Barthes developed in *S/Z* to a "Blondie" comic strip. He then proceeds to draw out and analyze some of the implications for mass culture criticism of the transition to late capitalism and postindustrialism, maintaining that the order and coherence once promised by narrative are replaced to a great extent by spectacle, incoherence, and a kind of "weirdness" that has yet to be confronted and theorized. Polan also insists, as do many of the writers here, that a feminist perspective must strongly inflect any theory of mass culture that would seek to account for our "complicated contemporaneity."

Andreas Huyssen's article, "Mass Culture as Woman: Modernism's Other," which ends the section and the book, provides a historical and theoretical rationale for such a feminist perspective. According to Huyssen, modernism was formed out of a desire to distance the threatening "feminine" aspects of mass culture and the masses. Flaubert is the paradigmatic case here, professing to identify with his Madame Bovary—the woman destroyed by pulp novels—but "transcending aesthetically the dilemma on which she foundered in 'real life.' " Huyssen traces the history of the perception of mass culture as feminine from the nineteenth century to the present and ends on a note of optimism, claiming that, with the emergence of new kinds of women performers and with the increasingly visible presence of women in high art, "the old rhetoric has lost its persuasive power." Thus, for Huyssen, the kind of oppositional thinking which relegated both woman and mass culture to the position of despised "other" is a thing of the past.

Huyssen's optimism may not be shared equally by all of the book's contributors. Yet, I think, a certain positive attitude prevails. This is not because the problems of mass culture, of mass entertainment, are minimized and glossed over, still less because mass culture is now seen as "empowering." Rather, by analyzing a number of very different textual artifacts and calling into question the sometimes constricting theories that purport to encompass and explain so much disparateness, the writers have opened up spaces in which to think about and work for genuine cultural change.

## NOTES

Many of these papers were originally presented at the International Symposium on Mass Culture held at the University of Wisconsin-Milwaukee in April 1984. I would like to thank Kathleen Woodward and the Center for Twentieth Century Studies for organizing that symposium, as well as for the generous support provided in the preparation of this book. I am grateful to the Center staff—and in particular to Shirley Reinhold and Laura Roskos— for their help in this project. Special thanks go to Jean Lile, whose skillful word processing and ready assistance in a variety of tasks greatly eased the editorial burden.

1. See Max Horkheimer, "Art and Mass Culture," *Studies in Philosophy and Social Science* 9, no. 2 (1941):290–304. The classic humanist statement against mass culture may be found in Dwight MacDonald, "A Theory of Mass Culture," in *Mass Culture: The Popular Arts in America,* ed. Bernard Rosenberg and David M. White (Glencoe, IL: The Free Press, 1957), pp. 59–73.
2. Leslie Fiedler, *What Was Literature? Class Culture and Mass Society* (New York: Simon and Schuster, 1982), p. 84.
3. Ibid., p. 49.
4. Theodor W. Adorno (with the assistance of George Simpson), "On Popular Music," *Studies in Philosophy and Social Science* 9, no. 1 (1941):45–47.
5. Hans Magnus Enzensberger, "Constituents of a Theory of the Media," *The Consciousness Industry: On Literature, Politics and the Media* (New York: Seabury, 1974), pp. 95–128.
6. Fredric Jameson, "Reification and Utopia in Mass Culture," *Social Text* 1 (1979):130–48. Richard Dyer, "Entertainment and Utopia," *Genre: The Musical: A Reader,* ed. Rick Altman (London: Routledge & Kegan Paul, 1981), pp. 175–89.
7. Stuart Hall, "Encoding and Decoding in the Television Discourse," *Stencilled Occasional Papers,* no. 7 (Birmingham, England: Centre for Contemporary Cultural Studies, 1973)
8. Dick Hebdige, *Subculture: The Meaning of Style* (London: Methuen, 1979).
9. Lawrence Grossberg, "I'd Rather Feel Bad Than Not Feel Anything at All: Rock and Roll, Pleasure and Power," *Enclitic* VIII, nos. 1–2 (Spring/Fall 1984):94–110.
10. Ibid., p. 101.
11. John Fiske and John Hartley, *Reading Television* (London: Methuen, 1978), pp. 135–36.
12. Terry Eagleton, "The Revolt of the Reader," *New Literary History* 13, no. 3 (Spring 1982):452.
13. Janice Radway, *Reading the Romance: Women, Patriarchy and Popular Literature* (Chapel Hill and London: University of North Carolina Press, 1984), p. 211.
14. Fiske and Hartley, pp. 125–26.
15. The distinction between "application" and "implication" of theory is Shoshana Felman's. See "To Open the Question," *Literature and Psychoanalysis: The Question of Reading, Otherwise* (Baltimore and London: The Johns Hopkins University Press, 1982), pp. 8–9.

# I.
# TRADITIONS OF MASS CULTURE CRITICISM

# 1

# AN INTERVIEW WITH RAYMOND WILLIAMS

## Stephen Heath and Gillian Skirrow

HEATH: Raymond Williams's work over the last twenty years has been very influential for the way in which people have thought about culture and politics. In the course of that work he has had occasion many times to look critically at mass culture and he has written specifically about the media, notably television, in his book *Television: Technology and Cultural Form*. Gillian Skirrow and I talked to Raymond Williams about issues relating to mass culture. It seemed particularly important to do this as the book of interviews, *Politics and Letters*, in which he went back over his work, reassessing it from the perspective of the current situation, more or less omitted any reference to those issues—the book on television itself, for example, received only one mention. So what we wanted to do was to remedy something of that omission, to try to explore with him questions involved in "mass culture, criticism, and analysis."

Raymond, perhaps what we need first of all is actually to look at the term "mass culture" and gain some understanding of that, what we mean by it, its historical and political implications.

WILLIAMS: Yes, actually I've always opposed the term "mass culture." This may seem presumptuous since use of the term is so widespread, but the unnoticed associations it brings with it are what I wanted at least to draw attention to. "Mass" and "masses" are modern words ranging in meaning from "multitude" to "crowd" to "mob." And if you look at the development of various phrases derived from that, you will find that, in politics, for example, the term "mass" is very ambivalent. The right use it to talk about mass democracy, which is rather vulgar and unpredictable and volatile; and the left talk about

Transcript of a videotaped interview prepared for the conference on "Mass Culture," Center for Twentieth Century Studies, University of Wisconsin-Milwaukee, April 1984

mass action as showing solidarity, people coming together to change
their condition. Now, that's an important and real historical ambivalence. But when you apply it to culture, and specifically to modern
media, what it obscures is this: that the real institutions of mass culture
in any central sense predate the modern media. I mean, the mass
cultural institutions are the mass meeting and the mass demonstration,
where people are physically assembled in large crowds and where
certain modes of communication—the display of banners, certain
shouts, and so on—are wholly appropriate to that kind of physical
assembly. Now, it's almost too obvious that in television, where typically there may be a very large audience and mass in the sense of
multitude but where people are distributed over their millions in very
small groups or alone or in a family relationship, many of the actual
techniques seem to me to have been developed for a more personal
kind of speaking. Therefore, if we are to understand, as we must, the
modes of communication characteristic of these media, possible in
them, we have to distance ourselves from what is otherwise only the
imposition on the media of a notion of the mass market. Mass as
against quality market. This is a medium which because of its expense
and so on has to reach a very large number of people. The term
"mass" confuses too many questions. If it's just a label, OK, but I think
it's more than a label, and a lot of assumptions come with it, particularly from anti-democratic prejudices about anything that reaches or
is addressed to a large number of people.
SKIRROW: But there's another term in this debate, isn't there, which
is "popular culture?"
WILLIAMS: Yes.
SKIRROW: How do you make a distinction between "mass culture," in
any of the senses you've mentioned, and "popular culture"?
WILLIAMS: Well, "popular" follows the same history, of course, but
with some interesting differences. When it is applied to culture it
usually implies a certain difference from what has come to be called
high culture or learned culture or liberal culture. On the other hand,
it took on at least three meanings as it came through to the twentieth
century. First, it got mixed up with folk culture: although the German
term *volk* could have been translated "popular," it was translated
"folk." And this had the effect of backdating popular culture. Popular
culture was everything before the industrial revolution—so that was
quite inappropriate. Then there was "popular" in the simple sense of
something that was addressed to a large number of people, and the
term coming into the nineteenth century meant "well-liked by a large
number of people." But there are two other senses of "popular" which
I think are important: one, this persistent use of the people to mean
a body of people politically as opposed to a power, a government.

Popular culture now sometimes means to some of its practitioners that which represents a certain kind of interest or experience, as against the modes of an established culture or as against a power. But that can very easily be isolated because it's almost inevitably self-consciously oppositional. People often then say, "Well, that kind of popular culture may be real and a part of the history of people's conditions and so on, but that is just a political culture"—something like that.

But the other meaning, in which I've been particularly interested lately, takes up that whole range which never got recognized as culture at all within an old dispensation: that of a very active world of everyday conversation and exchange. Jokes, idioms, characteristic forms not just of everyday dress but occasional dress, people consciously having a party, making a do, marking an occasion. I think this area has been very seriously undervalued, and it isn't only that it is undervalued in itself. We're not yet clear about the relation of those things to certain widely successful television forms. There is a sense in which everyday gossip passes straight into a certain kind of serial. And there's an obvious relation between the whole joke world and certain kinds of comedy, and the question then would be whether such television forms are articulating those areas, or whether they're simply latching onto them and in fact displacing, manipulating, redirecting them. But "popular" means all those things, I think.

HEATH: So the relations between mass culture and popular culture are actually quite intricate today, the two in no way simply separate. This brings us on to something you emphasized in your last book, *Towards 2000*, which is important here inasmuch as it represents your view on future developments and possibilities, on political opportunities with regard to the media, mass culture, popular culture. You've just been talking about the popular culture of everyday life, which is clearly, I think, not just redirected but also informed by mass cultural productions. In the book, as I understand it, you identify two areas of popular culture which are in some sense surviving and resisting and developing today. One area is bound up with memory and the establishment of forms of historical memory which you say have been able to come through in certain kinds of television drama in Britain, for example. It would be helpful to have some instances of exactly what you had in mind. The other area is that of what I just called the popular culture of everyday life, which feeds through things like gossip and jokes and so on and which you say is clearly there in domestic drama, presumably in forms of domestic television drama, in forms of soap opera. Or is this wrong, a misleading extrapolation?

WILLIAMS: No, no, it's an absolutely correct extrapolation although it leaves a lot of questions unasked. I mean, take the first area: there's been a very conscious attempt to revive, as it were, a popular history, and it is true that there has been a kind of cancellation of the lives of the majority of people, even where the evidence was recoverable, in favor of quite other versions of the past. Now, I think there are difficulties inherent in that. If you think of the usual examples, *Days of Hope* and such, or if you think (which often presents fewer difficulties) of certain documentary memories, retrospective interviews of people who were in the International Brigade in Spain or people who were in the General Strike or something of this kind, there are all sorts of problems about the representation of those memories, and they raise very complex questions in the end. One of the difficulties is that the resulting piece gets that inevitably retrospective air. I mean, one has to go only a short distance from such works to *Upstairs, Downstairs*, which presents, as I think, a totally false version of those relationships because they are tidied up and glossed over and sentimentalized. But that same retrospective air—people listen to it not in order to say that this is a past which connects with our present, but almost inevitably in the manner of some of the presentations, that this is a past which doesn't connect with our present—"Oh, gosh, what clothes we wore then!" and that sort of thing.

The other area concerning the popular culture of everyday life raises even more difficult questions because one can at least see the dangers in this popular memory thing and work at avoiding them. With the other, one is moving into one of the most manipulative areas in all the media: domestic serials, soap opera, comedy, comedians, conscious comedy. Most intellectuals have said that this area is simply reproductive pap. I then ask why, in relation to what other kinds of culture, that has such a particular engagement. I ask the question about *Coronation Street*, which nobody would look at to understand northern working-class culture now or then. But nevertheless there is an engagement with, among other things, the sense of the continuity of human lives. Much of the more serious contemporary art, characteristically for its own good reasons, has dropped the generational succession of the nineteenth-century novel, has often focused on some crisis in a situation or a relationship. It's worked through intensively. The end. Now, I think there are human interests in what happens next to people which are often low-order gossip interests, but some are rather high-order interests, I think, rather central interests about people—what happened next, what took place a year later, whether it worked out in this way or that. Of course you can see that a lot of it is gossip and you can see that a lot of it is manipulated, just as you can see that a lot of the everyday idioms are mimed in commercials by people who don't share them; they are just put on and attached to an ice cream or whatever. But I think there's something important there which is also saying something about what has happened in the most consciously serious art.

SKIRROW: Just to stay with *Coronation Street* for a moment, I think it is no accident that this interest in continuity of life manifests itself on television in the form of soap opera, which is mostly watched by women and in which many of the main characters are women.

WILLIAMS: Yes.

SKIRROW: Women have of course been associated with the idea of continuity since the earliest times, when they represented earth and other basic elements, and even now they often stand for a certain relationship to time and everyday life which contrasts with that of men, and against which men can appear to be moving fast and changing things. While it might be progressive if women were making these programs about a different engagement with everyday life, the fact is that women are largely excluded from television production, and programs such as *Coronation Street* seem to me only to be reinforcing a reactionary segregation of interest within popular culture in terms of gender.

WILLIAMS: Well, I think what you say is very important because the analysis is right, and it is related to the fact that everyday work outside the home is nearly always excluded. And the meeting places are characteristically the pub and so on. There's a whole problem about the representation of men's work, because even in the radical popular culture it tends to be much more often the strike than the everyday experience of work that is represented. And while that is so, the segregation is going to be complete. And the way in which the men come back into that culture, if we're seeing the continuity through the women, back into the family which is obviously a very fraught matter in a changing social structure like this, is only half said if the work the men have come from has not been represented and if the women increasingly working outside the home are not seen in those work relationships. And it wasn't that I wanted to defend that; I was saying that there is a simple, almost unargued interest in what happens next, an interest which in fact is widely shared, and that is precisely the way it then gets inflected-deflected in these forms, which can be so easily parodied as a result.

HEATH: One of the things in talking about television and popular culture, about *Coronation Street* and so on, is that what one is then talking about is reception, not production. Reception is clearly an area in which the popular culture might determine meanings, a particular engagement. But that is then in relation to a mass cultural production, to keep to those terms for the moment. What are the problems in talking about the possibility of popular culture in connection with something which is, of course, in no way popularly produced? We're talking apparently about reception rather than production. What are the difficulties in that?

WILLIAMS: I think that when the newspapers started gaining a wider audience, a lot of people had to learn demotic style and popular idioms. As a result, professionals who shared nothing of the lives that they were reproducing learned to produce an extraordinary idiomatic facsimile of those lives. People learn this sort of trade; it's learned as much in copywriting as in television serials and in certain kinds of tabloid journalism—the ironic thing then often being that the professionals are speaking more like the people than the people. There is even a two-way process in which certain idioms that perform well or that some very popular performer takes up actually pass back into the everyday idiom. So we must not make the error of supposing that what is being represented is that. Rather, one is saying, the link is, that there is that unsatisfied interest and all sorts of problems about why it's unsatisfied. And it then gets these forms which offer to speak to it.

HEATH: This is a little like—and it may be interesting to think about this in relation to the book *Towards 2000* today—what Enzensberger says in the famous essay at the end of the 60s on "Constituents of a Theory of the Media." Basically what he said was that the left was too quick to reject forms of, as it were, popular mass culture, forms which were clearly latching onto not false needs but real needs, latching onto them exploitatively and appropriating them in ways which had to be resisted, yes, but real needs nevertheless. What the left had then to do, the argument ran, was effectively to explore the whole area of mass culture and find ways of productively moving from it in regard to the real needs that it clearly engaged, even though in some sense, in every real sense perhaps, it falsified and alienated them.

Now surely one of the difficulties with what you're saying is that we're continually brought back to this problem of the relation between mass culture and popular culture. There's a very pessimistic account of this which isn't simply the automatic rejection of mass culture as false needs but which also leaves little hope for the popular in the mass. I'll try to give a version of it in order to provoke you. Let's go back first, though, to popular memory. In the 70s in France, for example, there was a great deal of investment in the notion of popular memory, and as an indication of cultural-political action, it gave you an idea of what to do. There was something of a feeling that provided one could only go out and locate an area that had been shut out from the existing terms of representation and represent it, then that was a good in itself. But the problems of the medium by which it was represented, indeed the problems of the assumption that it was simply a *medium* which was representing it, were never faced. To put it crudely, what you could quickly end up with was a kind of left-wing ethnological investigation of things outside the existing terms of representation that were then brought into those exclusive terms in a kind of specular, almost voyeuristic way. The problems of the medium weren't posed just because it was taken as a medium and the trap then was the imagination of an identity of a popular culture which could suddenly be revealed through it, in what were still the same mass terms.

That's the problem of the popular into the mass culture but there's crucially too that of the mass culture definition of, determination of the popular. You've talked of domestic serials and the ways in which they give onto basic interests, real human experiences and concerns, but then precisely one of the aspects of the development of mass culture, in the sense of the production by a minority who control the means of production, the effective possibilities of social representations, with financial interests so determining, is that part of the development has included a continual containing of positions, of readings: mass images that allow for all sorts of different readings and appeal within the overall limits of this mass culture. Thus, for example, television producers, writers and so on are well aware that there's a lot of activity around women in our societies, new relations of women amongst themselves, new definitions by them of their identity as women; they're aware of women as a "problem" or a "concern" which is then built into programs. The programs respond, they recognize and produce possible new readings, new identifications, but all held together in what is fundamentally a continually repeated spectacle, the terms of which, beyond and through the alternative readings—the appeal to something popular, coming from people in the society—will always be run back into what is basically the construction of the mass, a confined version of the popular. This is opposed to real versions of the popular bound up with forms of community and group activity and so on and so forth. At one stage you include all sorts of things; at another what is endlessly reproduced is always a spectacle, the production of an inclusive mass, just because these other possibilities are coming in—indeed, they are its material. I've tried crudely to put the pessimistic view. What would you say to that?

WILLIAMS: I don't think it's pessimistic at all. That does define the problem because what I'm not saying or certainly not intending to say is that there can be as it were radical and popular versions, radical and popular in the positive senses, of existing popular forms. My argument was more that there were elements in those popular forms which explained things in terms other than the irredeemable vulgarity or triviality or lack of sustained attention of the masses. I've never believed that you can have radical or popular or left versions of other kinds of cultural forms. In the same way you can't say—although there are some problematic cases—"well, let's have a really good radical soap opera." Take simply the level of attention. You can't attend to human development or human crises on those finely calculated schedules of duration of attention, length of sequence, and diversity of groups. Look at it in one of its most polished forms in *Dallas*. You can time the duration of shots and you can see the diversity of groups so that if you hate him, don't worry because in two minutes you'll be looking at her or you'll be looking at yet another him. Although such programs latch onto people's interests in what others are doing, they have radically reduced the possibilities of receiving the kind of attention people devote to with their own lives. You can't say "let us put some new content into this form"—this is radically the truth about form—so then whether it's pessimistic depends on whether one thinks it's pessimistic to face the kind of transformation that would be involved almost anywhere in this social order and it is a much larger job than is generally supposed.

What strikes me, what I want to emphasize most without hostility to the people but with frankness, is that this retrospective mode was not an accident. This endless nostalgic reconstitution. And it exists partly because the left for reasons of its own believed that somewhere if it could be tapped there was an essence of the people, an essence of the popular world which had somehow been lost but could be reconstituted by reconnecting it with its past. Whereas in reality—and this is certainly where the cultural analysis connects with the political one—this essence has been changed so much by actual history, that the only significant connection would be strictly contemporary not only in material, but in manner, in the way it is done, whatever period is being dealt with. The greatest danger is to have fantasies about a past consciousness which, if it could only be revived and given a few contemporary trimmings, would transform the present. It precisely would not. I mean, this belief is an example of one of the insufficient kinds of opposition that led to where we are now.

HEATH: We're moving towards issues relating to audiences and the construction of audiences. Indeed, we have to ask whether "audience" is a very good term when we talk about popular culture. We can see the kind of things it means with regard to mass culture, the construction of audiences there, or at least we think we can. What is the reality of audiences today in popular culture? In mass culture? How do they come together? What do we say about audiences today given the possibilities of the whole series of new technologies that are being rapidly developed? I know you resist very strongly ideas of technological determinism. You might want to say a few words about that and about how we can work through mass culture into alternative forms of audience.

WILLIAMS: I'm against that version of technological development and its future which supposes that inherent elements of any technology determine its use. I think this is plainly not true of any of the technologies you take. This should not, however, be understood to mean that a given medium does not have specific properties crucial to understanding how it works. But very often this is not what is meant by people who say a technology like cable television, to take the crudest contemporary case, necessarily implies home banking and video shopping, because I could at once list twenty alternative uses of precisely the same technology. Those are political and economic choices; they're not carried by the technology. It's quite hard when a technology has been developed in a certain way for people to say it could have gone a different route. But when a new technology is coming through, it's crucial to be aware of its possible alternative uses.

In thinking about audiences, I keep coming back to this notion of the constitution of a false nation. There's almost now a false transatlantic community within the English-speaking world. People say "isn't it wonderful that 17½ million of us were watching this ice-skating last night"—it's a shared national experience. It doesn't matter in that sort of case. It matters very much, however, when the program shows retired admirals and generals playing with models of war ships and airplanes over a map of the South Atlantic. Because they can't get any film of the war and this is the whole nation planning its collective military enterprise with these puppets. Now I would welcome anything which would break up this quite false sense because this idea of the nation, of the area of relevant concern, of people whom we "recognize," excludes the majority of people of the world whom we don't recognize and watch on television.

Indeed, I think these false images have only been developed because of certain specific problems in this society, problems of people knowing where they belong and how they relate. And so I am against the notion of public service broadcasting claiming to represent such ideas as the national interest or the public interest, all of which, I think, are false constructions. But I wouldn't want to rule out the possibility of actual alternatives to these ideas in terms of more real communities which needn't only be physical communities but communities of interest, physically spread out from each other. And certainly I think then a different mode of address would happen because, to come back to your earlier point, if the broadcaster believes that he is addressing the nation he starts talking in certain ways which are bad for him, bad for us. Even if people get used to it. Because they're false ways in that all he's really looking at is a camera and people in a studio and all he's otherwise learned is a convention, usually a false one, in its most developed form. Here's an example that I first noticed in popular newspapers. "You write," was printed above the reader's letters. *I* hadn't written, *you* hadn't written, but "you write" was printed because you're all "you." And they say on television programs now, "and next week you will have a chance to take part." We won't conceivably, if there are millions of us. But it means, this and this one we'll select: all you. This is a way of thinking. We are so much more diverse, much more specific.

HEATH: That's the creation of the instantaneous mass in relation to which television clearly works at the moment. One of the interesting things about what you've said, the reference to the nation and so on, is that, of course, the examples you've cited are those of "great historical moments": the Falklands War, the royal wedding, and so on which are presented as great images of the nation and unity. But actually most television doesn't seem to be concerned with that. In fact, it doesn't seem to be so much bound up with the nation as with the "internation." It isn't clear to me that mass culture is necessarily bound up with images of nationalism; indeed, versions of television in relation to nation would appear to be found (talking about industrially-developed countries) precisely in countries which have resisted as much as they can the extension to television. France is an obvious example of a country which has tried very powerfully to keep its television under direct state control as an instrument of the national ideology (the control is weakening now to some extent under the socialist government, though there's also an irony in that the terms of the weakening are those of a privatization and commercialization of televison). There you get a very powerful notion of trying to protect television from mass culture where mass culture means an international version of things, to protect it against that in the name of the nation.

WILLIAMS: I think that's right and I think that the medium requires us to make political judgments and avoid adopting more abstracted models of the people being addressed. Because they substitute for that, the nation which is this notional community with all this falsehood in it but which has certain connections to otherwise observable political reality.

SKIRROW: Earlier in this discussion you made a distinction between elements of the technology which might be supposed to determine certain kinds of use, and political and economic choices which determine the uses of the technology. But in thinking about the construction of notions of community in relation to the development of satellite television, one might argue that this distinction becomes insignificant because the expense of the technology is what will determine certain political choices, and so certain kinds of use.

WILLIAMS: I suspect that with the development of a cable system, satellites should really be looked at as the technical back-up to the areas that it is not possible to cable.

SKIRROW: Satellites will carry channels of mass entertainment which are sold to cable, and cable will then probably have one local access channel which will become a ghetto among, say, sixty other channels. And it won't be on a press button so you'll have to tune it in, making access in fact inaccessible.

WILLIAMS: That's not the technology telling us that but the people in power, the people making these decisions, the people giving the licenses. I mean, it's been decided who will dig up our streets to lay what cables. And our civic sense that there are streets to dig up and that we should have some say about what they're dug up to do is what is overborn now, and the opposition clusters far too much around maintaining the residual forms. So people are defending the BBC against cable. The real thing they've got to do is to think of other uses for which it could be developed. I'm not saying it would be anything but a really hard fight which in many places would be lost. But I think the other cause is much more substantially lost because then you're left forever with this declining asset and you can see cable developing in that way and BBC becoming what would soon be called the quality channel as the rest will have gone tabloid. This isn't bad in the sense that it's diminishing what's generally available. It is bad, as I've watched it over the years, for what's called the quality channel, precisely because that space is so massively occupied.

SKIRROW: Well, do you think the fight then is for regulation? We have to use this term because it seems to oppose the fashionable concept of "deregulation" although it is not at all clear how communications technology could be deregulated. Obviously it is going to be regulated in some way; the question is whether such regulation will promote commercial or social interests.

HEATH: I don't see deregulation as an issue. What in effect deregulation does is let the financial interests triumph.

SKIRROW: Which means it's regulated for profit.

WILLIAMS: I find I think increasingly about the level at which you can have regulation without it becoming one of these grand advisory bodies or government appointed things attempting to define in advance the limits of the decent or the truthful or the possible. I find myself thinking more and more, particularly in Europe, of a civic tradition, because I think that this is one area where I could just conceive regulation to be possible. I don't think it would be possible for a nation the size of Britain to arrive through discussion at some grand rules and conventions governing cable use. But I can imagine a city doing it and, interestingly, there are signs now in Europe that the importance of the city is increasingly being recognized, although it's still very problematic. After all, throughout the history of European culture, civic responsibility has often been more important than national responsibility. And since this would affect the use of these technologies,

I think it's something that should be very closely looked at and it's already happening. This would carry the possibility that you would have different stuff in one city from another and that would be a good thing because it's depressing to think of going from one city to another and finding the same stuff.

HEATH: Well yes, in the United States you could have different stuff from city to city but what you get mostly is exactly the same stuff, and we come back once again to ownership, to who is actually determining the possibilities and the limitations of our choice. But I suppose the question to you at this point is that of resistance. In one sense what you're saying is that we should resist mass culture, all along the line: the assumptions built into it, the terms of its production . . . though recognizing that mass culture now carries elements of a popular culture, that it also produces representations that do make connections, that can be read in other ways, subcultural developments and appropriations, for instance. But nevertheless, would it be right to say that we should resist mass culture? And then, a further question from the perspective of work as a critic or analyst: what kinds of things should we be doing; how should we be looking at mass culture?

WILLIAMS: Well, the resistance of course I agree with. As for analysis, I think there needs to be developed many different kinds of analysis which are in touch with each other. I think that the least developed— although it happens that in our particular conversation it wouldn't be the least developed—is that which tries to understand precisely the production of certain conventions and modes of communication right inside the form. I would put this at the top of the list not because it could answer all the questions on the table, but because it's the least likely thing to happen. People study audiences; they study the history of the institutions; and they study the technologies—something that ought to be done by more than technologists, because it isn't terribly difficult to understand enough about a technology to see the diverse possibilities, rather than just taking the publicity handout. People have always studied effects, though I've never been a great fan of this approach because I know of no social or cultural norm against which supposedly divergent effects might be measured. Concentrating on deviant effects conceals the effects of the norm. I would put top of the list, simply because it's the least developed, critical analysis of particular presentations and analysis of new presentations and political discourses. Hopefully such analysis would influence production. We have to understand right inside the productive process how these difficult modes of address and forms are actually constructed. It's been 26 years since I first did anything on television in Britain and the second thing I was asked to do, which I refused to do in the way suggested, was to discuss an education report, tear it up, and say, "this is rubbish." I said I won't do it, and the answer came (and who has not heard it since in studios across the world): "That's television." It's not any more television than anything else is television.

HEATH: One of the things that comes out of what you've just said in relation to criticism and analysis and the work we might do is the matter of quantity. What you said bears more especially on the analysis and criticism of particular aspects of television, particular modes, particular programs. But then one of the central issues is the sheer quantity of television, the volume of what we're talking about in any consideration of mass culture. Now when you did the television book, it is evident that you looked analytically and critically at quantity, which was brought into the argument qualitatively as what you called the experience of flow in television. Are there any ways in which you'd want to change that analysis now or suggest other possibilities for dealing with quantity?

WILLIAMS: You raise an important question. I think that the whole tradition of analysis has been of the discrete single work and while something can be done with that approach, it would be rather missing the point of the normal television experience. I first realized this when I thought what a very curious word we use for some unit of television: program, which is defined as a whole sequence of events that kind of follow. And there is a sense in which from the planning stage now television is constructed in terms of the sequence, and there are, as people properly say, "slots." And really the professional reviewer or the professional analyst who examines this sequence is able to get at some important questions but there are others which wouldn't be discussed at all. Yet there's great difficulty I think; I was rereading the analysis of flow I gave as examples. I think it needs to be much more developed. Where it seemed to me to work very clearly was in the flow of miscellaneous news items, or miscellaneous news items with commercials—which I have always argued don't interrupt the programs, they help to constitute them. And I think that we should resist the habits that have been learned from analysis of particular literary works, particular paintings and so on, and confront this notion of flow because it really does belong to the medium in the sense that you don't know the transmittor is there unless there's some sort of signal. So there's a continuity of the signal, that is to say, the first constitution of flow.

HEATH: It's like a telephone answering machine. You dial and it always answers.

WILLIAMS: That's right. And then you qualify, heavily qualify it by this notion that you mustn't leave the screen blank for a moment or somebody will switch channels, go over to your rivals. Producers plan programs to capture the audience at certain times of the evening. This doesn't follow from the notion of medium, but the continuity of the signal does. And then the continuity of the signal becomes the flow. I think that this allows us to analyze news differently, to ask more than about biased reporting. Questions about the nature of the news and the relevant area of information can only be answered in terms of flow. There's a lot of development in that, I would hope.

SKIRROW: I think your own work has been and continues to be a model of how intellectuals can work on popular culture and mass culture without being above it or outside it, or defeatist or pessimistic about it. But does it not worry you that—perhaps particularly in relation to *Towards 2000*—your optimism can be incorporated into the discourses that are around at the moment—and coming from a conservative government—about communications being the sunrise industry, cable providing instant community, and the new technologies representing progress for "the people"—discourses which are all part of the "gee whiz" syndrome?

WILLIAMS: Yes, it worries me. I've talked a lot about incorporation and I suppose it's because I watched this process operating on me as well as operating on others. I don't think I've been in any situation since I could think in which I haven't been aware of the positive attempts at incorporation, many of which I have to say have succeeded. Anybody who regards me as looking insufficiently outside of my cultural period would know that. Of course I see the danger. But there's no risk of my not saying what needs to be said against the really quite specious optimism you describe. Those people are playing with fire in so many ways that it's not difficult to distance one's self from them. Of course it's a risk. On the other hand, I wouldn't want to get into the position of many of my long-standing friends in this argument who are belatedly saying how good the BBC is and so on.

We have a conception of programming which I really do want to break up, to come back to the previous answer. Talking to some graduate students in Cambridge in a seminar, people who didn't normally work much on the media, I asked them to imagine a situation in which they went to the library each week, and a very nice librarian, a charming person, the most intelligent person in the back office said, "We've got a very interesting selection of books for you to read this week. We've got a historical novel, a history, a do-it-yourself thing, a thriller and a gardening book," and all they had to do was to take away the books. It's preposterous to anyone who values books, but this is precisely the convention which has become so naturalized in television. Good, nice people prepare a selection in a package for you . . . and then you can compare their package with other packages. And I certainly don't want to go along with those of my friends who are defending the old style packaging for fear of something worse. I think that position will be overborn in any case. It's like every other political situation: a merely defensive battle is going to lose.

SKIRROW: One voice has been consistently against the technological euphoria and also against the joy of destruction which seems to have invaded all kinds of technology, including video games—and which I think you alluded to in *Towards 2000* as an almost self-destructive force arising from the expectation that the whole world is going to be destroyed soon anyway—and that voice which has been consistently against all this has been the women's movement. There are also other voices such as the ecology movement, but these voices have not generally been taken into account in academic debates about popular or mass culture. Do you see that there are some signs of optimism in that kind of opposition which can point us toward developing new communication systems and, if so, how is it that work on that has been lacking? For example, in descriptions of popular culture there's very little on its relation to gender. Do you think that's because women have not engaged with it? Should it be left for women to engage with it, or is there something that people like you, for example, could do to engage with this argument?

WILLIAMS: I think this is the right question. It is a difficult business to learn to think and speak in new ways, and the best evidence of this re-education process is coming from one of the tendencies inside the women's movement. There is one voice within the movement which is of an ecological kind and which can connect with the more general ecological case. The technologies can take us beyond certain social blockages we now have—absurdities of aggregated cities and dense impossible traffic systems and so on—if they connect with the new thinking about settlements and relationships that is occurring in the women's movement, in the ecology movement and in a few associated groups. Such thinking is not happening in any orthodox political parties which are reproducing the present form and with it the present means of communication and their content.

HEATH: I suppose that's at least an area for possible development to end on. I hope we've touched on some issues in your work, Raymond, that perhaps haven't been brought out quite as directly before. Thank you.

WILLIAMS: Thank you.

# 2

# THEODOR ADORNO MEETS THE CADILLACS

## Bernard Gendron

> First you harmonize, then you customize.
> —Wilson Pickett

### I.

In the summer of 1955, the Cadillacs enjoyed their first musical success with the modest regional hit "Down The Road." They did not realize then that, as pioneers of the doo-wop style, they were part of the first wave of the rock 'n' roll revolution. Except for two minor national hits, the rest of their career was an accumulation of errors, broken promises, desperate searches for the right formula, and constant changes in personnel. Today they are a legend and a favorite among record collectors.

"Down The Road" appeared fourteen years after the publication of Theodor Adorno's classic diatribe against popular music. When Adorno was writing "On Popular Music" (with the assistance of George Simpson), the airwaves were filled with the music of the big bands—either in the swinging style of Tommy Dorsey or in the sentimental style of Guy Lombardo—music which, though somewhat different in sound and format, worked quite comfortably within the Tin Pan Alley system of songwriting that had dominated popular music since the turn of the century.[1] In this essay and in his subsequent writings, Adorno never veered from his construction of popular music as nothing more than Tin Pan Alley or some jazzy derivative of it, even though his death came at least a decade after the birth of rock 'n' roll.[2] At any rate, we can be sure that he never heard the Cadillacs.

This omission on Adorno's part has done much to damage the

credibility of his work on popular music. Many in the present generation of culture theorists took part in the radical movements of the sixties, which turned to rock 'n' roll as their primary means of cultural expression and turned to the Frankfurt School for their first lessons in culture theory. Not surprisingly, these new theorists display an ambivalence toward popular culture that is virtually nonexistent in the work of Adorno, Marcuse, and the rest. Although they agree that the products of the culture industry play a crucial role in buttressing the domination of patriarchal capitalism, they insist that in the right circumstances these products can also be put to a subversive use. For many, rock 'n' roll's appearance at a particular juncture of class, generational, and cultural struggle has given it a preeminent role among mass cultural artifacts as an instrument of opposition and liberation.[3]

This explains in part why Adorno's work on popular music elicits more expressions of opprobrium from left-wing culture theorists than anything else produced by the Frankfurt School. It is usually rejected out of hand. There is the almost universal feeling that however correct Adorno may have been in his attack on Tin Pan Alley (most rock critics share his antipathy), the results of his analysis cannot legitimately be applied to rock 'n' roll. So in discussions of the politics of rock 'n' roll, Adorno's work is usually reduced to a place marker at one extreme of the spectrum of views. Critics mention it as an example of how excessive left-wing criticism of popular music can be, and then drop it in favor of a more balanced position.[4]

This is unfortunate. Despite its failures and excesses, Adorno's 1941 essay "On Popular Music" remains in my opinion one of the two or three most penetrating pieces on the subject; it addresses many important questions which are often neglected by those who tend to dismiss Adorno's work. Moreover, I think it can be shown that if Adorno's critique works against Tin Pan Alley, it also succeeds against rock 'n' roll. Rock theorists have accepted too uncritically the myth of the great political and aesthetic gap between rock 'n' roll and Tin Pan Alley. We need to take a fresh look at Adorno's questions, recasting his 1941 essay in a rock 'n' roll setting. This is where the Cadillacs and their doo-wop confreres come in. They constitute the court exhibit.

## II.

Adorno attempted to expose the politically and aesthetically destructive ways in which the capitalist mode of production affects popular music. For him it all came down to one thing. "A clear judgment concerning the relation of serious to popular music can be arrived at only by strict attention to the fundamental characteristic of popular music: standardization. The whole structure of popular music is standardized even where the attempt is made to circumvent standardization" (p. 17). Adorno was not speaking of all kinds of standardization, only of that kind which has emerged with the capitalist industrial system.

In the broadest sense of the term, standardization is an almost universal fact of human production. At any given time or place, because of prevailing techniques, artifacts of the same kind tend to be produced in the same way, or in only a small variety of different ways. For example, at the turn of the nineteenth century, before the industrial revolution reached the firearms industry, gunsmiths had at their disposal the techniques and resources for constructing a wide variety of gun locks: the match lock, the wheel lock, the flint lock, and the percussion lock. Once the percussion lock was perfected, however, there were no longer any good reasons for producing the highly awkward, unreliable, and inefficient match lock, or any of the other competing forms. The percussion lock became the standardized form. Such standardized uniformities of practice and technique inform preindustrial music as well as manufacturing. It is sometimes said of Vivaldi that he composed the same concerto 500 times. Haydn was not averse to composing according to formula, nor were any of the anonymous contributors to the largely invariant tradition of the English folk ballad.

But what Adorno wanted to attack in the cultural sphere was not standardization in general. He was primarily concerned with two traits which only emerge in full force with industrial standardization: part interchangeability and pseudo-individualization, traits which are easily discerned in the large-scale manufacturing and marketing of such functional artifacts as the American automobile. For example, virtually any mechanical part from any 1956 Cadillac Eldorado (e.g., a carburetor) can be substituted for the corresponding part in any other 1956 Eldorado without disturbing the functional unity of the overall mechanism. Between the 1956 Eldorado and the 1956 Cadillac Sedan de Ville, the level of interchangeability is lower—the former was marketed as a classier car with greater horsepower—but most of the corresponding parts of these two cars are the same, as are the corresponding parts of lower-level Cadillacs and higher-level Oldsmobiles of later years. Interchangeability extends significantly, though not perfectly, beyond brand-name boundaries.

Interchangeable parts need not be qualitatively indistinguishable, though they usually are. All that is required is that the mechanism, after part substitution, continue to function in an integrated manner. For example, stereo speakers belonging to different systems may be interchanged, however much they may vary in design, size, and appearance, without disrupting these systems' ability to produce recorded sound. On the other hand, few pairs of pre-industrially crafted products have interchangeable parts. In the eighteenth century, the odds were exceedingly low that the lock of one hand-crafted gun could be successfully replaced with that of another to effect a functional fit with the former's stock and barrel. Precision machinery can be used to produce interchangeable locks and barrels; skilled hands and tools cannot. The eighteenth century gunsmith had to spend considerable time filing each lock-barrel pair to bring about a proper fit; thus, no two locks had exactly the same kind of fit to their respective barrels.

Pseudo-individualization is the indispensable capitalist complement to part interchangeability. The latter has to do with the inner essential mechanisms of industrial products, the former with their external trappings. The latter accounts for their basic similarities, the former for their apparent (and illusory) differences. Part interchangeability results from the drive to minimize the cost of production; pseudo-individualization results from the imperative to maximize sales. The system of advertising seduces us into believing that differences in packaging reflect differences in essence. Pseudo-individualization glamorizes style over the real inner content.

The 1956 Eldorado was the first Cadillac model to sport the famous tail-fin. To the mid-fifties consumer, all other Cadillac models paled in comparison, though their innards were virtually the same. Not surprisingly, the rest of the Cadillac fleet followed suit with wholly revamped tail-fin models in 1957, though mechanically they showed little improvement. In that brief period, pseudo-individuality within the Cadillac line operated both synchronically (for different models in the same year) and diachronically (for the same model in different years). For working-class youth, the fifties Cadillac was the most glamorous car on the American market, its body style standing for elegance, power, flash, adventure, movement—indeed, for having it all without drudgery or effort. The Cadillacs—the rock 'n' roll group—turned to General Motors for permission to bask in the glory of the name, and other groups had to content themselves with the names of particular models: the Fleetwoods, the Eldorados, the Sevilles.

Yet one who chose the more expensive Cadillac over the Oldsmobile was paying primarily for differences in style rather than mechanical quality. Even the Cadillac's equally expensive competitors outside of General Motors—the Lincoln Continental and the Chrysler Imperial—differed from it mainly in external wrapping, not engineering design. The fact that the Cadillac and the Chrysler and Lincoln had few if any interchangeable parts was more an artifact of marketing than of technology: the automobile corporations wanted to be the exclusive sellers of spare parts for their own models.

Pseudo-individualization tends not only to disguise part inter-changeability but also to distort it, thus transforming it into near-interchangeability or pseudo-noninterchangeability. Thus, the minute design differences in Cadillac and Lincoln carburetors, by subtly undermining interchangeability, further enhance the illusion of essential qualitative differences between the two makes.

## III.

Adorno claimed that popular music is as constrained by capitalist industrial standardization as any mechanical product of the assembly line. Let us examine this analogy between text and mechanism.

Assuming that in each popular song it is possible to distinguish between the core (the musical skeleton) and the periphery (the musical embellishments), Adorno argued that in popular music the central core is either invariant or subject to part-interchangeability. The variant periphery is contrived either to appear like a variant central core or to disguise the invariance or interchangeability of the central core. "In popular music, position is absolute. Every detail is substitutable; it serves its function only as a cog in a machine" (p. 19). One may interchange rhythms, chord progressions, speeds of execution, melodic fragments, riffs, lyrical formulae, and various vocal and instrumental devices. Meanwhile songwriters search incessantly for the pseudo-individualizing "hook" which will make the song appear unique and organically whole. The hook is to songs what the fin was to the 1956 Cadillac Eldorado. For Adorno the "so-called improvisations" in jazz provided the "most drastic" (and deceptive) example of pseudo-individualization in popular music (p. 25).

Adorno believed that good "serious" music does not suffer from this defect. "To sum up the difference: in Beethoven and in good serious music in general . . . the detail virtually contains the whole and leads to the exposition of the whole, while at the same time it is produced out of the conception of the whole. In popular music the relationship is fortuitous. The detail has no bearing on a whole, which appears as an extraneous framework" (p. 21). As an example, Adorno cited Beethoven's *Fifth Symphony*. One may get the superficial impression of interchangeable parts insofar as the symphony follows the four-movement formula, with the third movement being a scherzo in ABA form. Nonetheless, according to Adorno, one could not lift this scherzo out of the *Fifth Symphony* and place it, say, in a Haydn symphony without dramatically altering its meaning, since it was constructed to lead subtly into the fourth movement. The meaning of the scherzo in this case is inextricably tied to its relation to the fourth movement (pp. 20–21). For Adorno it followed from this that while

in popular music the mere recognition of the form virtually guarantees full understanding, in serious music one does not achieve full
understanding until one has struggled with the concrete inter-
connections of the text—recognition of the form is merely the first
step. Industrially standardized popular music is predigested, serious
music is not (pp. 32–33). Adorno pushed his thesis of industrial standardization in popular music to the very limits of plausibility. Industrial standardization for him operated not only within genres but also
between genres, diachronically as well as synchronically, in the long
run as well as in the short run. He saw no significant differences
between swing music and the sentimental ballads of the late thirties,
no significant development from the "hot" small combo jazz of the
twenties to the cooler big band jazz of the thirties. In effect, he believed
that nothing ever changes in popular music (pp. 26, 30).

According to Adorno, this dismal state of affairs in popular music
reflects and reinforces the deterioration of consumer taste within advanced capitalist society. The assembly line that produces the standardized automobile also produces a bored, numbed, and passive
worker. Workers are as customized by the capitalist production system
as the commodities they are hired to produce (p. 38). Industrial standardization in the culture industry both satisfies the consumption
needs of bored, passive workers and contributes further to their pas-
sivity. Bored consumers need constant stimulation; therefore, the industry creates pseudo-individualized hooks in music and the constant
illusion of novelty. Benumbed as they are, the workers have neither
the inclination nor the capacity to struggle intellectually with the cultural products they consume. The products must come to them completely predigested. This need is met by musical homogeneity and
part interchangeability; however, this uniformity must remain hidden
if the illusion of novelty is to be sustained. But the stimulative power
of each record palls very quickly, recreating the condition of boredom
it was meant to relieve. The only antidote is the constant production
of new recorded sounds (pp. 37–39).

In effect, "there is a justification for speaking of a pre-established
harmony today between production and consumption of popular music" (p. 38). Industrial standardization reflects not only the requirements of production for the musical text but also the demands of
consumption. It extends to the workers' leisure time the sort of control
that capital has over their labor time.

## IV.

Adorno's extraordinary claims made considerable sense in 1941
when he published "On Popular Music." It is well known that the

structure and musical content of Tin Pan Alley songs had hardly changed in the twenty years before the paper's publication. The overwhelming majority of these songs were composed in the 32-bar AABA format. Most songwriters never deviated from the simplistic harmonic paradigms in circulation, or from the "June-moon-spoon" rhyming formulas. There were notable exceptions in the more unpredictable harmonic devices and clever lyrics of Cole Porter, George Gershwin, and Jerome Kern, though these were not sufficiently intricate and avant-garde to satisfy Adorno.

The rock 'n' roll revolution may have mercifully put Tin Pan Alley out of its misery, but it did not bring to an end the industrial standardization of music. This is especially clear in the work of the Cadillacs and other doo-wop groups.

Doo-wop is a vocal group style, rooted in the black gospel quartet tradition, that emerged on inner city street corners in the mid-fifties and established a major presence on the popular music charts between 1955 and 1959. Its most distinctive feature is the use of background vocals to take on the role of instrumental accompaniment for, and response to, the high tenor or falsetto calls of the lead singer. Typically, the backup vocalists create a harmonic, rhythmic, and contrapuntal substructure by voicing phonetic or nonsense syllables such as "shoo-doo-be-doo-be-doo," "ooh-wah, ooh-wah," "sha-na-na," and so on.

For structural and harmonic guidance, doo-wop musicians relied almost exclusively on the tried-and-true paradigms and formulas that had existed for decades in the Tin Pan Alley and rhythm and blues fields. This is clearly a case of diachronic standardization. About 75 percent of the doo-wop songs were structured in the 32-bar AABA fashion typical of Tin Pan Alley; the remaining 25 percent followed the 12-bar AAB fashion typical of rhythm and blues. The blues-derived doo-wop songs adhered for the most part to standard blues chord progressions: I (4 bars), IV (2 bars), I (2 bars), V (1 bar), IV (1 bar), I (2 bars). Those in the 32-bar format in most cases followed the simple chord progression so familiar to children who learn to play duet versions of songs like "Heart and Soul" by ear: the I-vi-ii-V progression with two chord changes per measure. In 1955 the Moonglows, a doo-wop group, recorded "Sincerely," a song which is structurally and harmonically little different from Larry Clinton's 1938 recording of "Heart and Soul." For Adorno they shared the same standardized core. Similarly, the Silhouettes' 1958 doo-wop recording of "Get a Job" incorporates the structural and harmonic core of Big Joe Turner's 1944 blues classic "Rebecca."

It could be argued with equal plausibility that there is a high degree of synchronic standardization within the doo-wop genre itself. Most of the thousands of doo-wop songs composed during the late fifties closely resemble each other. But even their dissimilarities follow the principle of interchangeable parts. As an illustration, imagine a number of decks of cards, each of which represents a range of options within one doo-wop musical function. In one deck, the cards represent different doo-wop phonetic syllables, in another different call-and-response patterns, and so on: different melodic fragments for the lead voice, different counterpoint fragments for the background voices, different rhythms, speeds, vocal embellishments, lyrical fragments (e.g., "Gimme some lovin', some turtle-dovin' "), and gimmicks (a humorous bass voice, the sound of bells, a prepubescent singer). In most cases, one could create a credible doo-wop recording by simply picking one card from each deck. Thus, from any two doo-wop songs one could create two new songs by interchanging between them the strings of background vocal phonetic syllables (with proper adjustments in key signatures and rhythm). Imagine interchanging the "Shoo-Doo-Be-Doo-Be-Doo"s of the Five Satins' "In the Still of the Night" with "Dum-Dum-Dum-Dum-Dum-Dum-De-Doo-De-Dum" 's of the Dell-Vikings' "Come Go With Me." Where such interchanges are not immediately possible, certain amendations could make them work. But this only indicates that with certain doo-wop songs, interchangeability applies only proximally or is transformed into pseudo-noninterchangeability. Some doo-wop songs are as similar as two different Cadillac models; others are as unlike as a Cadillac and a Lincoln. Standardization and pseudo-individualization nonetheless prevail in both kinds of cases.

What is true for doo-wop also holds true for other rock 'n' roll genres: rockabilly, heavy metal, funk, etc. Consider how punk has standardized the musical sneer. There is also some standardization between rock 'n' roll genres (doo-wop and surf music, punk and rockabilly). So Adorno's analysis of popular music is not altogether implausible, and applies as well to the Cadillacs and the Sex Pistols as it does to Guy Lombardo and the Andrews Sisters.

## V.

I have tried to present Adorno's analysis of popular music in the best light, in order to eliminate the more facile and unfair objections usually leveled at it. Now I would like to discuss some of the failings of his theory. Adorno argued, successfully I think, that industrial standardization is an important feature of popular music, and must be taken seriously in any political assessment of the form. But he greatly exaggerated its presence, especially at the diachronic level. Secondly, he gave the wrong explanation for the music industry's predilection toward industrial standardization. This misconstruction of the role of the music industry affects the validity of his political critique, so I will discuss it first.

Adorno was not sufficiently sensitive to the crucial differences between the production of functional artifacts (e.g., the automobile) and the production of textual artifacts (e.g., the rock 'n' roll record). Thus he was too easily led to assume that, on the production side, the conditions which require industrial standardization in the culture industry are similar to those which require it in the rest of capitalist industry.

In functional artifacts, part interchangeability is largely a consequence of the technology of the assembly line. In this system of production, every whole (e.g., the automobile) is assembled out of qualitatively different parts, each of which is taken at random from qualitatively indistinguishable batches. Of course, different competitive brands (e.g., the Cadillac, the Lincoln) will emanate from qualitatively different assembly lines. But as long as state-of-the-art technology is allowed to flow freely, it will tend to prevail in all firms of a given industry, thus leading to a convergence of production techniques: assembly lines for Cadillacs and Lincolns will differ only marginally and contrivedly.

Technology does not put the same constraints on the production of recorded musical sounds. If anything, it greatly expands the possibilities for variation. For example, rather than supplanting the acoustic guitar, the electric guitar simply added to the rich variety of timbres obtainable with guitars. Nor do the technical constraints of production explain why doo-wop recordings typically use the saxophone for instrumental breaks, why doo-wop songs are usually cast in a 12- or 32-bar framework, or why doo-wop groups did not seize upon the potential of experimental tape editing, a technique which was later exploited by avant-garde composers (e.g., Stockhausen) and adventurous pop performers (e.g., the Beatles).

Adorno was aware that assembly line technology has little to do with the industrial standardization of popular music. He took this as a sign of the backwardness of the music industry, where "the act of producing a song hit still remains in the handicraft stage" (p. 23). In order to locate the industrial source of musical standardization, he turned from the sphere of production technology to that of production and marketing organization, where the music industry had already reached an advanced level of "industrialization," that is, oligopolistic concentration and cartelization. The story he tells is a rather familiar one. When the music industry was competitive and decentralized, many standards of popular song competed until one won out momentarily (synchronic standardization). But once the industry became concentrated and oligopolized, whichever form of music was dominant at the time was frozen permanently into place and "rigidly enforced" (diachronic standardization). Presumably this is not unique to the music industry (p. 23). Great market concentration anywhere means greater standardization.

This explanation is altogether unsatisfactory. For one thing, the modern recording studio is not technologically backward—it is at least as sophisticated as the assembly line. Furthermore, Adorno greatly underrated the dynamic character of capitalism in its oligopolistic forms. One need only look at AT&T's technologically innovative practices over the past few decades to see this. Although it may be true in the abstract that oligopolies and monopolies tend more toward rigidification than do competitive industries, we must not neglect the symbiosis existing between these two sectors. In the oil industry, the wildcatters take most of the risks in the search for new oil, and the major firms then buy up the proven wells. The personal computer was developed by small firms, and then the large firms moved in to consolidate. The music industry behaves similarly. Most of the early rock 'n' roll records were produced by the small record companies that emerged after World War II, like the obscure Josie label—whose only claim to fame was that it recorded the music of the Cadillacs. Once rock 'n' roll was established, the major recording companies captured most of its markets, although small firms kept reappearing to clear the air, occasionally supported by the big companies.

Adorno came away empty-handed in his search for a general industrial model for standardization in popular music. His analysis ignored the inherent differences between text and functional artifact. A text (whether written or oral) is a universal, whereas a functional artifact is a particular. However, to be marketed and possessed, every universal text must be embodied in some functional artifact (paper, vinyl discs). There were two quite distinct products involved in the 1955 release of the Cadillacs' "Down The Road" on the Josie label. The first—a universal—was the recorded sound resulting from the Cadillacs' studio performance and consequent re-mixing. The second was the moderately large batch of vinyl discs which, as particulars, embodied that sound. The processes used to produce the first are quite different from those used to produce the second. The vinyl discs of "Down the Road" were produced in great numbers, and thus were amenable to the disciplines of the assembly line, whereas Josie did at most only four or five recorded takes of the song, only one of which found its way onto wax. One simply doesn't mass produce universals. In 1955, Josie sold hundreds of thousands of discs, but generated only fifty to a hundred recordings—hardly a sufficient quantity to warrant the techniques of mass production. Even a large company like RCA, which may have sold over 50 million records that year, produced no more than a few thousand recorded takes. Thus, whatever the technological state of the culture industry, the assembly line is simply an inappropriate model for the production of texts-as-universals. This is not to say that the production of musical texts (as compositions or as performances) cannot be technically rationalized to maximize the power of management—such rationalization occurred, for example, in the Brill Building "song-writing" factory of the sixties. It does mean that it is and always will be a mistake to look to the techniques of mass production or the economics of market concentration for an explanation of industrial standardization in the culture industry. Whatever they are, the factors accounting for standardization in the production of musical texts must be significantly different from those which account for standardization in functional artifacts. Adorno's analysis is undermined by his failure to attend to these discontinuities.

## VI.

Adorno's theory runs into further difficulties when we move from the sphere of production to that of consumption. Adorno maintained that the pseudo-individualized components of each recording must camouflage its commonality and interchangeability with other recordings. However, he failed to appreciate the fact that records accentuate their commonality and interchangeability just as much as they do their individuality. This state of affairs seems to result from the *sui generis* characteristics of the commercially produced text, characteristics to which Adorno was clearly insensitive.

I do not buy records like I buy cans of cleanser. If I like my first can of Comet I will be willing to buy another can of Comet that is qualitatively indistinguishable. But if I like my record of the Cadillacs' "Down the Road" I will not go out and buy another copy of it. I will, however, want something of the same genre. For the music industry I fall into a particular market, and it will want to alert me to the presence of other such recordings. Direct advertising won't work, as it does for Comet, since it would require that record companies make a different ad for each different recording—an excessive drain on resources. The solution for the recording industry is to devise each record so that it advertises itself, particularly when it is played on the radio. The record must tell me, before I change the dial, that it is really the sort of record I like. A doo-wop record will highlight its "doo-wopish" features very early and very clearly. At the same time, it will alert me to its "hook"—that is, to what makes it unique. Both the interchangeability and individuality factors will be equally highlighted.

The typical doo-wop record starts with an eight-bar introduction, without lyrics or lead melody, establishing its doo-wop character and harmonies while showcasing the background nonsense vocals that distinguish it from other doo-wop records. Of course, given the time constraints, the record must advertise its genre in a highly simplistic and cartooning manner. But the genre that the record denotes in self-advertisement is also the genre that it embodies. A record that advertises its genre in a caricaturized way itself becomes a caricature of that genre.

Adorno often criticized the lack of nuance that accompanies standardization in popular music, but his failure to explain its uncamouflaged manifestations undermines his political criticism of musical standardization. It is probably due more to my being a hurried consumer than a passive consumer that the record industry resorts to simplistic self-advertisement. However undesirable this situation may otherwise be, it is not obviously dangerous politically. Indeed, even on aesthetic grounds, one could conceivably argue that some of the best "hooks" (e.g., the background vocals on the Cadillacs' "Speedo") have a legitimate evocative power which few musical devices can duplicate.

But much of this is pure speculation. We know very little about the roots of musical standardization, especially on the psychological side, in part because the subject has been virtually neglected since Adorno's first awkward attempts to make sense of it. In both its traditional and its industrial forms, standardization is such an important feature in folk, elite, and popular music (one notable exception being modernist experimental music) that it must be connected somehow to deep and entrenched psychological dispositions (whether socially or genetically acquired). In a surprising passage, even Adorno alluded to the conservativeness of the human ear whose musical preferences are shaped and rigidified by early childhood experiences—"the nursery rhymes, the hymns [one] sings in school, the little tunes [one] whistles on [one's] way home from school . . . Official musical structure is, to a large extent, a mere superstructure of this underlying musical language" (p. 24).

It seems that we must consider standardization not only as an expression of rigidity but also as a source of pleasure. How else do we explain the behavior of doo-wop collectors who scour through rummage sales and oldies record stores to add to their hundreds or thousands of like-sounding records? They take as much pleasure in the recognition of sameness as they do in the discovery of minute differences in recently acquired vintage doo-wop recordings. This pleasure resembles the "repetition compulsion" so characteristic of childhood behavior. Until these practices and pleasures are better understood, we will not be in a position to make any reliable political and aesthetic assessment of musical standardization in either its traditional or contemporary forms.

## VII.

While industrial standardization is an important characteristic of popular music—especially on the synchronic level—Adorno's analysis seems mistaken in attributing to it a dominant role on the diachronic level. Indeed, since popular music appears frequently to undergo significant and even radical changes, we might well ask why Adorno was led to say that it never changes.

Adorno's position presupposes an essentialist conception of the musical text. As I have shown, he seems to have thought that one can objectively or ahistorically distinguish between the core and the periphery of any musical text. Here I think he was again misled by his industrial model. In any functional artifact defined in terms of its function (e.g., "vehicle"), one can easily distinguish between the core and the periphery. The core is indispensable for the carrying out of the function, the periphery is not. For the 1956 Eldorado, the motor was obviously part of the core, and the fins were part of the periphery. But for the musical text, either as published or as performed, there is no clearly defined function that enables us to distinguish between core and periphery. Depending on the musical conventions or traditions to which one appeals, one may arrive at any of several different judgments. Adorno approached popular music from the point of view of Western "classical" music; if we view popular music in terms of its own conventions, the line between core and periphery will be drawn quite differently.

Connee Boswell scored a hit with "Blue Moon" in 1935. The Marcels, a doo-wop group, did the same with their version in 1961. If we compare these two recordings from the vantage point of classical Western notation, as Adorno did, we will unhesitatingly conclude that they share the same musical core, with the same melodies and chord progressions. This is another case of diachronic standardization. However, there are also very noticeable differences between the two recordings which might be of importance from another vantage point. Boswell gives us a muted torch song, while the Marcels do an upbeat number in which the soloist is constantly bombarded with an amazing variety of doo-wop sound from the backup singers. The melody and harmony may be the same, but the sounds are radically different. Correspondingly, the connotations are quite different, though the lyrics are the same. The first is a song of pining world-weariness, the second a let's-have-fun song, resplendent with the innocent (though vaguely threatening) enthusiasm of fifties teen pop culture. The first song conjures up images of art-deco nightclubs; the second song, images of urban street corners.

It all comes down to this. If we put melody and harmony in the core, and timbre and connotation in the periphery, we will see a radical sameness between the Boswell and Marcels recordings. If we put timbre and connotation in the core, and relegate melody and harmony to the periphery, we will see a radical difference. Western classical music focused on melody and harmony, whereas contemporary pop music focuses on timbre and connotation. Within the conventions of popular music, major changes in sound and connotation (e.g., the rise of rock 'n' roll) are considered to have much more revolutionary significance than changes in harmony.

How then are we to draw the line between core and periphery in popular music? A historical materialist would explicate change or advancement in a particular musical tradition in terms of its own conventions and practices, not in terms of some more favored tradition. To do otherwise is to open one's self to charges of ethnocentrism and elitism—exactly what happened to Adorno when he analyzed change in popular music.[5] It would be absurd, for example, to conclude that traditional Western African music is backward because its harmonic and melodic schemes are considerably more elementary than those of European classical music. Harmony is simply less important in African music than are rhythm, vocal expressivity, and participation. An African ethnocentrist might well condemn European music for its lack of sophistication in the latter three categories. Adorno complained that popular music never went beyond the tonal system of the Romantic Age (Liszt, Tchaikovsky) and could never accommodate any of the new systems of atonality. But this is altogether beside the point. Because the conventions of popular music only partially overlap with those of classical music, one must also consider the conventions of Afro-American music which have always been operative to some extent in American popular music. The fact that popular music borrows from the musical traditions of classical music does not subject it to the standards of progress of the latter. In this century a number of "serious" Western composers (Cage, Stockhausen) have turned to Eastern music for inspiration. Are we to say that in borrowing from old forms of Eastern music Western music has proved itself to be 1000 years behind the latter?

## VIII.

If we study popular music diachronically, in terms of its own conventions rather than those of an alien tradition, we will confront issues

different from those which preoccupied Adorno. The question is no
longer why popular music always remains the same, but why it changes
as often and as significantly as it does. Although a complete answer
to this question would take us beyond the music industry, since rapid
change seems to be an essential feature of modernism in both high
culture and popular culture, there *are* characteristics of music production which further reinforce this tendency. Certainly the constant
shifts in musical genres constitute at least *prima facie* evidence that
important transformations occur in the history of popular music. Before rock 'n' roll, people listened to ragtime, dixieland, swing, croon-
ing, be-bop, and rhythm and blues, among others. Whatever their
harmonic and melodic similarities, these styles differed quite substantially in timbre, evocation, connotation, and expressiveness. With the
coming of rock 'n' roll, the pace of change has accelerated. The thirty
years of the rock era have seen the coming and going of doo-wop,
rockabilly, the girl group sound, surf music, the British invasion, psychedelic rock, folk rock, heavy metal, and punk, to name just a few.
While it might be argued that these have only been fashion changes,
and hence merely surface changes, this sort of response simply fails
to attend to the important differences noted earlier between textual
and functional artifacts. In the latter, the fashion can change while
the mechanism remains the same; fashion is at the periphery, the
mechanism at the center. In the text, there is no mechanism to distinguish from the fashion, since a text is all style or all fashion. A
radical change in philosophic or literary fashion is a radical change
in literature and philosophy *tout court*.

Doo-wop displayed greater longevity than most rock 'n' roll styles.
It appeared on the pop charts in 1954, peaked in 1958, and continued
as a force into the early sixties. Rockabilly on the other hand enjoyed
only three years in the sun, while British punk and psychedelic rock
each had only two.

One can wonder what these rapid changes in style do to the music
consumer's sense of the flow of cultural history. The music industry
seems constantly to be reinterpreting or reinventing the musical past,
goading the consumer either toward outright rejection or nostalgia.
The first step, of course, is to disown the immediate past—to belittle
it, distance it, even to forget it so that the consumer typically becomes
embarrassed by her former musical preferences. Even the immediate
past seems in cultural time to be very far away, as if it were a former
self that liked what is now disdained. The British Invasion in rock
music finished the doo-wop style for good, and in the light of the
Beatles and Bob Dylan, the doo-wop genre appeared even to its erst-
while fans to be naive, repressed, silly, and inept.

The past, however, is not forever put aside. A wave of nostalgia soon sets in. In 1969, the industry and its consumers rediscovered the fifties. Producers scoured the countryside in search of former members of disbanded doo-wop groups and packaged them in "roots of rock 'n' roll" TV programs complete with film clips purporting to show how revolutionary early rock 'n' roll was and how stupid and repressed the establishment was that tried to suppress it. But even as the fifties rock revolution was glorified, it was being trivialized: the age of heroism was simultaneously portrayed as an age of utter innocence. While the media told us that we wouldn't be where we were musically if the doo-wop groups hadn't done what they did, they also reminded us that culturally we had long outgrown them and everything they stood for. Even when the media favorably mythologize their historical past, they depict it as distant and primitive. The music industry produces standardized and cartooned histories of the production and consumption of its own standardized and cartooned products—it gives us cartoons of cartoons. These matters require the sort of sustained investigation that Adorno failed to give because of his misconceptions of the dynamics of fashion changes within the music industry.

There is no easy explanation for the rapid turnover of popular music styles. It won't do to appeal to something as facile as planned obsolescence. The automobile industry in its heyday could plan obsolescence, because it had reasonable expectations that any model it produced would garner substantial (if not always profitable) sales—the crucial exception being the Edsel. Thus it could set new styles (and make the old ones obsolete) simply by introducing new models. The record industry works differently. Only 20% of all record albums break even or make a profit, and 60% of all singles are never played by anyone. Obviously, the industry cannot plan for obsolescence when it is uncertain as to which records will sell and which will not. If anything this uncertainty reinforces stylistic conservatism, since in such chaotic circumstances record executives tend to value stability.

Yet this hit-and-miss approach to record production leads quickly to genre exhaustion (and market saturation), and thus subverts stability. Between 1955 and 1959, approximately 125 doo-wop records appeared in the top 40. But for every doo-wop hit, there were hundreds of songs that failed. It is estimated that thousands of doo-wop groups were recruited from the streets to make records, many of which were released on long-forgotten record labels that lasted no more than two years. The Cadillacs were among the most successful of these groups, yet for each of their two modest hits they produced thirty failures. Thus, over a very short period of time, a very large number of qualitatively distinct doo-wop records were produced. Given the imperatives of self-advertising and cartooning, doo-wop, like most forms of popular music, was a highly simplified genre, not open to much variation, and soon the product was exhausted.

## IX.

The central political question about rock 'n' roll today is: who creates the meaning of the rock 'n' roll record? Most rock critics, not surprisingly, fall under the sway of the *auteur* theory. According to them, rock 'n' roll meaning is created primarily by performers, songwriters, arrangers, and producers—that is, the artists most intimately involved in the production of recorded sound. The Birmingham School of Culture Theory in England has provided us with the only recent antidote to that approach. Dick Hebdige, for example, has argued that one cannot understand the meaning of any rock 'n' roll record without situating it within the youth cultures which most typically consume it. In effect, he is telling us that greasers, mods, hippies, and punks "rewrite" the recorded text they consume by recontextualizing it within their practices and rituals.[6] The doo-wop style was not, in terms of its sounds and lyrics, intrinsically threatening to the mid-fifties parent culture. But because it was an important element of the rock 'n' roll revolution along with the music of Little Richard and Elvis Presley, and because rock 'n' roll was first associated with youth underclasses (blacks, greasers, and delinquents), doo-wop acquired a mythical veneer of sex and rebellion.

The Birmingham approach is certainly a refreshing alternative to the reviewers' constant glorification of the artist. Yet it has the same political effect, which is to legitimize rock 'n' roll culture. If either the artist or the consuming community is the primary creator of its meaning, then rock 'n' roll does have the liberatory power so often claimed for it.

Meanwhile, no one is addressing directly the question of the industry's role in the creation of meaning in rock 'n' roll, perhaps because of the difficulties involved. The music industry is really an elaborate complex of many industries—radio, TV, records, publishing, publicity—whose integration is difficult to conceptualize. It is considerably more difficult to articulate theoretically how this convoluted system contributes to the creation of rock 'n' roll meaning—one must combine political economy and semiotics, and there is no established way of doing so. Rock 'n' roll theorists who attend to political economy—and they are few—don't attend to semiotics.[7]

This is where Adorno's work can be of service. With his theory of industrial standardization in music, he combined concepts of both political economy and semiotics, drawing on analogies between the industrially-produced functional artifact and the industrially-produced cultural text. He failed, however, in not being sensitive to the limits of the industrial model. Thus he exaggerated the extent of standardization in popular music, and arrived at the wrong explanations for its occurrence. He paid insufficient attention to sources of musical standardization lying outside the capitalist mode of production. His elitism led him to musical essentialism, and his modernism to a too uncritical stance toward the ideology of aesthetic rebellion and anti-standardization.

Nevertheless, we cannot let Adorno's intolerances and mistaken explanations deter us from attending to the important questions he has raised. No theorist who focuses on rock 'n' roll from the "reception" side claims that youth cultures are capable of completely revamping the meaning of the records they consume. The rock 'n' roll record cannot function for them as an alien object which they may interpret altogether independently of the codes of the dominant culture. There is no doubt that some semantic contribution of the music industry survives the youthful consumers' final rewriting of the rock 'n' roll recorded text. What is at issue is how much survives and whether it undermines the youth subculture's own political contributions. To use Barthesian terms, is the rock 'n' roll record primarily a "readerly" or a "writerly" text?

Perhaps nothing is as resistant to consumer reinterpretation as the standardized forms, sounds, and verbal devices operating at the conventionalized core of the popular song. Because of their intimate association with constant repetition, plugging, and self-advertisement, these standardized components probably evoke the entrenched codes of the dominant culture much more powerfully than do the nonstandardized components. For example, most of the doo-wop songs that are clearly romantic and sentimental in the traditional Tin Pan Alley sense are usually cast in the 32-bar ballad form (with I-vi-ii-V harmony) so characteristic of Tin Pan Alley. The doo-wop songs cast in the blues AAB form are usually more upbeat, more ironic, or more lusty. Here certain standardized forms clearly call forth certain entrenched codes. Did the industrially-generated romantic and sentimental meaning of the doo-wop songs subvert or overcome the sexual and rebellious meaning produced by youth-cultural recontextualization?

There is in sum a constant struggle at the meeting point of production and consumption between the evocation of entrenched codes and the insinuation of alternative meanings. The tendency of the music industry is to employ in the production of musical texts devices, like standardization, that automatically call the dominant codes into play. Recent writers who have focused on reception in popular music have been insufficiently attentive to the power of these devices, and thus have tended to exaggerate the semantic creativity of the consuming subcultures. I believe that a reappraisal of Adorno's work can contribute significantly to the removal of these theoretical deficiencies. To further our understanding of the complex political stances of rock 'n' roll, we must now engage Adorno's productivist approach in a constructive dialogue with the more recent and fashionable reception approaches.

## NOTES

1. Theodor W. Adorno, "On Popular Music" (with the assistance of George Simpson), *Studies in Philosophy and Social Sciences* IX (1941):17–48.

2. See, for examples, Theodor W. Adorno, *Prisms*, trans. Samuel and Shierry Weber (London: Neville Spearman, 1967); *Introduction to the Sociology of Music*, trans. E. B. Ashton (New York: Seabury, 1976).

3. I have in mind Simon Frith, *Sound Effects: Youth, Leisure, and the Politics of Rock 'n' Roll* (New York: Pantheon, 1981); Dick Hebdige, *Subculture: The Meaning of Style* (London: Methuen, 1979); Greil Marcus, *Mystery Train: Images of America in Rock 'n' Roll Music* (New York: Dutton, 1982); Dave Marsh, *Born to Run: The Bruce Springsteen Story* (Garden City, NY: Doubleday, 1979); Robert Christgau, *Any Old Way You Choose It: Rock and Other Pop Music, 1967–1973* (Baltimore: Penguin, 1973); Jon Landau, *It's Too Late to Stop Now* (San Francisco: Straight Arrow, 1972); Ellen Willis, *Beginning to See the Light: Pieces of a Decade* (New York: Knopf, 1981); *The Age of Rock: Sounds of the American Cultural Revolution*, ed. Jonathon Eisen (New York: Vintage, 1969); and Lawrence Grossberg, "I'd Rather Feel Bad Than Not Feel Anything at All: Rock and Roll, Pleasure, and Power," *Enclitic* VIII, nos. 1–2 (Spring-Fall 1984):94–110.

4. See, for example, Simon Frith, *Sound Effects*, pp. 43–48.

5. This line of criticism was suggested to me by John Shepard in John Shepard et. al., *Whose Music? A Sociology of Musical Languages* (London: Latimer, 1977).

6. See, for example, Dick Hebdige, *Subculture*.

7. See, for example, Steve Chapple and Reebee Garofalo, *Rock 'n' Roll is Here to Pay* (Chicago: Nelson-Hall, 1977).

# II.
# STUDIES IN TELEVISION

# 3

# TELEVISION/SOUND

## Rick Altman

With the exception of a few lucid pages by John Ellis, critics have systematically steered clear of TV sound, preferring instead to dwell on narrative, industrial, or image-oriented concerns.[1] Yet a strong case can be made for the centrality of the sound track in the American commercial broadcast system and in other national systems that closely resemble it. In order to develop this hypothesis I shall first examine two received notions of television criticism: the first is Raymond Williams's widely accepted notion of "flow"; the second is the well known contention that broadcast networks compete for viewers, with the ratings of the A. C. Nielsen company charting their rates of success. This analysis will reveal that, in structure and economy, American broadcast television differs from most other national systems. As symptom and vehicle of that difference, the sound track of American television employs numerous strategies for capitalizing on and maintaining the reception configurations and industrial practices particular to American TV. Six of these strategies are detailed later in this article.

I.

For Raymond Williams, "the central television experience [is] the fact of flow."[2] Declining to discriminate between television systems, Williams claims that "in all developed broadcasting systems the characteristic organization, and therefore the characteristic experience, is one of sequence or flow. This phenomenon, of planned flow, is then perhaps the defining characteristic of broadcasting, simultaneously as technology and as a cultural form" (p. 86). Developing a teleological account surprisingly similar to André Bazin's version of cinematic realism,[3] Williams proceeds to outline the seemingly necessary and natural development of flow in British and American broadcast television, stressing "a significant shift from the concept of sequence as programming to the concept of sequence as *flow*" (p. 89). Reflecting ontologically, Williams eventually relates the notion of flow to "the television experience itself" (p. 94), as if the technology itself were sufficient to assure a similarity of situations across cultures and industrial systems.

The notion of flow has already proved to be extremely appropriate to the analysis of American television. I intend to criticize not the notion itself, but the claim that it is characteristic of television in general. I propose that the notion of flow depends on a specific cultural practice of television, that it cannot be properly understood without reference to the parallel notion of household flow, and that the sound track is specifically charged with mediating the relationship between these two flows. Williams himself lays the groundwork for this analysis when he recognizes significant differences between British and American practices, as well as between commercial and public systems. At every point, however, he is content to interpret those differences in terms of the degree of actualization of the medium's true nature. The British are "behind" the Americans, public television lags behind the commercial sector, but all are going in the same direction, because they all partake of the same technologically determined essence.

Looked at from this vantage point, a nascent national broadcasting system providing one program per evening is simply not sufficiently developed to support a fully operative flow; give it time and eventually that flow will appear. But what of those broadcast or cable systems that, unlike the American and British industries on which Williams' analysis depends, impose and maintain programming restrictions which specifically preclude the development of a full-fledged flow?

Two alternative models are quite clear here. Either we explain the difference in level of flow by a difference in the stage of development of a particular television system, as Williams does, or we recognize the extent to which such differences in flow correspond to differences in the function of television as defined by a particular culture. Provisionally, I would suggest the following hypothesis: flow replaces discrete programming to the extent that 1) competition for spectators is allowed to govern the broadcasting situation, and 2) television revenues increase with increased viewing. In short, flow is related not to the television experience itself—because there is no such single experience—but to the commodification of the spectator in a capitalist, free enterprise system. We thus find the lowest level of flow in Eastern Bloc countries where programming is carefully controlled and dispensed in measured doses at appropriate times. In heavily socialized Western European countries like France, where television is produced and programmed by quasi-governmental, quasi-independent institutions, the level of flow is somewhat higher, but it is still clearly limited by state decisions. Television in Britain, which began as it did in France, has succumbed much more rapidly to commercialism. The situation there is still mixed, but as the two BBC channels move closer to emulation of the two commercial stations, and as the system as a whole moves toward imitation of its American counterpart, the coefficient of flow grows apace. Even within the United States, there is a radical difference in flow: networks, which compete openly and directly for spectators, foster a high level of flow, while public channels and local access channels, which have a radically different mission, maintain an entirely different coefficient of flow. But let a big-city public channel become overly aware of its ratings (as in New York, Chicago, or Los Angeles), and the flow begins again.

It should come as no surprise that the countries with the highest level of flow are also those with the most highly developed ratings systems, since flow is linked to profit motives and spectator commodification. Unlike the film industry, which sells programming to audiences, commercial broadcast television sells the audience to advertisers. Just as cinema spawned a complex industry devoted to evaluating the quality and attractiveness of its products, so the commercial television industry has created a method of evaluating first the quantity and then the quality of its product. Cinema's secondary industry concentrates primarily on films themselves, and thus expresses itself largely as newspaper and radio reviews, as Oscars and other awards; television's evaluation service, however, has been more concerned with television's quite different product: the audience itself. Like academic scholarship in the field of television studies, the evaluation of television audiences has been expressed almost exclusively in numeric terms. Of primary importance among evaluation devices are the ratings published by the A. C. Nielsen company. Of course, there has always been some controversy as to what Nielsen actually measures. While Nielsen claims that its meter/diary combination provides a clear picture of the viewing audience, numerous studies have suggested that Nielsen's model of attentive television viewing may need some revision.

Following up earlier studies by Robinson and Allen,[4] many portions of the 1972 Surgeon General's Report on Television and Social Behavior directly address the problem of viewer attentiveness to television programming.[5] Not surprisingly, Foulkes et al. found that eye contact dropped enormously when adolescent boys had an opportunity to enjoy alternative attractions such as games, books, and toys while watching television.[6] LoSciuto found that 34 percent of the programs listed in viewing diaries as "watched" were in fact intermittently watched or only overheard as the respondent engaged in other activities (in order of frequency: work, housework, eating, talking, reading, child care, sewing, personal care, hobbies, and schoolwork).[7]

The most important of these studies involved the videotaping of families who were also asked to respond to questionnaires about their viewing. Conducted by Bechtel et al., this study revealed that for much of the reported viewing time, families were not actually viewing—even though the television might have been on.[8] Expressed as a percentage of the time the set was actually on, the results are still striking: programs were actually watched from 55 percent of the time (commercials) to 76 percent of the time (movies) while the set was on.

This study led the authors to conclude that "globally, the data point to an inseparable mixture of watching and non-watching as general style of television viewing behavior."[9] Indeed, the editor of Volume Four of the Surgeon General's Report, Jack Lyle, felt compelled to add to his introductory comments an appendix reflecting on the continued tendency toward overestimation of viewing time in commercial and academic studies. Attention time is not limited to eye contact time, he pointed out, but surveys continue to act as if it were.[10] Only recently have a few analyses corroborated Lyle's intuitions.[11]

The Nielsen rating system—as well as several current studies on television aesthetics—assumes that active viewing is the exclusive model of spectatorship, yet there is a growing body of data suggesting that intermittent attention is in fact the dominant mode of television viewing. This practice of intermittent spectatorship influences programming decisions and the construction of the sound track. Since network strategists aim not at increasing viewership but at increasing ratings, and since those ratings count operating television sets rather than viewers, the industry has a vested interest in keeping sets on even when no viewers are seated in front of them.

The sound track thus begins to take on an active role. In order to keep those sets operating while all viewers are either out of the room or paying little attention, the sound track must perform some quite specific functions:

1) The auditor must be convinced that the sound track provides sufficient plot or informational continuity even when the image is not visible. For example, it must be possible to follow the plot of a soap opera from the kitchen—or the score of a football game from the bathroom.

2) There must be a sense that *anything really important* will be cued by the sound track. This notion grows in part out of the continued identification of television programming with live presentation; it is at its height during all-day live coverage of such popular events as the Watergate hearings, election returns, or prolonged sporting

events like the Olympics. If we can be assured of being called back for the important moments, then it remains worthwhile to keep the set on even when we cannot remain within viewing distance.

3) There must be recognizable continuity in the type of sound and material presented throughout individual programs or over succeeding programs. Radio stations achieve this by promising the same style of music and/or talk throughout the day. Television does it by sliding from one supposed women's concern to another throughout the day (at least until mid-afternoon, when the children's continuum starts), or from one sport to another on weekend afternoons. While this is mainly a negative criterion (if a break in continuity occurs, the set risks being turned off), it should be recognized that the whole system is predicated on negativity: the goal is not to get anyone to watch the television carefully (as in certain other countries and on my university channel), but to keep people from turning the television off (which is what Nielsen reports, and thus is what determines network income).

4) The sound itself must provide desired information, events, or emotions from time to time during the flow—time of day, weather, school closings, news briefs, prize awards, emotional crises, etc. Even the straight news, sports, and film channels have solved this problem by scheduling updates on a more or less regular basis, or by interrupting one kind of program constantly with a short version of another. The CNN Headline News interspersed throughout regular WTBS programming is the most obvious example of this practice, but the news briefs in the middle of the Olympic coverage and the Olympic updates between standard network favorites are sufficient proof of the generalization of this practice. This principle is as true of fictional programming as it is of real-life reporting. A program featuring silent images of skullduggery, heroism, fainting, true love, naked love, and the naked truth still requires audible evidence of these important occurrences to maintain the interest of the intermittent viewer.

In short, with only one out of two switched-on televisions actually being watched (this is a rough average of the figures advanced by the various studies mentioned above), the sound track becomes the major mode of mediation between what Williams calls "programming flow" and what I will term "household flow" (with the full understanding that this second flow can just as well occur in a bar, a student union, a fraternity house, a doctor's waiting room, or the break room of a factory or business[12]). Earlier, I suggested that the notion of flow is not a natural concomitant of television technology, but the result of a particular consumption configuration. The significance of that rather enigmatic claim is now evident: in a system where the audience is the ultimate commodity, and where the size of the audience is measured not by the number of persons actually watching television but by the number of sets turned on, television must be organized in such a way as to harmonize with the household flow on which it depends. Thus, programming is fragmented into short segments which reflect the limited continuous viewing time of anyone caught up in the household flow. At the same time, renewed emphasis is laid on the message-carrying ability of the sound track, which alone remains in contact with the audience for fully half the time that the set is on. To put it another way, the presence of flow is dependent not on competition between channels, as Williams claims (p. 93), but on *competition with household flow*. In systems where programming flow is minimal, there is a similarly low interplay between the television and the household. In the many national systems where films occupy whole evenings of broadcast programming unencumbered by either intermissions or commercial breaks, the relationship between household flow and television programming is not unlike that which exists between household flow and theatrical film exhibition: when it's time to watch the film, you leave the household behind.[13] Such is decidedly not the mode of television viewing in this country, because the development of programming flow is inseparably linked to the interpenetration of household flow and television programming—a connection which is strongly supported by the tendency of measurement systems to confuse viewers with auditors.[14] The most obvious result of this process is the investment of the sound track with the special responsibility of making sure that no potential auditor turns off the set, thus assuring that the well-known over-reporting of viewing will continue.

## II.

American commercial networks have developed the following six important functions and techniques for the television sound track.

1) *Labeling*. Where competition has led to a high level of flow, the typical television texture is that of the short segment. This is obviously true of commercials, *Good Morning America*, the evening news, variety shows, quiz programs, and the *Wide World of Sports*. It may not be as obvious in narrative fiction programming, but the same fragmentation is nevertheless operative. *Dallas*, for example, is organized not only according to a novelistic hermeneutic, but also around an intricate menu of topics which for some viewers are experienced by character (J.R., Bobby, Sue Ellen, Pam, Cliff, Miss Ellie, etc.), and for others by theme (sex, love, power, etc.). Because it is presented to us as "segmentation without closure," to quote Jane Feuer, *Dallas* does not expect to subordinate all our attention to the linearity, directionality, and teleology of a goal-oriented plot.[15] Instead, it recognizes from the start our desire to choose the objects of our attention on other grounds

as well. Whereas the level of audience attention to a given Hollywood film scene may be roughly dependent on the importance of that scene in resolving the plot's dilemmas, attention to a given *Dallas* scene depends also on the topic and characters present. In recognition of this difference, we might say that attention to classical Hollywood narrative is in large part *goal-driven*, while attention to American television narrative is mainly *menu-driven*. For the spectator firmly planted in front of the television, the menu is made clear by the images. For the half of the audience whose eyes are not glued to the tube, however, the sound track must serve to *label* the menu items.

2) *Italicizing.* In *Visible Fictions*, John Ellis points out that "there is hardly any chance of catching a particular program 'tomorrow' or 'next week sometime' as there is with a cinema film" (p. 111). Whether the events transmitted by television are live or not, the television experience itself is thus sensed as live by the home viewing audience. Just as the camera has to be on the spot to record a live news event, the potential spectator must make sure that her eyes are on the television when something important happens—or risk missing it forever. Paradoxically, this is even more true of a canned fiction program than it is of a live news or sports program; the latter may be covered in the late news, whereas a moving fictional event is lost forever to anyone who fails to return to the screen at the appropriate time. (I suspect that, contrary to expectation, the practice of time-switching by VCR does little to lessen this sense of potential loss. In my experience, time-switching is used not for those programs that are viewed intermittently, but instead for those programs that the viewer is dedicated to watching carefully from beginning to end.)

The characteristically irreversible exhibition situation of broadcast television provides a general link to a wider range of irreversible, unschedulable forms, all of which compensate for the inability to go back and see the same thing over again by ensuring a repetitious, quasi-ritual approximation of sameness in the next material to appear (oral epic and pastoral forms do this, as do the serial novel, the comic strip, and radio and television drama). Television programming itself thus takes on the attributes of irreversible reality. *We* cannot decide when to watch a particular type of programming, nor can we decide when a particular event will occur within a program. We must be attentive to the programming on a non-stop basis in order to make sure that we miss nothing, in the same way that a babysitter automatically monitors the reality of the house and children for which she/he is responsible. Here the italicizing function of the sound track takes over. We cannot always keep our eyes focused on the set, but we have learned to listen for certain sound cues which say, "this is the part you've been waiting for, this is the exciting moment, this is the great play, this is the time when the program you are tuned to delivers up its basic stuff."

The news announcer speaks; his heightened objectivity requires a neutral image—nothing special, nothing unusual, no changes from minute to minute, from day to day, from month to month. But the sound changes constantly—in fact it is for this very change that we are always listening, even when we can't be viewing. But to what end are these verbal italics used? Uniformly, they serve to call us to the image, to let us know that something is happening that we dare not miss; in short, something *spectacular*. The word is well chosen because it reveals the extent to which the italicizing function of sound serves to identify that which is worth *looking at* rather than just hearing. Television contributes directly to a notion of life in which daily events are hardly perceived. Treated as life's uneventful, audible, continuous filler, our daily flow gains meaning only when it points to the spectacular—an event in which by definition we cannot participate, but which, if seen, can give our lives meaning. By italicizing certain parts of each program, the sound track thus leads us back to the image, to the television set itself, and in so doing places us permanently in an aesthetics and an ideology of the spectacular.

3) *The sound hermeneutic.* Sound has a hidden advantage over all other appeals, because in the Western world sound is nearly always taken to be incomplete; it seems to call for identification with a visible source. Television has accustomed us to a high degree of return on our audio-visual investment; we are quite confident that television will show us the source of the sound, if only we rush in from the kitchen fast enough. We are used to the sense of wholeness that this arrangement assures. When we hear a sound, we find its source on the screen, thus giving us a sense of presence, of resolution.

It is revealing to compare this situation to the common film arrangement. In an article in the *Cinema/Sound* volume of *Yale French Studies*, I demonstrated how off-screen sound, or, to be more precise, sound without a visible source (what Michel Chion calls "acousmatic sound"), creates a "sound hermeneutic": the sound asks the question "Where?" to which the image, upon identifying the source, eventually responds "Here!"[16] In other words, the sound track initiates the spectator's involvement, with the camera either complying or not complying with the spectator's desires.

In television, however, the spectator/auditor takes the place of the camera in the sound hermeneutic. When the sound piques my curiosity, I can be nearly sure of satisfaction simply by turning my gaze to the screen. Instead of depending on the camera and the director, who may make me wait to see what is making that noise, I alone exercise control. By raising my eyes and glancing toward the screen

I discover the sound source on my own, thus experiencing the wholeness that it implies.

Unlike film spectators, who rarely have any illusions about their ability to control the film they are watching, television spectators are led to believe that they have power over the image. But in fact the labeling and italicizing that trigger the sound hermeneutic are carefully controlled and follow a prescribed path, thus creating for the TV subject an ideological positioning different from that of the cinema counterpart, one that the illusion of liberty manages to conceal even more fully.

4) *Internal audiences.* When we hear the voice of a favorite star, we turn toward the screen to complete our sense of the star's presence. That star may be an actor, a political personality, a sports hero, or just a cute face in a commercial. In all these cases, we have a degree of control over the kinds of sound we choose to follow to the screen. A far more common situation robs us of that power altogether: what we hear is not a mark of a particular visual presence on the screen, but a sign that someone else thinks an important phenomenon is taking place on the screen. In fact, few techniques have a greater influence on television's overall inner dynamic than the nearly perpetual presence of the internal audience, which is sometimes in the image but is always on the sound track. Commonly, the sound track serves to editorialize even when it is matched with live images. Live sporting events are in fact live images accompanied by a very few live sound effects, with the rest of the sound track devoted to voice-over commentary; even the short snatches of sync-sound dialogues are only relays from the announcer's speech, like direct quotation in a historical novel.

No matter how live the image, the sound continues to serve as presentation, as commentary—in short, as audience to the image. Carrying out its italicizing function, the sound track serves a value-laden editing function, identifying better than the image itself the parts of the image that are sufficiently spectacular to merit closer attention on the part of the intermittent viewer. The operative model for an understanding of television's audio-visual complex is thus not the one which would be appropriate to a truly live presentation of events. It would be reasonable to expect that the spectator at such an event hears and sees both parts of the spectacle simultaneously. In contrast, the TV viewer's vision of the live event is typically filtered through the sound track, which speaks for an interposed interior audience. It is certainly not by chance that this is the preferred arrangement in most studio-shot television: the camera looks over the heads of the studio audience at the spectacle that they are consuming. Whether the sound track carries simultaneously recorded studio applause or only an added laugh track, the sound is engineered to convince us that the applause or laughter emanates from a spot closer to us than the spectacle itself. It is striking to note how often newscasts and sports update programs, not to mention *Good Morning America* and other breakfast shows, include internal monitors, usually located behind the announcer so that the announcer has to look slightly away from the audience in order to see the on-screen monitor. In so doing, the announcer clearly establishes visually the general configuration of TV's internal audience: in order to get to the promised images, we must look over, through, or around an internal spectator who may or may not be seen, but who is always heard, and who is always ready to tell us what we "need to know" about those images.

The most common internal audiences are well-known and frequently used: the newscaster, the sports announcer, the studio audience (or its laugh track substitute), the stadium crowd, the users of advertised products. A more complex situation occurs in the increasingly frequent "location narratives" (as opposed to the "studio narratives" shot with an audience either actually present or implied by the sound track). Adult soaps or action shows, largely restricted to the later prime-time hours, these location narratives look and sound more like Hollywood films than other TV products: with no announcer, no studio audience, and no satisfied consumers built into the sound track, it would seem that they alone of all television programming are utterly devoid of the influence of an internal audience. Yet these programs are often specifically built around a series of highly visible events and characters, for whom other characters serve as an internal audience. In *Dallas*, for example, Ray and Donna play the role of the show's "good conscience," existing more to provide a model moral reaction to J.R.'s shenanigans than to initiate their own activity. J.R.'s various bedmates—especially Merrilee Stone—play the opposite role of gloating over his immorality. Poor, pretty Afton is little more than a constant audience for Cliff Barnes and his ambitious ineptitude.

When a program cannot comfortably fit an internal audience into its own cast, or when greater intensity is needed, music provides the answer. In some ways, the music for location narratives seems to begin where Hollywood leaves off, but we should not be fooled by this surface resemblance. To be sure, both are programmatic, but the path taken by television music is far more commentative, far more likely to identify even the slightest incident for the savvy listener in the next room. The movements of film music are long and general, as compared to television music's attention to every high and low point. Just as the laugh track must guarantee a certain number of laughs per minute, so the music for a location narrative must provide a detailed road map for the housespouse trying to follow the program from the kitchen and unable to rush out for just anything. Though the method is different, the result is the same: the sound track provides an internal audience guiding the viewing choices of the external audience.

5) *The sound advance.* Lodged within the claims I have already made is a significant contradiction. On the one hand, television tends toward live or "live-on-tape" presentation, with internal audiences reacting to internal spectacles in real time; on the other hand, television sound serves to call the intermittent viewer to see either the source of the sound or the reason for its emission. The problem is a simple one: how can the prospective viewer be sure of seeing the spectacle which has caused audience applause when that applause has been caused by an activity which took place before the applause, and which may thus no longer be available to the external audience coming in from the kitchen or looking up from the daily paper? The image performs, the miked audience reacts, but by the time the television audience looks, the spectacle may have disappeared. Logically, this is what should happen, but in fact we often find something quite different. In order to serve its own logic, network television commonly reverses the natural progression. The miked internal audience is made to react, drawing the external audience's attention, before the spectacle is revealed. On the surface of things, this arrangement sounds preposterous. How can the audience react to something it has not seen? It can't, and that's just the point: the internal audience must react to something that *we*, the external audience, have not yet seen. Consequently, there must be a delay between the time when the internal audience witnesses the relevant spectacle and the moment when that spectacle is revealed to the external audience.

In studio recording, this is extremely simple. The most obvious expedient is simply to wave the "APPLAUSE" card in front of the audience just before the emcee appears. A similar result may be obtained by bringing the "star of our show" in from the side, in such a way that the studio audience sees and recognizes him before he is on screen. And what if a panelist were to fall over a microphone cord, eliciting howls of spontaneous laughter from the studio audience? No problem, for as a television-trained actress, the panelist will undoubtedly remain in the undignified position for several seconds, mugging long enough to make sure that the camera—along with the home audience—has picked up her graceless but newsworthy pratfall. Through the use of audience cue cards, clever set designs or mixing patterns, programmatic music, and instant replays, the intermittent viewer is given time to return to the set and witness the excitement, thanks to the fact that the sound is followed, from the point of view of the external audience, by the cause of which it is the effect.

What is the end result of this reversal? What earlier looked like

natural causality (objects make sounds) now takes on a magical air
(reaction produces action). Sound and image are presented back-
wards, transforming the casual auditor into a spectator as well. The
insertion of the auditor into spectatorship, of household flow into
television flow, thus takes place through the reversal of accepted logical and temporal relationships between sound and image. The sound,
which is a reaction, must be recast as a prediction, so that the image
to which I am being called might instead seem to be made especially
for me.

6) *Discursification*. Hollywood narrative film is mainly non-discursive.
It refuses to recognize the presence of the viewer, making that viewer
adopt instead the stance of the voyeur, a stance that depends on a
dependable and continuous level of attention. With TV the audience
is not secure. Television competes with surrounding objects of attention just as the products it advertises do; it is thus far more discursive
as a whole, addressing the audience and involving spectators in dialogue, enjoining them to look, to see, to partake of that which is offered
up for vision.

The use of sound to call the intermittent spectator back to the set
has wide-ranging effects on the discursiveness of sound and image
alike. For the film spectator, Mamoulian's famous dropped vase ex-
plosion in *Love Me Tonight* is a joke, an exaggeration, or a mismatch,
but a similar sound event on television would be a call to return to
the set, a call to switch from sound as *histoire* (the sound tells me what's
happening) to sound as *discours* (the sound tells me to look in order
to find out what's happening). In a similar way, American TV news
has moved increasingly toward the presentational, merging a primary
level composed of a neutral announcer image and a highly charged
presentational sound with a secondary level composed of a highly
charged image and tributary sound. The truth is thus recognized,
paradoxically, as double: the announcer tells us the truth ("Today Mt.
Elba erupted again, producing a lava flow which destroyed two vil-
lages, cut three roads, and took at least ten lives"), but that is historic
truth, an event which took place elsewhere involving others, and which
thus does not involve us. But if I could see the events, if they could
be reoriented from their historic position into a new slant where they
would be played for me, then they would change form and function,
becoming part of a discursive circuit. The deeper, paradoxical truth
of our television is this discursification of the world. It is not that
seeing is believing (an earlier assumption of TV audiences), but that
images collected just for us give us a sensation that no flat, historical
account could possibly give. And only the prior announcement on the
sound track can make those images seem to be made just for us.

The instant replay is perhaps the ultimate example of this discursive
syndrome. Suppose I'm in the kitchen getting a beer. Suddenly I hear

cheering and an announcer screaming about the utter perfection of the throw and the acrobatic grace of the catch. Up until this point, the players have been playing to win, i.e., for themselves, according to the objective, impersonal rules of the game. They may showboat from time to time for the stadium crowd or even for the telespectator, but when they are playing, their actions are primarily aimed at disarming and defeating the opponent. Now, when the crowd roars, I rush from the kitchen to catch the end of the play, but of course it is over, done, gone forever as a play. But the instant replay saves the day. It shows *me* exactly what *I* just came from the kitchen to see. With multiple cameras and variable slow motion, it seeks out the most extraordinary angle, or the one view that reveals the offensive interference that made the catch possible. The replay thus stands in the same relationship to the play as the process of representation has to the present. Formless, uninterpreted, lacking in direction, the present takes on its meaning—its "for-me-ness"—only in the process of re-presentation. The memory of television is thus not the memory of a whole game, but the combination of a certain liberty of circulation (beer, phone, john, newspaper, etc.) with the paradoxical knowledge that the game is summed up for me in the right shot at the right time.

Strikingly, the sync sound that called me to the set has disappeared by the time the instant replay appears; the sound has spent itself in calling the wandering spectator. By bringing a specially made image together at this specific time with a spectator especially desirous of seeing that very image, the sound has succeeded in involving both the spectator and the image in the discursive circuit which it directs. On the one hand the TV flow, on the other the household flow. Only when the sound track succeeds in bringing image and spectator together do they fulfill their mission. Charged with calling me to the image, the sound track uses every weapon at its disposal: labeling, italicizing, the sound hermeneutic, internal audiences, sound advance. But the ultimate argument, as well as the final goal, remains the notion, fostered continually by the sound track, that the TV image is manufactured and broadcast just for me, at precisely the time that I need it.

## NOTES

I want to express my appreciation to Sam Becker, Eileen Meehan, and Paul Traudt, colleagues at the University of Iowa who helped initiate me into the bibliography of what was for me a new field.

1. John Ellis, *Visible Fictions: Cinema, Television, Video* (London and Boston: Routledge and Kegan Paul, 1982), especially chapter eight, "Broadcast TV as Sound and Image," pp. 127–44.

2. Raymond Williams, *Television: Technology and Cultural Form* (New York: Schocken, 1974), p. 95.

3. For a critique of Bazin's approach to film history, see Jean-Louis Comolli, "Technique et idéologie: caméra, perspective, profondeur de champ," in *Cahiers du cinéma*, (May–June 1971 ff.):229, 230, 231, 233, 234–35, 241.

4. John P. Robinson, "Television and Leisure Time: Yesterday, Today and (Maybe) Tomorrow," *Public Opinion Quarterly* 33 (1969):210–22; C. L. Allen, "Photographing the TV Audience," *Journal of Advertising Research* 5 (March 1968):2–8.

5. *Television and Social Behavior*. A Technical Report to the Surgeon General's Scientific Advisory Committee on Television and Social Behavior, ed. Eli A. Rubinstein, George A. Comstock, and John P. Murray (Washington, DC: U. S. Government Printing Office, 1971).

6. D. Foulkes, E. Belvedere, and T. Brubaker, "Televised Violence and Dream Content," *Television and Social Behavior*, vol. 5, pp. 59–119.

7. Leonard A. LoSciuto, "A National Inventory of Television Viewing Behavior," *Television and Social Behavior*, vol. 4, pp. 33–86.

8. Robert B. Bechtel, Clark Achelpohl, and Roger Akers, "Correlates between Observed Behavior and Questionnaire Responses on Television Viewing," *Television and Social Behavior*, vol. 4, pp. 274–344.

9. Ibid., p. 298. It is important to note that this study includes as "watchers" many individuals who are simultaneously involved in other activities, thus suggesting a possible overestimation of active viewers. The categories used are 1) participating, actively responding to the TV set or to others regarding content from the set; 2) passively watching; 3) simultaneous activity (eating, knitting, etc.) while looking at the screen; 4) positioned to watch the set but reading, talking or attending to something other than television; 5) in the viewing area of the TV but positioned away from the set in a way that would require turning to see it; 6) not in the room and unable to see the set or degree of impact of visual content. Categories 1–3 are considered "watching" while categories 4–6 are considered nonwatching. It is instructive to compare this approach to the more traditional categories offered by Jon Baggeley and Steve Duck in *Dynamics of Television* (Westmead, England: Saxon House, 1976). Their *lowest* level of attention, "at which there is a totally passive involvement in the imagery's simple novelty value" (p. 68), corresponds to level two in the scheme of Bechtel et al., who list no less than *four* lower levels of attention.

10. Jack Lyle, "Television in Daily Life: Patterns of Use Overview," *Television and Social Behavior*, vol. 4, pp. 26–28.

11. A convenient review of this literature is available in George Comstock, Steven Chaffee, Natan Katzman, Maxwell McCombs, and Donald Roberts, *Television and Human Behavior* (New York: Columbia University Press, 1978), pp. 141–72. In addition, see especially Helen Leslie Steeves and Lloyd R. Bostian, *Diary Survey of Wisconsin and Illinois Employed Women*, Bulletin 41 (Madison: University of Wisconsin-Extension, 1980). The data collected by this study, which suggests that working women view television without engaging in some simultaneous activity only 35.2 percent of their "viewing" time, serve as a base for a forthcoming article by Samuel L. Becker, H. Leslie Steeves, and Hyeon C. Choi, entitled "The Context of Media Use." See also the various reports of Television Audience Assessment, Inc., an alternative to Nielsen's and Arbitron's Audimeter approach established by the Markle Foundation in 1979 with the help of the Ford Foundation. According to a preliminary report, 49 percent of the total audience surveyed reported additional activities during

"viewing" time; 42 percent of those reported that they were distracted from viewing by their major additional activity, even though only prime-time viewing was surveyed. See Elizabeth J. Roberts and Peter J. Lemieux, *Audience Attitudes and Alternative Program Ratings: A Preliminary Study* (Cambridge, MA: Television Audience Assessment, 1981). Perhaps the best reflection of intermittent viewing from a fictional point of view is provided by Michael J. Arlen's short story "Good Morning," in *The View from Highway 1* (New York: Ballantine Books, 1976), pp. 13–19. Part of the historical context of early network strategies for promoting intermittent viewing patterns is included in an unpublished paper by William Boddy, "The Shining Center of the Home: Ontologies of Television in the 'Golden Age.' " Boddy points out the extent to which intermittent radio listening served as an early model for television spectatorship.

12. On television viewing outside the home, see the work of Dafna Lemish, "The Rules of Viewing Television in Public Places," *Journal of Broadcasting* 26 (Fall 1982):757–82, and *Viewing Television in Public Places: An Ethnography*, unpublished dissertation, Ohio State University, 1982.

13. Available cross-cultural data strongly support this claim. In *The Use of Time: Daily Activities of Urban and Suburban Populations in Twelve Countries*, ed. Alexander Szalai (The Hague: Mouton, 1972), Robinson and Converse report the following figures, which I have regrouped into broad political/economic categories:

|  | Total minutes daily viewing | Viewing as primary activity | Viewing as secondary activity | Secondary activity as a percentage of total |
|---|---|---|---|---|
| Eastern Europe | 59 | 51 | 8 | 14 |
| Western Europe | 88 | 70 | 18 | 21 |
| USA | 129 | 92 | 37 | 29 |

Though these figures were collected in the late sixties, and thus need updating, they clearly suggest a positive correlation between intermittent viewing and the American advertising-oriented, ratings-based model which Western Europe has resisted only in part. It should be noted that in the case of simultaneous activities not identified hierarchically by respondents, this survey classifies half of each activity as primary, half as secondary, thus assuring an *overestimation* of viewing as a strictly primary activity. For information on data collection guidelines, see Robinson, "Television and Leisure Time," pp. 210–22.

14. Just as I have argued against including all television systems in a single and undifferentiated "television experience," I would argue that American broadcast television must be broken down into appropriate time sectors, each corresponding to a different level of competition with household flow. As early as 1945, a CBS publication on *Television Audience Research* (New York: CBS, 1945), argued that "Television's daytime programs . . . can be constructed so that full attention will not be necessary for their enjoyment. Programs requiring full attention of eye and ear should be scheduled for evening hours when viewers feel entitled to entertainment and relaxation" (p. 6). The Allen study mentioned in note four provides the following data, broken down into daily time sectors:

|                                         | Total | Morning | After-noon | Evening |
|-----------------------------------------|-------|---------|------------|---------|
| Hours set in use per week               | 31.8  | 3.5     | 9.7        | 18.6    |
| Non-viewing with set in use             | 12.8  | 1.8     | 4.5        | 6.5     |
| Non-viewing as percentage of time set is in use | 40    | 52      | 47         | 35      |

The period with the lowest percentage of intermittent viewing thus corresponds both to the period of lowest competition with household flow (children in bed, housework done) and to the period characterized by the highest quotient of self-contained, goal-driven narrative programs. The daytime hours, which reveal a markedly higher rate of intermittent viewing, are traditionally associated with female and children viewers. Szalai et al. report that viewing TV as a secondary activity is more than twice as frequent for American housewives (38%) as it is for employed men (18%). More recently, Roberts and Lemieux identify women aged 18–39 as the group least likely to give a program full attention (only 31% of women 18–39 remained in the room throughout a full program). What is shocking about these figures is the fact that Roberts and Lemieux conducted all surveys *in prime time only* (thus missing the periods of high intermittent viewing by women) and that Szalai et al. report that 36% of all TV viewing by *employed* women is secondary to some other activity—just 2% less than for housewives. These figures point to two related but nevertheless separate phenomena in American broadcasting and its consumption:

1) network programming choices are carefully correlated with household flow patterns, producing a coefficient of television flow which, while remaining high as compared to other national systems, decreases during evening hours.

2) cultural patterns have created a substantially higher level of intermittent viewing for female adults than for male adults.

Both of these hypotheses call for further research, perhaps along the lines of Tania Modleski's "The Rhythms of Reception: Daytime Television and Women's Work," in *Regarding Television: Critical Approaches—An Anthology*, ed. E. Ann Kaplan (Frederick, MD: University Publications of America, 1983), pp. 67–75.

15. Jane Feuer, "The Concept of Live TV: Ontology as Ideology," *Regarding Television*, pp. 15–16.

16. Rick Altman, "Moving Lips: Cinema as Ventriloquism," *Yale French Studies* 60 (1980):67–79; Michel Chion, *La voix au cinéma* (Paris: *Cahiers du Cinéma*/Editions de l'Etoile, 1982).

# 4

# THE TELEVISION NEWS PERSONALITY AND CREDIBILITY

## *REFLECTIONS ON THE NEWS IN TRANSITION*

## Margaret Morse

Television remains the most credible of the media no matter how public opinion is measured. This credibility is distinctly television's own making. . . . And at its heart are two features embodied in television—the visual coverage of events and the display of news personnel. These two are the reasons most frequently advanced by those who rate television as first in credibility. Those who rate newspapers first cite different reasons, such as completeness of coverage. This discrepancy hints not at difference on a single standard but the application of two different sets of values. Before television, no one would have attached such notions to credibility. Experience with television may be slowly reshaping the public's concept of truthfulness in news.

—George Comstock in
*Television in America*

### News from Somewhere

The news is a privileged discourse, invested with a special relation to the Real. In our mobile, fragmented society, it also performs a cohesive function, linking people together and connecting the isolated

and increasingly deinstitutionalized private realm of experience to the
public world outside. Thus the news has become an indispensable
ideological tool in modern Western societies; in the United States it
is considered to be "a staple of democracy." Though other news media
still play a more important role than television in conveying information, television news serves as the symbol of the news per se and
as an indicator of public attention to issues of concern to American
society. In order to function as a cohesive social force, the news must
above all be worthy of belief. In the decades since the advent of news
programming on television, the news has undergone a significant
change in the forms and values which maintain its credibility. In this
essay I locate these changes in a shift that has occurred in the balance
between objective and subjective modes of the construction of the
news. In critical discourse, only the journalistic, objective model of
the news is legitimized, while news in a subjective mode is generally
considered nothing but an aberration or degradation of news values,
deplored as "show biz," "glitz," and "glitter" atypical of the news
profession.[1] However, news in a subjective mode can have a far more
powerful impact on what we perceive as "real" than the old news based
on print.

## I. A Shift Away from Objective Forms:
### The Construction of a Subject of the News

The difference between television news and the print news of the
past lies in the answer to the question, "who is speaking?" Print news
developed a mode of narration, a style, and content which suppressed
the subjective origin of the news "story" in favor of a "reality" which
seemed to possess a voice of its own. Although television news grew
out of, and still offers allegiance to, this older mode of address—what
in linguistic theory is called "story"—it has gradually developed its
own mode of address, resembling "discourse." "Discourse," in the
words of Emile Benveniste, is "every utterance assuming a speaker
and a hearer, and in the speaker, the intention of influencing the
other in some way. [It comprises] all the genres in which someone
proclaims himself as the speaker and organizes what he says in the
category of person."[2]

In the course of the historical development of print news, an ideology of objectivity or impartiality transformed what were at one time
reports from and for particular interest groups into "objective reports"
addressed to the general public and accepted as general knowledge.
Since the 1830s *the news* as a singular rather than plural notion has
been commonplace in America[3]; since then there have been many
newspapers but only one *news*. Along with criteria for the content of

news stories (balance, fairness, etc.), commensurate social roles (i.e., the reporter) and techniques (i.e., interviewing sources) were developed. These techniques for producing "objective contents" were supported and made possible by the earlier technological innovations of print and an "objective" narrative mode (used in courts of law as well as in novels) in which the person of the narrator was suppressed as far as possible. Stories seemed to come from nowhere.

The Word and the Image were able to assume objective authority because of the separation of the speaker from the message and its transmission through the automated processes of the press and camera. Even the voice, that prime instrument of human subjectivity, seemed to come from some transcendent source in radio news. It was ghostly, disembodied, and specially cadenced to achieve an exalted tone.[4] The newsreel, though an audio-visual form like television, obeyed rules for presenting the news that were quite unlike those later developed for television. On the newsreel team, the cameraman had primacy, reporters were invisible workers behind the scenes, and the public smiled and performed self-consciously for the lens. The source of the newsreel's authority was the visual presentation of an event, supplemented with a booming voice-over narration.

Today it does not seem strange to us to have a triumvirate of network anchors or "national" news broadcasts. Nor does the host of conventions governing the format of television news seem strange. The emotional keys lent to the newsreel by music and post-synchronized sound effects, for example, have been virtuously expunged from television news, while presenters have become visible and the public has been prohibited from looking at the camera.

No longer a report issuing from apparently anonymous processes, television news appears to emanate from a limited and well-defined set of familiar subjects, or "anchors," who have earned our trust through the display of various qualities and through the regularity and intimate circumstances of their appearance on television.[5] The term "anchor" came out of the 1952 presidential conventions, where it was borrowed from the name of the strongest runner of a relay team, the anchorman, who runs the final leg of the race. The name, however, suggests "stationary positioning,"[6] and indeed the anchor centers the discourse of the news and himself occupies a zero-degree of deviation from the norm. But anchors do not merely deliver or report the news (what Eliseo Veron calls "the ventriloquist model").[7] They have become personalities who seem to be responsible for its enunciation. Among all the news personalities, the three network anchors are the supersubjects of the news as a totality and possess a national role and identity. Thus, as Jessica Savitch put it, "anchors have become as newsworthy as the stories and personalities they cover"[8]—a notoriety attained by "newsreaders" in European television as well.

This was not always the case. As Barbara Matusow has pointed out, anchoring evolved from "relatively humble figures who read the news"—such as John Cameron Swayze on *The Camel News Caravan* and Douglas Edwards on *World Tonight*—to a "pantheon of individuals who profoundly influence the world in which we live."[9] The newsreader of the past could be a humble figure because the reader's authority came from the paper, and from the transcendent source which wrote ("printed") on it. In several European countries, television has retained newsreaders "who make no pretense of involvement with the material they read," thereby "de-emphasizing personality" (Matusow, p. 51). In some instances, different individuals will read on different days so that the public does not come to associate the news with a single source.

By contrast, not only is the American network anchor responsible for the unity of the news because of his own familiar presence; he is, according to Walter Cronkite, "the only person who really knows what is in the broadcast."[10] Furthermore, he has gradually emancipated himself from the authority of the page and adopted a discourse of his own.[11] Today it seems as though the anchor speaks on his own authority as an overarching presence, as a subject of the news who vouches for its truth.

The symbolic position from which the anchor speaks influences the construction of our cultural values. According to Walter Cronkite, "We must be able without reference to written works to pull from our heads the background of a given story, complete with the historical reference when relevant. We have to balance the moral and the immoral, the acceptable and the grossly inappropriate, the acceptable and the offensive, the right and the wrong even as facts are tumbling in upon us, and there are no second guesses."[12] The network anchor is required to know all the facts, and to be able spontaneously to place information in a generally valid value system; the anchor's role is that of a general subject, rather than a particular individual. The knowledge required is no longer simply the knowledge of or acquaintance with the "facts," which had been part of the reporter's cloak of objectivity, but seems now to include the knowledge of personal experience and enlightenment in a way that blurs the distinction between the two.

Unlike local news personalities, who comprise a "team" representing parts of the community in terms of gender, ethnicity, and race and who are individually responsible for just parts of the news, the network anchor is a supersubject by himself. He is not merely the representative of the news per se, or a particular network, or television as institution, or the public interest; rather, he represents the complex nexus of all of them. The network anchor has thus become a "symbolic representation of the institutional order as an integrated totality,"[13] an institutional role on a par with that of the president or of a supreme court justice, although it originates in corporate practices rather than political or judicial processes.

The network anchor is a very special variety of star—subdued, constructed through reduction and simplification, and authorized to speak the truth. The influence of the "evening star" seems personal, but it is really positional. The backlighting, the desk in a place "above the world," and the relay center—the exchanges between the anchor, reporters and public (which will be described in more detail later)—all enhance his credibility.[14] As is well known, the position of the network anchor as "enunciator" of the news has come to be extremely well-paid, reflecting the value of the image of the news personality as a commodity. However, in line with its somewhat sacred character and the "positional" source of its power, its value is not freely exchangeable. As Walter Cronkite put it in a television interview with Barbara Walters, the personal influence of the anchor can't be " 'cashed in' without casting doubt forevermore on all newspeople as to whether they are telling you the truth on the evening news, whether their integrity is intact, or whether they are building a base to eventually run for office."

Though his influence is positional, the anchor must be seen as a subject, one who "speaks the truth as he sees it" with inner conviction; otherwise, he would lack the charisma required for the impression of credibility.[15] In our effort to understand the significance of news delivered by a subject, linguistic theory helps by identifying the two kinds of news—objective and subjective—as messages in which two different modes of enunciation predominate. The anchor, or "I," as the subject of the audio-visual news message, is analogous to the "I" in a sentence: we see him in the television image and we hear him tell the stories and invite reporters to deliver their news "packages." Yet he "enunciates" the news only in the most literal sense of the word (we see his lips move and we hear his voice). The act of enunciating the news is actually performed by an entourage of news professionals, as well as by the TV producer and crew. The network anchor is the visible representative of this speaking collective subject (in television terms the anchor is "talent"). The anchor as "talking head" is the link between the message or utterance and the enunciation of the news. Interestingly enough, the part of the news consisting of "tell stories" was called "the magic" by Walter Cronkite. Indeed, it is the speaking subject *in* the news message that performs the "magic" of binding so many elements and cultural institutions together to form a coherent "reality."

Thus, the talking head represents an individual who is the subject of enunciation of 1) *the news*, 2) his own interiority, 3) the respective television networks, and 4) the *public* and its interest in the surveillance of government, the economic sphere, and the natural world.[16] The swivel chair which shifts the anchor's gaze to other news personalities and to the viewer is matched by a central subject of enunciation swiveling between institutions.

Though the national network television news format is a contradictory mixture of subjective and objective modes of news presentation, subjective news values—the results of news personalities presenting themselves as believable subjects—now dominate. (The phenomenon also plays an increasingly important role in print).[17] This shift toward the subjective is unlikely to be easily reversed, since the fiction of objective news has itself become problematic in the general decline of the legitimacy of objectivity as an ideology.[18] The basis for the construction and legitimation of objective news has been undermined by twentieth-century revolutions in science and philosophy, which have tended to deny the very possibility of truth and objectivity. Even at the level of common sense, the general public seems to believe that partisan values and particular interests lurk beneath the professional institutional practices of news organizations. Oddly enough, the answer of subjective news to this charge is to make the "impression of credibility" evoked by the newsman himself the guarantee of truth. Yet whatever doubts have surfaced about the news, there remains a sense not only that we need the news, but that we also need to believe in it. The construction of a supersubject of the entire news discourse— innocent, all-knowing, and sincere—begins with a visible subject of enunciation of the news *in* the news narration. What are the sources of credibility invoked by that subject?

## II. Credibility and Being Here: Anchors as Paracletes[19]

The gaze of the news personality is directed at the camera, as if in face-to-face contact with the viewer. Carolyn Diana Lewis reports that the newscaster is directed as follows:

> "Relate your story in a direct, intimate and conversational manner. When you look into the camera, you have to believe that it is not a camera at all, not a dead object like a stone or a building, but something alive. If you look and see only a dead camera, your eyes will develop a glazed look that can set up a barrier between you and the viewer. However, if you can see a living viewer in your mind's eye and speak *to* him instead of *at* him, you will find the right tone for reaching him."[20]

What the news personality—anchor, reporter, or commentator— recreates on the impersonal television screen is the first order of social reality, the face-to-face situation.

In *The Social Construction of Reality*, Peter Berger and Thomas Luck-mann write, "The most important experience of others takes place in the face-to-face situation, which is the prototypical case of social inter-action. In the face-to-face situation the other is fully real. This reality is part of the overall reality of everyday life, and as such massive and compelling. . . . Indeed, it may be argued that the other in the face-to-face situation is more real to me than I myself" (p. 29). This face-to-face reality "imposes itself upon consciousness in the most massive, urgent and intense manner"—a here and now of the body and the present, an intersubjective world objectified by language. "Reality," however monolithic it may appear to us, is a constructed, relative, and fragile objectification with which a subject precariously and incom-pletely identifies. There are also different levels of this "reality": Ber-ger and Luckman argue that if face-to-face conversation is the primary social reality, it is also the primary means of "reality mainte-nance"(p.21).

The news as subjective, spoken by a person *to* me, adopts the form of this paramount reality, obscuring the boundaries between everyday life and mediated or "secondary experience." (By comparison, the news in print is a more distanced symbolic legitimation of "reality," a secondary ordering process of naming, filling in gaps, and establishing hierarchies. It is at its most "real" as the impersonal printed page which accompanies breakfast or the morning commute.) Face-to-face conversation seems more real than objective news stories; it is also subject to different truth conditions: since discourse is not represen-tation—a mode of the real—but an act in reality itself, the news as discourse enjoys a different linguistic and, by implication, ontological status. The referent of discourse is itself; its own time, place, and subjects are its "reality." Thus, it is not subject to the same verification as the referent of a story or even of a photograph, a represented world. Face-to-face conversation need not match or resemble "re-ality"—it *is* reality.

Moreover, this reality can seem to possess spiritual resources, par-ticipating in the realm of what the theologian Martin Buber calls the "I-Thou." We might speculate that the news personality, as a trans-parent soul addressing the viewer face-to-face, draws upon a powerful cultural potential for a reality of spiritual communion. Of course, this differs from the I-Thou situation, which occurs in a shared place and time, in that the viewer's own subjectivity is inhibited. As a result, the subject who speaks to the viewer face-to-face on television may even seem more "real" than the viewer seems to him/herself. Since the newscaster is not actually present, the conversation is one-way; there is no actual feedback, and no recognition of the immediate experience or concerns of the viewer—reciprocity is impossible. However, television news has evolved various ways of creating the impression of "being here," in the virtual time and space of language realized between subjects. The telecaster is not *here*, but the impression of presence is created through the construction of a shared space, the impression of shared time, and signs that the speaking subject is speaking for himself, sincerely.

*Shared space.* The actual space of the telecast production—the image on the screen—and that of the viewer are absolutely separate from each other. But the newscaster's direct gaze and lips talk to a position which is not anchored in material space (the camera lens in the studio), but in a virtual relation in discourse. The anchor's shifts of gaze between the viewer, other newscasters, and sources play the role of linguistic shifters such as "I" and "you"; shifters "do not refer to 'reality' or to 'objective' positions in space and time but to the utterance, unique in each time, that contains them" (Benveniste, p. 219). The stare of the newscaster is directed at the position which can be filled by any viewer.

The visual field has shifted the balance toward discourse by means of the direct gaze and the "magic" of lips speaking the words of the news. The anchor's utterance is an assembly of mismatched parts—the language, narrative, and news voice are inherited from objective news and linked to a fictitious discursive performance and phantom subjective presence. The material of TV news still originates in the impersonal print world of news syndicates, and so does its language. Though TV news narrative affects an oral style, it is still written—and it is usually far pithier, more clearly structured, and more conclusively stated than is true conversational style. The language of the news is still largely narrative, suppressing the use of "I" and "you" in favor of third-person statements (along with an occasional "we"). It is an impersonal language, delivered in a heightened "news voice" borrowed originally from radio. Furthermore, television news is read.

On the other hand, it is read *as if it were not read*, as if it originated spontaneously with the newscaster in conversation with the viewer. This convention clouds the distinction between the newscaster in his official role as reporter and the newscaster as a person who speaks for himself; rather than simply reporting the news as a mouthpiece for other agencies, the newscaster seems to "know" the news in the sense of personal knowledge.

*Shared time.* The sense of a "present" discourse is created primarily by the representation of moving lips "producing" the news message as it is uttered. We see that the time of the act of enunciation *as represented* in the utterance is equivalent to the time of the utterance or message itself; in this sense, television news is "live."

There are degrees of "liveness." For example, the news report which is uttered, transmitted and received simultaneously as the news event happens ("real time reporting") seems the most "live." (The term "liveness" also connotes that such a report is less edited and therefore less censored and more credible.) But even if that "live" report were taped and transmitted an hour, a day or even years later, the report remains "live" in a self-referential sense, i.e., the time of the act of enunciation and of the utterance coincided in a present tense when the report was originally produced. It also retains the credibility of spontaneous utterance. "Live" does not necessarily mean that the act of reporting has to be simultaneous with the event reported or with the reception of the report. In any specific news show, the anchor speaking in the studio adds a crucial element of "liveness" to events already in the past tense—even if the transmission of his performance is delayed for viewers in other time zones. Ultimately, the time of the act of enunciation as it took place in actuality is not as important as the virtual shared time created by the news utterance itself. The one crucial element is the presence of a subject *in the utterance* shown speaking the words issuing simultaneously from our television set "to us."

The temporal referent is not time in the world (note that dates are seldom used in TV news), but time in relation to the time of speaking (today, yesterday, tomorrow). Stories in the past are enclosed and related to the present of the utterance (in a photo, for example, there is a significant temporal gap between the time of the event and the time of its photographic presentation to the viewer, the conjunction of here/now, there/then of which Roland Barthes wrote; it is this gap which the image of moving lips bridges). The ideology of "liveness," which Jane Feuer has examined in relation to television as a whole,[21] is based not only on the electronic technology of simultaneous recording and transmission, but also on virtual forms of discourse that were once realizable only in conversation sustained by a community in contiguous space and "real" time.

*Sincerity.* The chief test of the truth of discourse (as opposed to the truth of representations) is whether or not the utterance is sincere. Does I = I, that is, does the subject of enunciation match the subject of the utterance? Does the subject believe what he/she says? Sincerity is a difficult achievement, signifying a congruity of interior mental life with external expression. Conclusions about sincerity can be based only on observable characteristics, behavior which lends the impression of credibility. These primarily non-verbal signs are thought of as transparent: the news personality must be charismatic as well as sincere, seeming to offer through personal magnetism and this transparency of subjectivity spontaneous access to what Victor Turner calls "*communitas*": "a realm of direct, immediate and total confrontations of human identities."[22]

Sincerity then is the unification of social role and personal belief, as well as the unification of the speaking subject and the subject in the sentence which our own twentieth-century cultural experience tells us is *imaginary*. But these subjects of knowledge and belief, of speaker and language, and of person and a social role are not only different—they can never coincide. Even the most successful socialization is incomplete; social roles are never exactly equivalent to personal identities. Psychoanalysis, too, tells us of the split-subject, of the gap between the conscious and the unconscious, between the self and the "I" of language. The news as institution, however, does not admit this disparity (which, to use Lionel Trilling's terms, would mean being "authentic" rather than "sincere"). It posits instead a subject who embodies "a shared viewer fantasy, a collective need"[23] for what has come to be, according to former CBS President Richard Wald, "the traditional sense of what an anchorman is: in effect, the all-wise, all-seeing mouth, that person who knows everything and will tell it to you. That person never really existed. . . ."[24] That person may be constructed, however, and will function to maintain the cohesive cultural fictions which are held as knowledge, serving as "the one who believes" in the news so that we can offer belief despite our better knowledge.

This all-seeing, all-knowing, god-like person is, of course, male and white. White women, and men and women of other races—except for a brief sojourn by Max Robinson on a three-man ABC team and a team-up of Barbara Walters with Harry Reasoner—are left to the margins of the morning and the nightly news. Instead, the current anchors are, in the words of an ex-President of a cable news network, "all three tall, white, Anglo-Saxon Protestants with dark hair coiffed very carefully, thin faces with an intelligent look. You know it's Tom, Dan and Peter. . . . Sometimes I think they're all the same guy. They must move from studio to studio."[25] The anchors also display a very restricted range in sartorial codes: "When they took over their forebears' swivel chairs, they borrowed their old suits as well.—'You must remember, they are in a job of information and credibility that unfortunately allows them narrow fashion parameters.' "[26] The acting codes are similarly restricted and subdued, a careful balance of patriarchal authority and middle-aged accessibility.[27] Some slight bemusement and irony are allowed (think of John Chancellor or David Brinkley), but the distance created is from the world itself, not from the news discourse. The effect is to create a collusive understanding with the viewer and intensify the discursive force of the presentation.

The problem with making personality the basis for the construction of reality (and social control) is that the news then depends on particular people. These people become the legitimate bearers of general knowledge as types and occupiers of an institutional role. The "magic" of the anchor position virtually guarantees a god-like aura—but the position is filled, naturally, by ordinary men. That ordinariness is not the Achilles heel, but another source of the "reality" of the anchor: he is a real and accessible person who "knows everything and will tell it to you." If "that person never really existed," he is *here* nevertheless.

### III. Credibility and Disavowal in Television News: "Display of News Personnel" and "the Visual Coverage of Events"

Knowing the news in the sense of being acquainted with it and knowing it in the sense of accepting its truth value are not the same. Both knowledge of the news and belief in it are promoted by a chain of fictions in which news personalities and television viewers collude. The "truth" of the news is generally thought of in terms of its referential value: how well does it match events in the world? A prime example of such referential proof is the news photograph, which provides evidence that "looks like" the event (iconic evidence) and which indicates that someone was there (indexical evidence). Symbolic messages, conveyed in words and other conventional symbols, are not as convincing in this sense, because they refer to the system of shared meanings in our culture more strongly than they do to the world "out there." Although the visual aspects of the news can relate to the world in any of these ways, we tend to think of these aspects as iconic, resembling the "really" real.

"Objectivity" in the news is produced by a set of techniques which are meant to render the news utterance, and the subjectivity of the person who utters it, as transparent as possible, so as to show the world "out there" in the most accurate and unbiased manner. We have already examined how the subjectivity of the news reporter, regarded as a source of bias in objective news values, can both be a source of "reality" and possess a truth value. To attach "the reality of discourse" to television, however, requires a willing suspension of disbelief on the part of the audience in several areas relating to the visual display of news personnel.

If psychoanalysis tells us of the split-subject, it also tells us of the split-belief—our capacity to believe and not believe at the same time, a necessary capacity particularly in reading fiction. Analogously, "artificial innocence" is necessary in believing the news. It is, of course, unlikely that anyone believes completely in the news; socialization is never *that* successful. Instead, we bring a degree of belief to it, and even that belief is tempered by some recognition of the constructed nature of the news, and of its possible special interests. We offer news a split-belief, divided between an identification of the news with the imaginary (a regression to an earlier state of neutral life in which signs were identified with the things themselves) and a recognition of its symbolic nature.[28] This mixed state of mind is known as disavowal; a good indication of it is the expression, *I know . . . but nevertheless.*[29]

The points in the news which are "imaginary," and thus necessitate disavowal, include the following: the creation in the image of the news personality of a "symbolic representation of the institutional order as an integrated totality" (Berger and Luckmann, p. 76; I have already discussed this); the disavowal of the real barrier of the television screen; the existence of the fourth wall or imaginary line of demarcation *within* the represented space on the screen; the acceptance of the visual coverage of events as a reservoir of "objective" news values; and the coherence of the news discourse, which is largely an effect of the relays between news personalities.

*The real barrier of the TV screen.* The first disavowal is of the machine, the television set itself, which, like print, is impersonal. The personal element is available to us only as an image and a voice, a talking head on the screen. To make that image a presence, we must disavow the glass screen of the television (or the camera as mediator in the studio) as an absolute barrier between the public world in the news and the private realm in which we receive it. In the cinema, the screen acts as a fourth wall or imaginary barrier between the world of discourse and the "elsewhere" world of story; in television, it is treated as transparent and porous. The bridging of this spatial separation between the viewer and the representation of the news personality is formally repeated at several levels in the television production system itself. The control room, for instance, is absolutely separate spatially, but it is connected electronically via monitors to the sets where "the talent" performs before the cameras.

*The fourth wall.* The question as to why news personalities represent the public and its interests is seemingly answered with reference to the history of news practices (beginning in the print media) and the ideologies that link the news institution to democratic values. In practice, however, television news "represents" the public differently than does news in print. The anchor and his delegates, the on-air reporters, represent the public in a formal way; at the same time, the public is split into an object "out there" in the public realm and an audience in the privacy of the viewing situation. The mechanism for this splitting is the "fourth wall" within television's representational image. Though the physical barrier of the screen is ignored in television news, another fully imaginary barrier akin to the fourth wall in the theater is established—a "wall within" which moves closer and farther away within the illusory depths of the tube.

The "fourth wall" is established within the depths of the television picture through the averted gaze and the admonition, "Don't look at the camera!" This prohibition is applied to everyone but representatives of television as an institution, news personalities and other presenters, and product representatives in advertising. The anchor can talk to us and to his delegation of reporters; reporters can talk to us through the anchor (the anchor relays us with a shift of gaze or a squeeze frame and segue, and we the viewers see the reporter as if in the anchor's position; we may then "occupy" the reporter's position in relation to the source). Reporters may interview the public, but the source, no matter whether he/she is an expert or representative of the general public, may not talk to us directly through the camera. This arbitrary convention allows us to be gazed at and talked to by a few privileged people only; those people who cannot talk to us, including those interviewed by news reporters and other representatives of the public, are somehow deemed "incompetent with the camera."

The most obvious reason for this convention is that it is a visual version of the journalistic convention of the reporter as messenger, in which a reporter's utterance is made to seem "objective" by quoting and attributing responsibility for all "subjective" views and opinions to someone else.[30] In actual fact, the display of news personnel has the opposite effect of making anchors and reporters into news personalities or subjects. As Carolyn Diana Lewis has put it, the interview is typically followed by the reporter "addressing her audience, and thus [she] becomes a distinct personality. The stand-up stamps the story with the reporter's imprimatur" (p. 40). The convention converts what is essentially conversation into story, essentially creating the news.

This "wall within" creates distance, which can be useful to established authority figures—"accessed voices" considered as experts, as well as government officials. Another reason for this fourth wall might be the need to "insulate" news personalities from the unpleasant messages they deliver, which in turn puts the viewer in a position of separateness and safety from the news. Whatever the reason for this convention, the result is that news personalities monopolize the "face-to-face" conversation, becoming more "real," at least in terms of our symbolic system, than we are to ourselves. The "wall within," along with the hierarchy between anchor and reporters, also establishes the anchor's gaze as the one through which all other "views" of the world must be relayed, including the public's view of itself.

The power of the "wall within" the news may become more visible when that wall is set in the context of other social boundaries. In an archival sample of one news day—August 6, 1968—on all three networks, issues connected with the civil rights struggles against segregation were linked to reports on the "Poor People's Campaign" of Ralph Abernathy and the Republican Convention. Two examples of the use of the "wall within" were particularly striking.

• On ABC news, Ted Koppel reported from the home of a poor

black family in Miami (the family was not introduced). The camera opened on Koppel addressing us about the U.S. Riot Commission's report on America's growing racial division into two societies, "separate and unequal." The camera slowly pulled back to reveal a black family watching TV in their apartment. While the family watched Steve Allen on television talking about the riot commission report Koppel asked us to put ourselves in the family's position. Commercials appeared on its/our TV screen intercut with shots of dirty dishes and cockroaches and the black family watching. Everyone in the family stayed silently glued to the television set. Even a little girl maintained her composure and didn't look at the camera coming in for a close-up of her. The story ended with Koppel's voice-over while the camera came through the screen door into the apartment and captured a series of close-ups on cockroaches.

Aside from the cooperative cockroaches, the striking thing about this report is that the black family was never asked to speak for itself; the family members never looked at the camera, at "us." The family wasn't even interviewed; the interview technique, in which sources answer a reporter's questions, would have obscured the family's lack of authorization to speak for itself to us. Since 1968, when this report was aired, sensitivity to practices of racial segregation has grown, making this conventional barrier more visible—and in this instance, less innocuous.

• On the same day, CBS's Ed Rabel reported on an incident in the small Southern town of Luverne, Alabama, where an elderly white man, once a member of the Ku Klux Klan, was being boycotted for hiring a black man who sent his child to county schools. This white man was also being ostracized by the rest of the white community for his civil rights activities. The report began and ended with a stand-up of Rabel at the edge of town in front of a sign calling Luverne "The Friendliest City in the South." Shots of the mill under boycott and an interview with its ostracized owner, Mr. Miller (who made free use of a term for blacks considered racist now and certainly even then in the North), followed a shot which (with Rabel's voice-over) attempted to show the Millers leaving church, being ostracized. The camera was "censored" with a tree branch by a churchgoer. After an interview with the minister, the narrative returned to the interview with the elderly Miller. Gazing directly into the camera, he pleaded for "working together" and learning to love one another, and then began to weep. This man, who was so naive that he couldn't foresee the ostracism he would bring upon himself by breaking a social boundary, broke another kind of convention—the "wall within" of television—and reached the audience in an emotionally moving and discomfitting way.

A different convention of news gathering, "monitor logic" (long in use on PBS and non-primetime network news), allows the anchor to conduct interviews himself through the use of monitors in the studio. This eliminates one layer of news personnel, but it has not brought with it a change in the fourth wall. Even though interviewees speak facing a camera and appear "face-to-face" on the monitor and our TV screen, they are shown first talking via monitor to the news personality. We viewers adopt the anchor's position when the monitor speaks to us. Ted Koppel of ABC's *Nightline*, a late night news program of interviews and analysis, explained in a newspaper interview why even guests *in* the studio do not share his physical space: "Control is crucial to Koppel's role of balancing several voices. He will not permit a guest to sit next to him. Guests in the Washington studio are in separate rooms in front of cameras. They cannot see Koppel and can only hear him through an earpiece. This way all guests are on an equal footing. It also puts me at a tremendous advantage. I am accustomed to the technology and most guests are not. In live programming, I'll take any edge I can get.' "[31] Note that guests must talk to each other via monitors as well; their blind "equality" does not extend to their relation to the anchor himself. Monitor logic is no different in discursive stance from older conventions of television news. All gazes must be relayed through the eyes of the central figure in the swivel chair, who effectively monopolizes the conversation as discourse. The anchor becomes the only "full" personality in a situation which reverses the usual way we think of centralized surveillance and social control, constituting a panopticon in reverse: Big Brother isn't watching us, we are watching Big Brother.

Given that the "live" parts of the news are accounted for primarily in the "magic" moments when the anchor speaks, how real is the speaking subject of the news to us as viewers? We appear to see the actual "enunciation" of the news, the words in the mouth of a speaking subject who is talking to us; at the same time we know we are not seen and not heard. We do not "believe" the news personality is *here*, but some viewers go so far as to return the salutations and valediction of the newscaster as if he were physically present. This is known as "parasocial behavior," which blurs the distinction between primary and secondary experience, between discourse and story.[32] However, viewer "talk-back" to the news personality is not a sign of total, delusional belief but of willing collusion in a fiction. This talk-back can be derogatory and rude, to the point where the other person is "switched off"—behavior that would clearly be unacceptable in a "real" conversation between peers. After all, it is really only an impersonal machine. In a sense, the viewer is not all "here" either. Though he/she is actually in the living room, the viewer does not fully attend to or respond to a monologue as if it really were a dialogue; or if he/she does, it is without responsibility or consequence.

*The visual coverage of events.* Here would seem to be an objective validation of the news report, with credibility based on "looking like" and "being there" in a coherent reference world. However, on closer examination, the visuals of television prove to be different from photos in a newspaper with an iconic and indexical reference to the world. With few exceptions—those moments in field reports when sound and image emanate from the world of the news story—the visuals are not based on the "realism" of a space rendered as an optical analogue of the visible world, a perspectival space which began with the Renaissance. Far from being a rationalized view of space, news visuals are a collage of items of incongruent types and scales co-existing within the television frame. Furthermore, the visual and/or aural presence of a narrating personality is all-pervasive, again with the brief exception of the "sound bite" in a field report where the world seems to speak for itself.

The visuals within the frame (the logos, the news set, the visuals from "outside") generally have a loosely symbolic relation to the world "out there." For example, in the animated logos which introduce the news, the magical appearance of abstract shapes gradually takes on the gestalt of letters of the alphabet and symbols, seen in a perspective and scale often impossible in "real life." These animated logos are a combination of rational, literate modes and the dream logic of primary process in which objects combine and transform themselves and in which words become "things."

The news set itself, visible behind the anchor in his opening salutation and in a tell story, shows the "speaking subject" against an abstract map or bank of monitors used as "wallpaper." Though verbal announcements and titles may indicate a city, the set signifies a "national nowhere" of narration somewhere out of and above the world. The hanging box insert over the right or left shoulder of the anchor in a "tell" story usually frames a symbol connected with the story topic. This symbol (piles of coins or a dollar, for instance, for stories on interest, the exchange rate, or rising building costs) bears an arbitrary relation to the visible world and a far more direct relation to the symbolic system of our culture with its labelings and groupings. The "window" shows "story space" to be ambiguously related to the interiority of the anchor. It is positioned like a thought balloon in the comics and appears in conjunction with his narration like a visual realization of his thoughts. Thus, another visual convention offers an odd proof that the anchor *really does* harbor knowledge inside him; he *is* sincere.

Visuals from "out there" presented in video or film would seem to be more patently referential, beginning often with a cityscape or landscape or a scene related to the reported event. A closer look, however, reveals that the visual background of the stand-up (for example, the White House, Capitol Hill, farm field, or overlook of Jerusalem) is a carefully chosen "icon," an image of something "real," the significance of which does not depend on any specific event but already exists independently. It functions as a symbol. When, for instance, Capitol Hill is carefully framed behind a reporter telling about an event in Congress, the reporter must leave "the scene" itself—the halls and offices of Congress—in order to locate himself "symbolically." The loose connection of the visuals to a world "out there" is, of course, related to the problematic conception of events as "things" which happen in the world, visible changes which can be made into "visual coverage." What makes an event is culturally defined and lent a significance in discourse. Perhaps more important, it may exist entirely in discourse. Even tangible or visible changes in the natural world are organized, and meanings are mobilized which orient and hierarchize them as events in the symbolic system much as they orient the symbolic system to the world.

Conversations between anchors and sources that are conducted through monitors would seem to be a recognition of the discursive nature of "events." The "reality of discourse" within monitor exchanges has already been discussed; the iconic and indexical reality of bodies in "face-to-face" conversation is oddly undermined as well. The monitor in which *one sees* and hears the partner in discourse can be displaced spatially from the camera and audio intake from where *one is seen* and heard. The image on the monitor is not usually in the same scale as a talking head in life, nor is it necessarily in a position where one normally would find a conversation partner (it is often on a huge screen high up above in the studio). The vectors of conversational logic are misplaced: people can be shown talking to each other as a stack of talking heads in monitors. Monitor logic then promises a disorienting "derealization" of the face-to-face situation of bodies in space.

*The coherence of the news discourse.* What then provides the news with coherence if not a referential world imaginable as a spatial and temporal unity? The narration of the news proceeds in three tracks—print-like titles, images of various kinds (including most graphics), and the sound-narration (plus "accessed voices") in verbal language. These tracks are in discrepant language modes for much of any one newscast. For example, the language of the newscaster is often in a *story* mode while his body is poised for face-to-face *discourse*, the moving lips literally synchronizing the visual and sound tracks into a coherent whole. Print and verbal language are also different orders

which occur simultaneously. Sometimes print-like titles will overlay
an image, repeating nearly verbatim the soundtrack, or will label the
image. They also can anchor the report from the field in a specific
place with a particular narrator, again repeating the sound and image
track. The titles, then, seem to play a redundant role, providing an
overlay of literacy, reiterating or anchoring the verbal-visual orders.
Mismatched visual, linguistic, and print orders (an occasional and
understandable occurrence, considering the complexity of the
"matching" process in the control room) can add to the ethos of "liveness," but several goofs can undermine the coherence, and hence the
credibility, of the news report and the personalities who present it.
Ideally, the news is a seamless, convincing whole.

There are several kinds of shifters which provide continuity of flow
between stories. The first and most important of the visual shifters is
the shift of gaze tossing the narration to another news personality and
place of narration. Graphics such as squeeze frames also provide a
"magical" sort of passage between spaces. The turn of the swivel chair
is of the same indexical order. While the gaze as shifter does move
right and left, this spatial indicator is not linked to a locus in "real"
space but is a "toss" of the position of subject in discourse.

One would think that the verbal links or "segues" between stories
would provide the opportunity to add a secondary logic of causal,
spatial, and temporal relations with appropriate linguistic connectors.
However, one often finds that connections between stories are based
on figures of speech and cliches rather than on any causal relation
between items—what Freud called superficial associations "by asso-
nance, verbal ambiguity, temporal coincidence without connection in
meaning, or by any association of the kind that we allow in jokes or
in play upon words."[33] Even here, television, that most "real" of media,
can and often does emulate a primary process rather than a secondary
logic.

But perhaps the two most important sources of coherence are as
follows: first, the constancy of the presence of the news personality
and the apparent origin of the news items in the single personality
of the anchor; and second, the regular time and limited duration of
news delivery. The regular appearance of the national news, "a collage
reaching 30 million people a night with a portrait of reality truncated
into twenty-two minutes,"[34] makes it a capsule which can be taken
daily with ease. The news also gains coherence simply from its limitation to a regular space and time. Updates and important breaking
news can override (or be superimposed on) regular television programming, a sign of the privileged nature of the news (these updates
have begun to take the form of teasers and self-promotion during
commercial breaks, especially on local news).

There is, however, a delicate balance between such intrusions and the integrity of the news package. During truly traumatic or ecstatic national events (the moon landing, for example), the expansion of the news into hours of coverage seems to serve the public in an attempt to come to terms with the challenge to a basic part of social reality. It is a way of stopping regular activities for a common catharsis. Such "crisis" news can vary considerably in format. In some instances, such as the memorable Senate hearings concerning Senator McCarthy and Watergate, the participants speak for themselves. In others, such as the Kennedy assassination and funeral and the Chicago Democratic Convention of 1968, the emotional reaction of the anchor is one of the important things people remember about the events (for example, Walter Cronkite's breaking out of his usual news cadences into tears or anger serves to underline the perception of his sincerity).

For a while, two models for the all-news cable channels existed, one based on constant updating and ever-changing stories, and the other, which we still have today in the Cable News Network,[35] based on rotating packages which allow the viewer to watch the news according to her/his schedule, a kind of time-shifting. The update model failed for many reasons, but perhaps primarily because as a model, the idea of a "news" which acts as a sort of parallel to reality, always running and always changing, tends to provoke anxiety. One could always be missing something important. Moreover, the program is impossible to comprehend or master. Displacing reality, it invites the incessant intake pattern of the news junkie, whereas network news is designed more like medicinal intake in capsule form.

It is clear that anxieties motivate news viewers. According to Av Westin, the first question any news broadcast should answer is: "is my world safe?" (p. 62). Any pleasure or entertainment value is probably contained in the phatic contact with news personalities and the poetic or formal attractions of the news for itself. This basic anxiety suggests why we, the viewers, need to know and believe in the news and hence why we may willingly offer our suspension of disbelief—though, as I have suggested, what is at stake is not just "my world" but a means of social control and a status check on our symbolic system. The balance between the news "package" and the "update" appears to be related to the threat to the symbolic system and the norm of social reality in a particular piece of news.

The role of the news in the delegitimation of political power is a complex subject in every instance. Conversely, the attempt to delegitimate the news with the charge of a "credibility gap" (by Spiro Agnew or the Moral Majority, for instance) is often a struggle for the mechanisms of power in the news, an attempt to "center" it more advantageously politically, rather than an analysis and critique of its credibility structure. The news in the West is about the *a*normal. It is almost always the "bad" news. It is about challenges to the symbolic system and its legitimacy. News can be both a means of incorporating and defusing change and a means of moving within symbolic systems, changing in response to the challenges of other systems and natural phenomena.

IV. The Function of the News as Transition: Ceremony or Ritual?

In summary, the rise of the news personality since the advent of television has brought changes in the mode of address and the bases of credibility of the news. My investigation of this news format has shown that it emulates the more "primary" aspects of life experience: the reality of face-to-face relations and conversation; credibility based on the "magic" and charisma of the speaking subject as well as on more traditional objective values; and visuals more influenced by primary process than a rationalized "realism" or analogue of the external world. The news, less as a separate genre than as part of television as a whole, is also an important means of socialization.

The news, or television, has not truly become a friend, conversation partner, private daydream or parent. Rather, it has blurred the boundaries between these primary experiences and the secondary means of constructing and legitimating social reality. Our reactions as viewers are also more blurred: our relation to the news personality can be parasocial, somewhere between a relation to a machine and one to a familiar person. Our "knowing" is not the "full" personal knowledge of the face-to-face encounter, but it is more than the *acquaintance with* that the news has always provided. Our "believing" is not "full," but is rather composed of various degrees of "I know . . . but nevertheless. . . ." We are willing to overlook the great variety of gaps in news form discussed above in favor of granting the news and the news personality the imaginary unity and fullness they represent.

In order to understand how the news functions, it is enlightening to consider *when* the news appears in television programming and in daily life. The major news periods in a sample weekday on the West Coast are in the morning from 7–9 a.m. (including network, local news, and news magazines), in the evening from 5–7:30 p.m. (including local and prime time network news), and in the late evening (11 p.m. local news; 11:30 p.m. ABC's *Nightline*).

The morning news begins the flow of daytime programming which includes soap operas, talk and game shows, and movies. The evening news acts as a punctuation mark on the daytime flow and a prelude to the prime time flow of news magazines at 7:30 p.m. and the fiction and entertainment programming underway by 8 p.m. Morning and prime time news occur at key thresholds in the day between work and leisure. Morning news precedes the transit from the privacy of the home, where one kind of reality prevails, to the realm of work, a reality with entirely different roles, hierarchies, and rules. Morning news can be used as an alarm and pacing device to speed the viewer/auditor into the rhythms of the work world; the news, however lightly attended, may also orient her/him in social reality. Jane Feuer has commented on the "family" set and structure of the relations between anchors of *Good Morning America*.[36] In contrast, the evening news has a more hierarchical "work" structure in its anchor-reporter relations, and the set, dress, and demeanor of the news personalities are from the world of work and its imposed roles. Yet the mode of address to us is personal and we are given to understand that a person, not a role, type, or individual is addressing us, heart and mind. The evening news is a mixed form, a decompression chamber which aids the transition between one reality and the other—between the attentiveness demanded by the world of work and the relaxation promoted by the TV fare of prime time drama and entertainment and the exhaustion of work (or, for that matter, of "consuming," another form of work).

In the transit, however, the news and the world of work maintain primacy over the dream-like reality of private life, becoming "more real than I am to myself." The news overrides not so much personal experience as our sense of its reality, establishing the primacy of dominant values and the world out there. The annexation of the primary forms of private interaction and the monopolization of address by the news personality (both with us and with those behind the "wall within") aid the legitimation of "social reality" conveyed in the news.

The news is a daily ritual of transition. While certainly not a religious phenomenon, it does seem to have special privileges—a kind of sacred status, if you will—and does appear regularly, like a liturgic ritual. Like a liturgy, the sequential dimension of which is ritual, its function is to "mend ever again worlds forever breaking apart."[37] Victor Turner writes that ritual almost always accompanies a transition to another state; it has a spiritual dimension and "communicates the deepest values of the group regularly performing it" (p. 83).

Turner, however, distinguishes ritual from ceremony: while ritual is a vehicle of transformation, a subjunctive of culture, ceremony is in the indicative, a way of ratifying the norm, order against flux. Ceremony "banishes from consideration the basic questions raised by the made-upness of culture, its malleability and alterability. . . . [It] seeks to state that the cosmos and social world, or some particular small part of them, are orderly and explicable and for the moment fixed."[38] Ceremony is, then, a means of social control which does not engage the person at the most subjective, relational levels, whereas narrative descendents of ritual are "the supreme [instruments] for binding values and goals . . . which motivate human conduct" (pp. 87–88).

The national news as we have it today, with an "anchor" of restricted rather than inclusive type, a monologic structure, and an indicative mood, is primarily ceremonial, "anchoring" norms and limiting response. It is hardly part of a "non-transactional order," but is itself a commodity, and exchanges its audience as commodity as well. It is neither reflective nor intersubjective. Yet the news does not become a "lived reality" without ritual; thus it is a hybrid form, which includes ritual aspects, alludes to higher values, and is itself full of indeterminacies and latent alternatives, aspects of culture recombined in grotesque ways, unprecedented combinations of the familiar. Whether crisis news or the daily norm bears more potential for transformation is a question worth investigating. It is also possible to imagine other more reflective, more intersubjective forms of the news. The resort to charismatic and primary forms in the news suggests also that it may be part of a larger cultural shift away from the forms of realism, literacy, and objectivity which have been dominant in Western culture since the Renaissance and the age of industrialization. Whether the news is a part, a symptom, or an instigator of this cultural transformation is an open question. The hybrid news form, a representation which addresses us as discourse, does not herald a return to an "oral" culture, but rather indicates the emergence of new cultural forms and redrawn boundaries of a complex nature.

## NOTES

The Vanderbilt Television Archives were of tremendous help in providing archival tapes, indices, and viewing facilities. I wish to thank the staff and the director for their help with both my research project at Vanderbilt University in 1982 and my continuing research, 1982–85. Kathleen Woodward, Director of the Center for Twentieth Century Studies, has my warmest thanks for both the invitation to participate in the Center's 1984 mass culture conference and the subsequent encouragement of this project.

1. News professionals experience the hybrid of objective and subjective news values on television today as a conflict between "the television end of the news and the news end of television" rather than as a contradictory mixture of different species of news (Judith S. Gelfman, *Women in Television News* [New York: Columbia University Press, 1974], p. 55). Ron Powers, in *The Newscasters* (New York: St. Martin's Press, 1977), attacks the influence of news consultancies and the transformation of "journalism" to "show biz."

2. Emile Benveniste, *Problems in General Linguistics* (Coral Gables: University of Miami, 1971), p. 209. Gerard Genette has applied Benveniste's

distinction between story and discourse to genre theory in "Boundaries of the Narrative," *New Literary History* 8, no. 1 (Fall 1976):1–15; and Roland Barthes has applied the model in "Historical Discourse," *Social Science Information* 7, no. 4 (August 1967). Barthes points out that the historical utterance is actually a "false performative"; that is, it calls forth into existence rather than represents. Distinctions between *story space, discourse space,* and an *intra-discursive* level in television and in the news specifically is developed in my essay, "Talk, Talk, Talk: The Space of Discourse in Television News, Sportcasts, Talk Shows and Advertising," *Screen* 26, no. 2 (March-April 1985):2–15.

3. From the 1830s on, news in the United States developed its own "zero-degree" style which expunged even more marks of its subjective origin; see Michael Schudsen, *Discovering the News: A Social History of American Newspapers* (New York: Basic Books, 1978) and Dan Schiller, *Objectivity and the News: The Public and the Rise of Commercial Journalism* (Philadelphia: University of Pennsylvania Press, 1981). However, these stylistic emphases occurred within the general objective framework of print and narrative, which separate the speaker from the utterance. The model for a subjective news must go further back in history, to a pre-industrial *tidings.* See John Hartley, *Understanding News* (London and New York: Methuen, 1982), p. 18.

4. William Gibson, in "Network News: Elements of a Theory," *Social Text* 3 (Fall 1980):94, reports that television adopted the "Institutional Voice of the News," which Robert MacNeil calls "half-sung, half-chanted." This stentorian "voice from the well" of radio (see Edwin Diamond, *Sign Off: The Last Days of Television* [Cambridge, MA: MIT Press, 1982], p. 68) is probably less pronounced in television, but listening to audio alone confirms an other than conversational pattern of inflection.

5. Against this view see John Fiske and John Hartley, *Reading Television* (London and New York: Methuen, 1978): "We can say that there is no single 'authorial' identity for the television communicator" (p. 83). The news genre is, however, "authored" by the chief news personality and his staff.

6. This reading of the word is disputed by Roone Arledge, noted in Marvin Barrett, *Rich News, Poor News* (New York: Crowell, 1978), p. 22. But see Savitch (p. 170); and Diamond, (p. 69 ff.).

7. Eliseo Veron, "Il est la, je le vois, il me parle," *Communications* 38 (1983):105 ff.

8. Jessica Savitch, *Anchorwoman* (New York: Putnam, 1982), p. 165.

9. Barbara Matusow, *The Evening Stars: The Making of the Network News Anchor* (Boston: Houghton Mifflin, 1983), p. 1 ff.

10. Walter Cronkite, in an interview with Lee Michael Katz, "Walter Cronkite, Anchorman at Rest," *Washington Post*, reprinted in the *San Francisco Chronicle* Jan. 8, 1984.

11. In a study of the "reading behavior" of television news anchors, using tapes from the Vanderbilt Television Archives, I examined a sample of newscasts from all three networks from 1968, 1974, and 1979 to determine whether or not "reading behavior" had changed in that decade. In 1968, newscasters were accomplished at glancing up to look at the lens while reading from notes on the desk. By 1974, glancing *down* at the desk was used primarily to make or emphasize a point, to indicate a quotation, or to close a story. That is, the newscaster was *pretending to read* notes when he was primarily using cues or a teleprompter. By 1979 glancing down and fingering papers were much rarer practices; today they are virtually nonexistent. Instead the anchor and other newscasters pretend *not* to read, but to speak directly to us. For further

research, see Henry R. Austin and William C. Donahy, "The Comparative Look-Up Ability of Newscasters on Television," *Journal of Broadcasting* 14, no. 2 (1971):197–205. In *The Work of the Television Journalist* (New York: Hastings House, 1972), Robert Tyrrell suggests an occasional look down, a practice now practically obsolete. For another view, see experimental work of Jon Baggeley and Steven Duck on the link between particular presentational techniques and the establishment of credibility. J. B. Baggeley, *Psychology of the TV Image* (New York: Praeger, 1979); and Baggeley and Duck, "La Credibilité du message televisuel," *Communications* 33 (1981):143–64.

12. Cronkite, quoted in Barrett, *Rich News, Poor News*, p. 185.

13. Peter L. Berger and Thomas Luckman, *The Social Construction of Reality* (New York: Anchor-Doubleday, 1967), p. 76.

14. See Av Westin, in his *Newswatch: How TV Decides the News* (New York: Simon and Schuster, 1982), for a very useful description of the introduction of various techniques in television news.

15. Max Weber, of course, developed this religious concept for sociology. Richard Dyer, in his section on "charisma" in *Stars* (London: British Film Institute, 1979), pp. 34–37, discusses Weber's concept of charisma as one means of legitimation of political order.

16. John Ellis, in *Visible Fictions: Cinema/Television/Video* (London: Routledge and Kegan Paul, 1982), gives an account of how television acts as a delegate for the viewer (pp. 133, 164). The imaginary of *objective* news is the coalescing of utterance and referent; the imaginary of *subjective* news coalesces the image of a visible subject moving his lips and the complex subject of enunciation analyzed here.

17. Fiske and Hartley view television as a whole as a contradiction between "bardic" and "literate" form and message (pp. 85–100).

18. See Robert A. Hackett's "Bias and Objectivity in News Media Studies," in *Critical Studies in Mass Communications* 1, no. 3 (Sept. 1984):229–59 for a discussion of these values and their roles in academic news criticism.

19. In *Sign Off*, Diamond writes that as the news developed, "looking authoritative became as critical as sounding authoritative." Richard Wald, now vice president of ABC News, once suggested the result of this combination: "anchorpeople cast in the form of paracletes, messengers of God" (p. 69).

20. Carolyn Diana Lewis, *Reporting for Television* (New York: Columbia University Press, 1984), p. 54.

21. Jane Feuer, "The Concept of Live Television: Ontology as Ideology," in *Regarding Television*, ed. E. Ann Kaplan, American Film Institute Monograph Series, Vol. 2 (Frederick, MD: University Publications of America, 1983), pp. 12–22.

22. Victor Turner, *From Ritual to Theater: The Human Seriousness of Play* (New York: Performing Arts Journal, 1982), p. 45.

23. Powers, p. 2.

24. Quoted in Barrett, *Rich News, Poor News*, p. 22.

25. Reese Schoenfeld, speaking on "The Anchor—and so it goes," aired on *Inside Story*, PBS, Feb 3, 1984 (PTV Transcript). But one can be *too* intelligent, *too* much an egghead (see Matusow on Roger Mudd). Or *too* old—as Mike Wallace apparently is now; or *too* young—Peter Jennings had to age for a while in Europe. One can be *too* good looking.

26. Editorial with a quotation from the designer Alexander Julian in "Dressing Down TV's Anchormen," *GQ* (Nov. 1982):100.

27. See Robert Stam, "Television News and Its Spectator," in *Regarding Television*, pp. 28–30.

28. The *imaginary* (prevalence of the relation to the image of the counterpart), the *symbolic* (structured like a language) and the *real* (a third but inaccessible order) are essential orders of the pyschoanalytic field, as developed in the work of Jacques Lacan.

29. Christian Metz applies disavowal to fiction film in his "The Imaginary Signifier," *Screen* 16, no. 2 (Summer 1975):14–76. It is applied to theatre and other cultural rituals in O. Mannoni's *Clefs pour l'imaginaire: ou l'autre scène* (Paris: Editions du Seuil, 1969). Mannoni stresses the identification of the spectator with "someone who believes" as a means of controlled regression.

30. See Bernard Roshco, *Newsmaking* (Chicago and London: University of Chicago Press, 1975), pp. 23–37.

31. Sally Bedell Smith, "Ted Koppel Off Camera," *New York Times*, reprinted in the *San Francisco Chronicle* Mar. 6, 1985.

32. Mark R. Levy, "Watching News as Parasocial Interaction," *Journal of Broadcasting* 23, no. 1 (Winter 1979):69.

33. Sigmund Freud, *The Interpretation of Dreams*, trans. James Strachey (New York: Norton, 1963), p. 568.

34. Jeff Greenfield, media critic, speaking on "Lead Story: The News on the Networks," aired on *Inside Story*, PBS, April 23, 1982 (PTV Transcript).

35. The Turner Broadcasting System, owner of the Cable News Network, bought out the Satellite News Channels, owned jointly by ABC and Westinghouse effective on October 27, 1983 for $25 million. *The New York Times* of October 13, 1983 reported that Satellite News had lost more than $40 million since it began.

36. Feuer, in *Regarding Television*.

37. Roy Rappaport, *Ecology, Meaning and Religion* (Richmond, CA: North American Books, 1979), quoted in Turner, p. 206. Gregor T. Goethals, in *The TV Ritual: Worship at the Video Altar* (Boston: Beacon Press, 1981), discusses the ritual aspect of television as a whole.

38. Sally Moore and Barbara Myerhoff, editors of *Secular Ritual* (Amsterdam: Royal von Gorcum, 1977), p. 87; quoted in Turner, pp. 16–17.

# 5

# SITUATION COMEDY, FEMINISM, AND FREUD

## DISCOURSES OF GRACIE AND LUCY

## Patricia Mellencamp

> Since we said "I do," there are so many
> things we don't.
>
> —Lucy Ricardo

> This is a battle between two different
> ways of life, men and women.
> The battle of the sexes?
> Sex has nothing to do with it.
>
> —Gracie Allen and Blanche Morton

During the late 1940s and the 1950s, linked to or owned by the major radio networks, television recycled radio's stars, formats, and times through little proscenium screens, filling up the day. Vaudeville and movies fed both of these voracious, domestic media, each reliant on sound, and each influential in the rapidly developing suburbs. With a commercial collage of quiz, news, music, variety, wrestling/boxing, fashion/cooking, and comedy shows, both media were relatively irreverent toward well-fashioned narrative and worshipful of audiences and sponsors. Television was then (and continues to be) both an ecology—a repetition and recycling through the years—and a family affair, in the 1950s conducted collectively in the living room, with the dial dominated by Dad. A TV set was a status symbol, a rooftop economic declaration, and an invitation to other couples to watch.

Like suburban owners of TV "sets," the four television networks were also concerned with status; thus "the news" was made a separate category of the real and legitimate, presumably distinct from "entertainment." At the beginning of the 1950s, the United Nations debates were prestigiously broadcast. The proceedings of the Kefauver congressional committee, which was investigating organized crime, were televised by WPIX in New York; the networks carried these "real life" dramas with good ratings. In April 1951, General Douglas MacArthur's speech to Congress was broadcast; his words attacked the "containment" and limited warfare policies of the Truman administration, revving up the paranoiac or conspiracy interpretation of not only world but also social events. In July 1952, the GOP convention was televised, and Stevenson and Eisenhower fought part of the subsequent election on television. The Army-McCarthy hearings began on April 22, 1954 and received high ratings for the many hours during which Senator Joseph McCarthy accused the military of "communist infiltration" and then was undone on live television.[1]

Coincident with these prestigious broadcasts of the "real"—events of power, politics, and "truth"—and the massive licensing of broadcast air and time, women were being urged to leave the city, work force, and salaries; move to the suburbs, leisure and tranquillity; raise children; and placate commuting, overworked husbands for free. In reality, of course, not all women did so. Most women over 35 remained in the paid work force; when allowed, instead of building battleships, they took other jobs. That TV and particularly situation comedies would, like radio, both serve and support the new, imaginary, blissful domesticity of a ranch style house, backyard barbecue, and a bath and a half seems logical—it is, of course, historical. "Containment" was not only a defensive, military strategy developed as U.S. foreign policy in the 1950s; it was practiced on the domestic front as well, and it was aimed at excluding women from the work force and keeping them in the home.

To argue that television was a powerful machinery for familial containment of women is hardly original. Yet the specifics of program strategies are intriguing and complex—hardly monolithic or perfectly generic, as most discourses presume. For me, two issues are central: the importance in early 1950s comedy of idiosyncratically powerful female stars, usually in their late thirties or forties; and the gradual erosion of that power that occurred in the representation of women within comedy formats. In situation comedy, pacification of women occurred between 1950 and 1960 without a single critical mention that the genre's terrain had altered: the housewife, although still ruling the familial roost, changed from being a humorous rebel or well-dressed, wise-cracking, naive dissenter who wanted or had a paid job—from being out of control via language (Gracie) or body (Lucy)—to being a contented, if not blissfully happy, understanding homebody (Laura Petrie). With this in mind, we need to review specific programs, particularly in TV's early stages. This paper is based on a general analysis of forty episodes of *The George Burns and Gracie Allen Show*, which was on the air Wednesday nights from October 1950 until June 1958, when Gracie left the show; and of 170 of the 179 episodes of "*I Love Lucy*," which was broadcast Monday evenings from October 1951 until May 1957. It also begins to rethink Freud's construction of the radical underpinnings and "liberating" function of jokes, the comic, and humor—perhaps yet another "foreign" policy of potential containment for U.S. women.

## I.

In fifteen-minute segments, broadcast live three times a week in 1949, Gertrude Berg—writer, producer, and star—disguised herself as Molly Goldberg, the quintessential Jewish mother, a melange of chicken soup malaprops and advice. Leaning out of her window, she would intimately confess to us: "If Mr. Goldberg did not drink Sanka decaffeinated coffee, I don't know what I would do—I don't even know if we'd still have a marriage . . . just try it once, and that's what I'm telling you." The program and its popularity were emblematic of the subsequent televised avalanche of situation comedies, a direct descendant of radio, vaudeville's "husband and wife" sketches, music hall, and *comedia del arte*'s stereotypical scenes and characters. The elision of program and star with sponsor was another version of television's corporate coupling/ownership.

In the 1950–51 season, *The George Burns and Gracie Allen Show* debuted, continuing in this tradition. Burns and Allen funneled their 1926 marriage, their vaudeville, radio and film routines, and their characters/stars into an upper-middle class situation comedy—a historical agglutination suggesting that what is monolithically termed "mass culture" is a process: a collection of discourses, scenes, or turns recycled from various media and contextualized within historical moments. Despite its similarity to the Molly Goldberg type of program, this show represented a new version of the happily married couple, featuring the zany, fashionable Gracie of bewildering *non sequiturs* and the relaxed, dapper George of one-liners and wisecracks living in suburban, affluent Beverly Hills. Gracie was certainly unlike TV's nurturing-yet-domineering mothers who dwelled in city apartments. Yet she was familiarly different as "Gracie." Derailing the laws and syntax of language and logic, her technique was a referral back to either the nearest or the most unexpected referent as a comic turn on the arbitrary and conventional authority of speech (and she would continually break her own rules just when her friends and we caught on). She baffled all the male and most of the female characters, concocting improbable stories and schemes that were invariably true in amazing circumlocutions which became that week's "plot."

The casual narratives of each week's program were used merely as continuity for vaudeville routines and existed primarily to be mocked by George. The scenario is often as follows: an ordinary event—shopping, going to the movies—would be "misinterpreted" and then complicated by Gracie, who would then connect a second, random event to the first. For example, their college son, Ronnie, needs a story for the USC newspaper; Blanche Morton, her next-door neighbor and confidante, wants new dishes. Linking these two unrelated problems, Gracie contrives a fake theft of Ronnie's wealthy friend's car. When the car is initially found in the Mortons' garage, Blanche's husband is so relieved not to have to pay for this "new" car, which he believes Blanche has bought, that he gladly buys the plates; and Ronnie scoops the story of the theft.

Adding to the shaggy dog quality of the plots were the many bewildered characters (including the postman) who would drop by the house and would then be involved by Gracie. The more unrelated the character, or innocent bystander to the plot, the better; a large measure of Gracie's comedy depended on the other characters' astonishment. Her naive, friendly *non sequiturs* rendered them speechless, reluctantly agreeing, finally reduced to staring in reaction shots. (This is diametrically the opposite of what occurs in *"I Love Lucy"* where Lucy is invariably given the last word or look, the editing indicating that different mechanisms of identification and spectator positioning are operative in each show.) Then, winking, George would either join in the linguistic mayhem or sort things out. His intervention was not, however, for our understanding, but for that of the confused, speechless characters; his Aristotelian analyses of Gracie's behavior and illogic left bystanders doubly amazed. Finally, at the end of each show, George would issue the imperative, "Say goodnight, Gracie."

Garbed in dressy fifties fashion, set in an upper-middle class milieu of dens, patios, and two-car garages, constantly arranging flowers or making and serving coffee but not sense, Gracie equivocally escaped order. Despite being burdened by all the cliches applied to women— illogical, crazy, nonsensical, possessing their own, peculiar bio-logic and patronized accordingly—in certain ways, she seemed to be out of (or beyond) men's control. Unlike the ever loyal and bewildered Harry VonZell, the show's and the story's announcer, and other characters in the narrative sketches, neither she nor her neighbor Blanche (who both loved and understood Gracie) revered George or were intimidated by his cleverness; in fact, Gracie rarely paid attention to him, or to any authority figure. She unmade decorum, she unraveled patriarchal laws, illustrating Jean Baudrillard's assertion through Freud:

"The witticism, which is a transgressive reversal of discourse, does not act on the basis of another code as such; it works through the instantaneous deconstruction of the dominant discursive code. It volatizes the category of the code, and that of the message."[2] The "dominant discursive code" of patriarchy tried, through benevolent George, to contain Gracie's volatization, her literal deconstruction of speech, and her tall tales of family. Whether or not the system won can be answered either way, depending on where the analyst is politically sitting—with George in his den, or in the kitchen with the women.

Gracie's forte was the shaggy dog story—either as verbal riff or as the very substance of the narrative: the first use led to illogical nonsense, a way of thinking definitive of Gracie's comedy; the second led to instigation and resolution of the week's episode. Furthermore, the shaggy dog event, preposterous as it was, would always prove to be "true." Take for example the following episode. The scene is Gracie's sunny, ruffle-curtained kitchen with table in the center, an auto-replenishing coffee pot, and numerous exits. The initial situation is explicated in the dialogue:

> GRACIE: Thanks for driving me home, Dave.
> DAVE: As long as I towed your car in, I didn't mind at all Mrs. Burns.
> GRACIE: There's some coffee on the stove. Would you like some?
> DAVE: I've been wondering, Mrs. Burns. How are you going to explain this little repair job to your husband?
> GRACIE: I'll just tell him what happened. I went shopping and bought a blouse and on my way home I stopped to watch them put up the tents and this elephant came along and sat on my fender and smashed it.
> DAVE: He'll never believe it.
> GRACIE: Of course he will. He knows a fender isn't strong enough to hold up an elephant. George is smarter than you think he is.[3]

To prove her story to George, Gracie will show him the blouse. Her idiosyncratic cause-effect connections have nothing (or everything) to do with physics, the arbitrary conventions of language, or common sense. In many ways, her style of speech is uncommonly funny because it is ahistorical, ignoring the speaker and the situation while obeying language's rules. Like Chico Marx, she takes language literally; unlike Chico, she is unaware of her effect on other characters.[4] Gracie delivers her deadpan lines without reaction or expectation, obliviously using the same expressive tone no matter what the terms of the discursive contract—which she ultimately reconstructs anyway.

The rest of this episode consists of retelling the story—first to Blanche, who then tells her husband, Harry; then to the insurance salesman, Prescott; and simultaneously to Harry VonZell and Stebbins, the circus man. George, basically a solo, narrative entrepreneur, keeps breaking and entering Gracie's dilemma of credulity with comments ("All I wanted was a little proof"), observations on life, and ironic maxims about marriage: "Married people don't have to lie to each other. We've got lawyers and friends to do that for us." George bribes Gracie with a promise of a mink coat for the "true" story, which, of course, she has already told him. The show culminates in a final courtroom scene with all of the participants sitting in the Burns' living room validating the truth of Gracie's initial story, which is confirmed by Dave, the "seeing is believing" mechanic. The truth of male vision verifying Gracie's words is endlessly repeated, both in the series and in this program. Dave says, "If I hadn't come down to the circus grounds to tow away your car, I wouldn't have believed it myself." During the last scene, he reiterates: "If I hadn't seen it with my own eyes, I wouldn't have believed it myself." During this conclusive trial, presided over by George, a new character—Duffy Edwards, the furrier—enters with Gracie's newly won fur coat and says to George: "I always watch your show. I knew you were going to lose." Unlike Lucy, Gracie always wins in the narrative, which thereby validates her story.

However, other codes are also operative: George is center-framed in the mise-en-scène and by the moving camera; he is taller than all the other characters; and he has access to the audience via his direct looks at the camera. He nods knowingly, with sidelong collusive glances at us (or perhaps at eternal husbands everywhere). In the end Gracie is frame left. She wins the narrative and the mink coat, but loses central screen space; perhaps most importantly, she never was in possession of "the look." Roland Barthes, placing power firmly in language, asks: "Where is speech? In locution? In listening? In the returns of the one and the other? The problem is not to abolish the distinctions in functions . . . but to protect the instability . . . the giddying whirls of the positions of speech."[5] The whirls are giddying; yet George Burns, the dapper entertainer as Hollywood gossip, critic, and golf partner of CBS president William Paley, presides over the show with benign resignation, a wry smile, and narrative "logic" firmly grounded in bemused knowledge of the frothy status of the situation, comedy, and television. Throughout each program, Gracie is blatantly dominated not only by George's looks at the camera and direct monologues to the audience, but also by his view of the program from the TV set in his den, and by his figure matted or superimposed over the background action as his voice-over comments on marriage, Gracie, her relatives, movie stars, show business, and the "story."

In his analysis of Freud's *Jokes and Their Relation to the Unconscious*, Samuel Weber suggests an intriguing reading of the Aufsitzer, or Shaggy Dog jokes—nonsense jokes which create the expectation of a joke, causing one to search for concealed meaning. "But one finds none, they really are nonsense," writes Freud. Weber argues that the expectation rests in the desire "to make sense of the enigmatic assertion with which the joke begins . . . such jokes 'play' games with the desire of the listener. . . . By rousing this 'expectation' and then leaving it unsatisfied . . . such jokes function in a manner very reminiscent of the discourse of the analyst, who refuses to engage in a meaningful dialogue with the analysand."[6] It is, however, difficult to apply Weber's insight to Gracie, to compare *her* rather than George to the analyst. After all, it is George with whom the listener is in collusion; it is George who hears Gracie from his tolerant, central, bemused vantage point. It is as if he occupies the central tower in the panopticon, or the analyst's chair behind the couch, unseen, with all scenes visible to his gaze.

As Weber writes, these jokes are "come-ons," taking us for a ride. "For at the end of the road all we find is nonsense: 'They really are nonsense,' Freud states, thus seeking to reassure us, and himself as well."[7] Perhaps *Burns and Allen* could be interpreted as a massive, male reassurance that women's lives are indeed nonsense. The Aufsitzer is a joke played on the expectation of a joke, and is clearly a complicated matter—in the case of Gracie Allen, it is a refusal of conventional meaning gleefully accepted and encouraged as rebellion by Blanche Morton and contained for the audience by the omniscience of George, who narcissistically strives as super/ego to "unify, bind . . . and situate [himself] as a self-contained subject."[8]

Nor should we be misled by the fact that George is the "straight man" and thus seems to occupy a slightly inferior position, which he himself describes as follows:

> For the benefit of those who have never seen me, I am what is known in the business as a straight man. If you don't know what a straight man does, I'll tell you. The comedian gets a laugh. Then I look at the comedian. Then I look at the audience—like this . . . That is known as a pause . . .
> Another duty of a straight man is to repeat what the comedian says. If Gracie should say, "A funny thing happened on the streetcar today," then I say, "A funny thing happened on the streetcar today?" And naturally her answer gets a scream. Then, I throw in one of my famous pauses . . .

But George was never *just* a straight man; the monologue continues:

> I've been a straight man for so many years that from force of habit I repeat everything. I went out fishing with a fellow the other day and he fell overboard. He yelled "Help! Help!" So I said, "Help? Help?" And while I was waiting for him to get his laugh, he drowned.

This gag defines quite precisely George's actions, as well as indicating their vaudeville origins. Inevitably, like the male leads in most situation comedies, he got the final and controlling look or laugh. Containment operated through laughter—a release which might have held women to their place, rather than "liberating" them in the way Freud says jokes liberate their tellers and auditors. As radical as the nonsense joke might be (when it comes from the mouth of the male), it's different, as is the rest of life, for the female speaker. The audience too is measured and contained by George, whom both the camera and editing follow: the husband as television critic, solo stand-up comic, female psychologist, and tolerant parent/performer. Yet, unlike in most situation comedies, it was clear that George depended on Gracie, who worked both in the series' imaginary act and the program's narratives. Thus, the contradiction of the program and the double bind of the female spectator and comedian—women as both subject and object of the comedy, rather than the mere objects that they are in the Freudian paradigm of jokes—are dilemmas which, for me, no modern critical model can resolve.

## II.

In its original version, "*I Love Lucy*" debuted on Monday, October 15, 1951, at 8:00 p.m. Held to the conventional domesticity of situation comedy, Lucy Ricardo was barely in control, constantly attempting to escape domesticity—her "situation," her job, in the home—always trying to get into show business by getting into Ricky's "act," narratively fouling it up, but brilliantly and comically performing in it. Lucy endured marriage and housewifery by transforming them into vaudeville: costumed performances and rehearsals which made staying home frustrating, yet tolerable. Her dissatisfaction, expressed as her desire for a job, show business and stardom, was concealed by the happy endings of hug/kiss (sometimes tagged with the line, "now we're even")/applause/titles/theme song. Her discontent and ambition, weekly stated, were the show's working premises, its contradictions massively covered up by the audience's pleasure in her performances, her "real" stardom. The series typified the paradox of women in comedy—the female performer caught somewhere between narrative and spectacle, historically held as a simulation between the real and the model.

As was the case with *The George Burns and Gracie Allen Show*, the entire series was biographically linked to the marriage of the two stars. Lucille Ball, movie star, and her husband Desi Arnaz, Cuban band leader, became Lucy and Ricky Ricardo; their "friends" appeared on programs as bit players or as "themselves." At the end of one episode, for instance, the voice-over announcer said: "Harpo Marx played himself." Image/person/star are totally merged as "himself," the "real" is a replayed image, a scene, a simulation—what Jean Baudrillard calls "the hyperreal." The most extraordinary or bizarre example of the elision of "fact" and fiction, or the "real" with the simulation, martialled by the "formal coherency" of narrative, was Lucy's hyperreal pregnancy. In 1952, with scripts supervised by a minister, a priest, and a rabbi, seven episodes were devoted to Lucy's TV and real pregnancy (without ever mentioning the word). The first episode was aired on December 8, timed with Lucy's scheduled caesarean delivery date of Monday, January 19, 1953. Lucy's real, nine-month baby, Desi, Jr., was simulated in a seven-week TV gestation and electronically delivered on January 19 at 8:00 p.m. as Little Ricky, while 44 million Americans watched. (Only 29 million tuned in to Eisenhower's swearing-in ceremony. We liked Ike. We loved Lucy.) As were all the episodes in the series, this one was given a children's book title, "Lucy Goes to the Hospital."[9]

But if the "real" domestic and familial details of the star's life were so oddly mixed up with the fiction, perhaps the supreme fiction of the program was that Lucy was not star material, and hence needed to be confined to domesticity. Thus the weekly plot concerned Lucy's thwarted attempts to break out of the home and into show business. Unlike Gracie's implausible connections and overt machinations, though, all of Lucy's schemes failed, even if failure necessitated an instant and gratuitous reversal in the end. Lucy was the rebellious child whom the husband/father Ricky endured, understood, loved, and even punished, as, for example, when he spanked her for her continual disobedience. However, if Lucy's plots for ambition and fame *narratively* failed, with the result that she was held, often gratefully, to domesticity, *performatively* they succeeded. In the elemental, repetitive narrative, Lucy never got what she wanted: a job and recognition. Weekly, for six years, she accepted domesticity, only to try to escape again the next week. During each program, however, she not only succeeded, but demolished Ricky's act, upstaged every other performer (including John Wayne, Richard Widmark, William Holden and even Orson Welles), and got exactly what she and the television audience wanted: Lucy the star, performing off-key, crazy, perfectly executed vaudeville turns—physical comedy as few women (particularly beautiful ones, former Goldwyn girls) have ever done.

The typical movement of this series involves Lucy performing for us, at home, the role that the narrative forbids her. She can never be a "real" public performer, except for us: she must narratively remain a housewife. In the episode entitled "The Ballet," for example, Ricky needs a ballerina and a burlesque clown for his nightclub act; Lucy pleads with him to use her. Of course he refuses. Lucy trains as a ballet dancer in one of her characteristic performances: dressed in a frothy tutu, she eagerly and maniacally imitates a dancer performing ballet movements which she then transforms through automatic, exaggerated repetition into a charleston. Whenever Lucy is confident that she has learned something new, no matter how difficult, she gets carried away. These are the great comic scenes, occurring after the narrative setup: pure performances during which the other characters show absolutely no reactions. This is the first "story" line, before the mid-program "heart break": "curtains" as halves of a heart lovingly open/close, or frame and divide each episode. Then, the second: Lucy will now train to be a burlesque comic. Her baggy pants clown/teacher arrives at their apartment, pretends she's a man, tells his melodramatic tale of woe about Martha and betrayal; Lucy becomes involved, says the Pavlovian name, Martha, and is hit with a pig bladder, sprayed with seltzer water, and finally, gets a pie in the face. The scene ends with Lucy saying, "Next time, you're going to be the one with the kind face"—in other words, the victim of the sketch. Then, as in all the episodes, and in this one more literally than in most, the two stories are condensed in a final, onstage performance. At his nightclub, Ricky is romantically singing "Martha" in Spanish. Ethel calls Lucy to inform her that Ricky needs someone in his act. She dresses up as the burlesque clown (not the needed dancer), and steps onstage with her wrong props. When Ricky sings the refrain, the word "Martha" is now her Pavlovian cue: she beats the male ballet dancers with the bladder; squirts the female ballerina with seltzer water; and, in a conclusion which uses up all the previous setups, slams a pie in the singing face of tuxedoed, romantic crooner Ricky. (The Saudi Arabian government detected an element of subversion in this series and banned it because Lucy dominated her husband.) This episode, like so many others, is a rehearsal for a performance, involving in the end a comical, public upstaging of Ricky. We are simultaneously backstage and outfront in the audience, waiting for Lucy's performance and Ricky's stoic, albeit frustrated, endurance; thus, expectation is not connected to narrative, but to anticipation of the comic—a performative or proairetic expectation.

An exemplary instance of Lucy's upstaging, or humiliation, of Ricky may be seen in the episode entitled "The Benefit," in which Ricky's attempts to be the comedian rather than the straight man are utterly foiled. In this episode Lucy, along with the audience, discovers that Ricky has re-edited their benefit duo, taking all the punchlines for himself. Fade. Onstage, in identical costumes of men's suits, straw hats and canes, Ricky and Lucy perform a soft-shoe sketch. Ricky stops, taps his cane, and waits for Lucy to be the "straight man." Of course, she won't. While singing "Under the Bamboo Tree" about marriage and happiness, Lucy, with the camera closeup as her loyal accomplice in the reaction shots, outrageously steals all of Ricky's lines, smirking

and using every upstaging method in the show biz book. Applause,
exit; the heart, this time as a literal curtain, closes. Lucy gets the last
word and the last laugh during this ironic "turn" on the lyrics of the
romantic song. It is interesting to compare Ricky, the would-be comedian forced by his partner/wife to be the straight man, to George,
the "straight man" who always gets the final, controlling laugh.

That Ricky can be so constantly upstaged and so readily disobeyed
is not insignificant, for with his Cuban accent (constantly mimicked
by Lucy), he does not fully possess language, and is not properly
symbolic as is George, the joker or wielder of authoritatively funny
speech. The program's reliance on physical rather than verbal
comedy, with Lucy and Ethel as the lead performers, constitutes another exclusion of Ricky. Unlike George, Ricky is not given equal, let
alone superior, time. He constantly leaves the story, and his departure
becomes the cue for comic mayhem and audience pleasure. Although
he is "tall, dark, and handsome," not the usual slapstick type, his
representation as the Latin lover/bandleader/crooner and slapstick foil
for Lucy's pies in the face suggests that Lucy's resistance to patriarchy
might be more palatable because it is mediated by a racism which
views Ricky as inferior.

In "Vacation from Marriage," the underside of situation comedy's
reiteration of the same is briefly revealed. Lucy, with Ethel in the
kitchen, is talking about the boredom and routine of marriage. "It
isn't funny, Ethel, it's tragic." The rest of this show and the series
make marriage funny and adventurous. Week after week, the show
keeps Lucy happily in her confined, domestic, sit-com place after a
23-minute tour-de-force struggle to escape. That neither audiences
nor critics noticed Lucy's feminist strain is curious, suggesting that
comedy is a powerful and unexamined weapon of subjugation. In
most of the programs' endings, the narrative policy was one of twofold
containment: every week for seven years, she was wrong and duly
apologetic; and while repeating discontent, her masquerades and es-
capades made Monday nights and marriage pleasurable. Allen, on the
same network, untied legal language and the power polarities implicit
in its command; Ball took over the male domain of physical comedy.
Both unmade "meaning" and overturned patriarchal assumptions,
stealing the show in the process; yet neither escaped confinement and
the tolerance of kindly fathers. "That's entertainment!"—for women
a massive yet benevolent containment.

## III.

As theorists of historiography have argued, discourses of "truth"
and the "real" move through a cause-effect, narrative chronology to
a resolute closure without gaps or discontinuities. There is something

at stake in this strategy, and it is related to power and authority. Narrative embodies a political determinism in which women find a subordinate place. But narrative in situation comedy is only the merest overlay, perhaps an excuse. As George Burns said, "more plot than a variety show and not as much as a wrestling match." This implausible, sparse "situation" exemplifies—in its obsessive repetition of the domestic regime, of marital bliss as crazy "scenes" and competitive squabbles—a social plaint if not a politics.

Situation comedy, with "gaps" of performance and discontinuities, *uses* narrative offhandedly. The hermeneutic code is not replete with expectation, not in need of decipherment, not ensnaring us or lying to us. Expectation of pleasurable performance—the workings of the comic and humor—rather than narrative suspense are currencies of audience exchange. Perhaps this system might challenge "narrative's relation to a legal system";[10] certainly narrative is not viewed as sacred or authoritative any more than husbands are. It is necessary but not equal to performance. In trying to determine how comedy works to contain women and how successfully it does so, theories of narrative will thus be of little help to us. It is necessary to turn to theories of the comic and humor.

I will hesitantly begin an inquiry into the consequences of Freud's assessment of the comic and humor in situations where both subject and object are women. In his study of jokes, particularly tendentious or obscene jokes, Freud assigns woman to the place of object between two male subjects. However, there must be a difference, perhaps an impossibility, when "woman" becomes the joke-teller. Also, given that the process between spectator/auditor and joker is, according to Freud, a mutually timed, momentary slippage into the unconscious, one wonders what occurs when that "unconscious" is labeled "female"—without essentialist or biological simplifications, but with historical and cultural difference in mind. Yet, while the "joke" comprises the majority of Freud's study, and while the joke is for Freud a more complicated process than is the comic, its structure is not applicable to the structure of either of these television series (with the crucial exception of the role of George Burns, for whom Freudian joke analysis works perfectly), possibly because the joke *is* such a strong male preserve.

Unlike the three-way dealings of jokes, the comic, for Freud, is a two-way process; it is not gender-defined, and it derives from the relations of human beings "to the often over-powerful external world."[11] We experience a pleasurable empathy with the person who is pitted against this harsh world, whereas if we were actually in the situation, "we should be conscious only of distressing feelings."[12] We laugh at Lucy's comic moments, yet I wonder whether women might not also have experienced a certain amount of distress, particularly given the constraints of the 1950s and the constant subtle and not-so-subtle attempts to confine women to the home. Freud notes that "persons become comic as a result of human dependence on external events, particularly on social factors."[13] Lucy is caught in her economic subservience to Ricky, as well as in the social mores of the fifties, a decade which covertly tried to reduce women to the status of dependent children. Lucy and Gracie are continually referred to as children; the women are "helpless" or economically dependent on males—particularly Lucy and Ethel, who do not have jobs as Gracie does. Thus it is interesting to note that what Freud calls the "comic of situation is mostly based on embarrassments in which we rediscover the child's helplessness"[14] (one thinks perhaps of Lucy's exaggerated crying when she is frustrated or thwarted in her desires). Moreover, just as one rediscovers the helplessness of children in the comic of situation, so too the pleasure that it affords is compared by Freud to a child's pleasure in repetition of the same story. Situation comedy endlessly repeats mise-en-scène, character, and story; this pleasure, like the pleasure derived from *most* television, must depend to a degree on weekly forgetting as well as on repetition of the intimately familiar. Freud concludes his meandering thoughts on the comic and its infantile sources: "I am unable to decide whether degradation to being a child is only a special case of comic degradation, or whether everything comic is based fundamentally on degradation to being a child."[15] "Degradation" is the crucial word here. Featuring the perennially disobedient and rebelliously inventive child, "*I Love Lucy*" hovers somewhere between the comic of situation and what Freud calls the "comic of movement"; or better, the "situation" (the external world) is the problem which necessitates the comic of movement of which Lucy is the master.

An appendage ten pages before the end of *Jokes and Their Relation to the Unconscious*, and a later, brief essay by Freud entitled "Humour," are especially interesting for our purposes. Freud's analysis of "humor"—epitomized by "gallows jokes," the clever, exalted diversions of the condemned victim just before the hanging—as a category distinct from either the joke or the comic better explains the female victim (both subject and object, both performer and spectator), her place in the internal and external conditions of "*Lucy's*" production. Endlessly repeating that she wanted to work, to perform, humor for Lucy was "a means of obtaining pleasure in spite of the distressing affects that interfere[d] with it." It acted precisely "as a substitute" for these affects.[16] Humor was "a substitute" produced "at the cost of anger—instead of getting angry."[17] As Freud observes, "the person who is the victim of the injury, pain . . . might obtain *humourous* pleasure, while the unconcerned person laughs from *comic* pleasure."[18] Perhaps, in relation to husband and wife sketches, and audiences, the sexes split right down the middle, alternating comic with humorous pleasure depending on one's view of who the victim is; this invocation of different pleasures suggests a complexity of shifting identifications amidst gendered, historical audiences.

Trying to revive Lucy for feminism, I have suggested that throughout the overall series, and in the narrative structure of each episode, she is the victim—confined to domesticity and outward compliance with patriarchy. Yet this series is complex; Ricky is often the immediate victim of Lucy, a role more easily accepted due to his Cuban rather than Anglo-Saxon heritage. Given this perhaps crucial qualification, Lucy is, finally, rebelliously incarcerated within situation comedy's domestic regime and mise-en-scène, acutely frustrated, trying to escape via the "comic of movement," while cheerfully cracking jokes along the way to her own unmasking or capture.

Importantly, humorous pleasure for Freud comes from "an economy in expenditure upon feeling" rather than from the lifting of inhibitions that is the source of pleasure in jokes—not a slight distinction. Unlike the supposedly "liberating" function of jokes, humorous pleasure "saves" feeling because the reality of the situation is too painful. As Lucy poignantly declared to Ethel, "It's not funny, Ethel. It's tragic." Or as Freud states, "the situation is dominated by the emotion that is to be avoided, which is of an unpleasurable character." In "I Love Lucy," the avoided emotion "submitted to the control of humour"[19] is anger at the weekly frustration of Lucy's desire to escape the confinement of domesticity. This desire is caricatured by her unrealistic dreams of instant stardom in the face of her narrative lack of talent: her wretched, off-key singing, her mugging facial exaggerations, and her out-of-step dancing. Her lack of talent is paradoxically both the source of the audience's pleasure and the narrative necessity for housewifery. Using strategies of humorous displacement (the "highest of defensive processes," says Freud—a phrase that takes on interesting connotations in light of 1950s containment policies) and of the comic, both of which are "impossible under the glare of conscious attention,"[20] situation comedy avoids the unpleasant effects of its own situations. The situation of Lucy was replicated by the female spectator—whether working as a wife or in another "job"—moving between comic and humorous pleasure, between spectator and victim, in tandem with Lucy.

In this later essay, Freud elevates humor to a noble, heroic status:

> [Humour] is fine . . . elevating . . . the triumph of narcissism, the ego's victorious assertion of its own invulnerability. It refuses to be hurt . . . or to be compelled to suffer. It insists that it is impervious to wounds dealt by the outside world, in fact that these are merely oc-

casions for affording it pleasure. Humour is not resigned, it is rebellious. It signifies the triumph of not only the ego but the pleasure principle . . . it [repudiates] the possibility of suffering . . . all without quitting the ground of mental sanity . . . it is a rare and precious gift.[21]

For Lucy, Gracie, and their audiences, humor was "a rare and precious gift." Given the repressive conditions of the 1950s, humor might have been women's weapon and tactic of survival, ensuring sanity, the triumph of the ego, and pleasure; after all, Gracie and Lucy were narcissistically rebellious, refusing "to be hurt." On the other hand, comedy replaced anger, if not rage, with pleasure. The double bind of the female spectator, and of the female performer, is replicated in the structure of the programs—the shifts between narrative and comic spectacle, the latter being contained within the resolute closure of the former—and the response of the spectator is split between comic and humorous pleasure, between denial of emotion by humor and the sheer pleasure of laughter provided by the comic of movement and situation of Lucy's performances. Whether heroic or not, this pleasure/provoking cover-up/acknowledgement is not a laughing but a complex matter, posing the difficult problems of women's simulated liberation through comic containment.

## NOTES

1. Eric Goldman, *The Crucial Decade and After: America, 1945–1960* (New York: Vintage Books, 1956 and 1960).

2. Jean Baudrillard, "Requiem for the Media," *For a Critique of the Political Economy of the Sign*, trans. Charles Levin (St. Louis, MO: Telos, 1981), p. 184.

3. The transcription was taken from tape.

4. See my "Jokes and Their Relation to the Marx Brothers," *Cinema and Language*, ed. Stephen Heath and Patricia Mellencamp (Frederick, MD: University Publications of America, 1983), for further explication of jokes and the comic within the wacky male world of the Marx brothers.

5. Roland Barthes, "Writers, Intellectuals, Teachers," *Image-Music-Text*, ed. Stephen Heath (London: Fontana/Collins, 1977), pp. 205–06.

6. Samuel Weber, *The Legend of Freud* (Minneapolis: University of Minnesota Press, 1982), p. 114.

7. Ibid., p. 114.

8. Ibid., p. 116.

9. Bart Andrews, *Lucy & Ricky & Fred & Ethel* (New York: E. P. Dutton, 1976). This book contains a synopsis of shows by air date and title which helped me to organize my textual analysis.

10. Hayden White, "The Value of Narrativity in the Representation of Reality," *Critical Inquiry* 7, no. 1 (1980): p. 10.

11. Sigmund Freud, *Jokes and Their Relation to the Unconscious*, trans. James Strachey (New York: Norton & Co., 1960), p. 196.

12. Ibid., p. 197.

13. Ibid., p. 199.
14. Ibid., p. 226.
15. Ibid., p. 227.
16. Ibid., p. 228.
17. Ibid., p. 231.
18. Ibid., p. 228.
19. Ibid., p. 235.
20. Ibid., p. 233.
21. Sigmund Freud, "Humour," *The Standard Edition of the Complete Psychological Works of Sigmund Freud*, Vol. XXI (London: The Hogarth Press, 1964), pp. 162–63.

# III.
# FEMINIST STUDIES IN ENTERTAINMENT

# 6
# WOMAN IS AN ISLAND
## *FEMININITY AND COLONIZATION*

## Judith Williamson

> Capitalism is the first mode of economy
> with the weapon of propaganda, a mode
> which tends to engulf the entire globe
> and stamp out all other economies,
> tolerating no rival at its side. Yet at the
> same time it is also the first mode of
> economy which is unable to exist by
> itself, which needs other economic
> systems as a medium and a soil. . . . The
> existence and development of capitalism
> requires an environment of non-
> capitalistic forms of production.
>
> —Rosa Luxembourg[1]

> The petit-bourgeois is a man unable to
> imagine the Other. . . . But there is a
> figure for emergencies—Exoticism.
>
> —Roland Barthes[2]

The concept of "mass culture" implies a *difference*: between "mass" culture and some other kind of culture. Just what this other culture is does not have to be defined, for the mere suggestion of an alternative allows us the illusion that our participation in mass culture is more or less voluntary. To study a culture presupposes to some extent that one is outside it, though it is fashionable to "slum it" culturally, rather as George Orwell did physically, among the masses. It is extraordinary but true that a recent proud admission among some left-wing academics was to have cried at *ET*. There is a perverse contradiction whereby the higher up the educational scale you are, the more fun is to be had from consuming (while criticizing) the artifacts of mass culture: camping on the other side of the field.

Two kinds of difference are necessary for meaning. One is the difference between terms. A word derives its meaning, according to Saussure, from being what all other words are not.[3] "Cat" is not "dog" or "horse"; "nature" is not "culture"; "mass culture" is not "academic culture." The other difference is that which exists between the term or sign and its referent: the word "cat" is not a cat, or it could not *stand* for cat, while the cat itself does not necessarily *mean* a cat, but could stand for something quite different, like good luck or witches. "Nature," the concept, has a meaning precisely because it *is* a cultural construct and is *not* undifferentiated nature, which must include everything in the world. And the referent of the term "mass culture" is not the artifacts themselves, the TV programs and so on, but the people who watch them, "the masses": people who must, to us in the academic world, appear as the "other" or we would not have an object of study but a *subject* of study—ourselves.

Looking beyond the differences which define the edges of "mass culture," we find a need for new terms, or possibly for old terms, of which I think the concept of ideology the most useful. We may feel we are free to slip in and out of "mass culture" in the form of movies, TV magazines, or pulp fiction, but nowadays we know better than to imagine we can exist outside ideology. The concept of ideology also brings with it, from Marxism, suggestions about power and function and class. Speaking broadly, the whole point about most of the ideologies manifested in mass cultural "texts" is that they are dominant or hegemonic ideologies, and are therefore likely to be intimately connected with that very class which is furthest from "the masses." The function of most ideologies is to contain difference or antagonism, and the most effective way to do this, as Laclau has pointed out in his discussion of populism, is to *set up* difference.[4] He argues that a populist ideology operates by creating a simple dualism between dominant and dominated groups, who then become defined purely by their mutual "difference" rather than by actual differences.

Living in liberal democracies, we are accustomed to "difference" appearing as a form of validation—whether in the form of "balance," as we are shown opposing points of view in controversial TV programs, or in the form of "choice," as we are able to choose between different brands of cornflakes when shopping. The whole drive of our society is toward displaying as much difference as possible within it while eliminating where at all possible what is different from it: the supreme trick of bourgeois ideology is to be able to produce its opposite out of its own hat. And those differences represented within, which our culture so liberally offers, are to a great extent reconstructions of captured external differences. Our culture, deeply rooted in imperialism, needs to destroy genuine difference, to capture what is beyond its reach; at the same time, it needs *constructs* of difference in order to signify itself at all. What I intend to focus on is not just the representation of difference and otherness within mass culture, but on the main *vehicle* for this representation: "Woman."

Psychoanalysis has examined the social construction of sexual difference, and psychoanalytic writers from Freud on have been careful to stress the distinction between the actual physical difference between the sexes and the psychical differences, which, although cultural rather than innate, can appear to be natural because they are "carried" by the biological difference: *He Shave. Me Immac.* But it is possible to go one step further, and, without taking "masculinity" and "femininity" as natural or given, to investigate the wider social meanings carried by these terms. Sexual difference, itself apparently natural, is used within ideology to "carry" other important differences, including that between "nature" and "culture." Psychoanalysis has focused on the signifiers of femininity. Yet the chain of signification never ends: femininity itself becomes a signifier of other meanings, many of them contradictory. I am going to consider not the psychoanalytic construction of sexual difference but the "differences" and expression of "otherness" that sexual difference carries in our particular Western bourgeois culture. Levi-Strauss shows how, in other cultures, natural systems of difference—those of plant and animal species, for example—are used to bear the significance of social differences and to organize the meanings of social structures.[5] A similar process works in our own culture. The "natural," or in this case the already "naturalized," is precisely what carries off the social meanings. Just as Freud said of a neurosis that there is nothing it likes better than a nice solid reality to hide behind, so with social mythologies, the more "real" the structures to which they are attached, the more tenacious they are.

In our society women stand for the side of life that seems to be outside history—for personal relationships, love and sex—so that these aspects of life actually seem to become "women's areas." But they are also, broadly speaking, the arena of "mass culture." Much of mass culture takes place, or is consumed, in the "feminine" spheres of leisure, family or personal life, and the home; and it also focuses on these as the subject matter of its representations. The ideological point about these areas, the domain of both "the feminine" and "mass culture," is that they function across class divisions. If ideology is to represent differences while drawing attention away from social inequality and class struggle, what better than to emphasize differences which cut across class—the "eternal" sexual difference—or those

How can new markets be opened up once the rest of the world has already been colonized? By creating new uses, new needs, new definitions; by finding new smells which require new deodorants, new kinds of stain which require *biological* attention, new and more functions, more divisions and subdivisions between products. If Immac is to distinguish itself, there must be more than one way of removing "unwanted hair"; and what better distinction to be made between functions, what more natural difference, than that of gender? Here we have "the feminine way to remove unwanted hair" differentiated from the masculine way, shaving, as naturally as male and female are distinguished in the jungle. The woman's difference and need for a different hair-remover are evidenced in her being carried by the man. The gender divide, naturalized by its association with the "primitive," itself carries the arbitrary division of functions that is necessary to make the product seem necessary.* In this way, one of the most *un*-natural activities, the removing of body hair, is turned into a natural, indeed primeval, attribute of femininity.

*There is a further division of functions *within* the sphere of feminine hair removal, as Immac appears in "cream, lotion or aerosol form" and provides "a special Roll-On pack" for underarms.

which are bigger than class, like nationality? The most likely Other
for a white working-class man, is either a woman (page-3 pin-ups are
the central feature of the highest circulation paper in Britain) or a
foreigner—in particular somebody black. It is *not* likely to be someone
from the class which controls his livelihood.

So one of the most important aspects of images of "femininity" in
mass culture is not what they reveal, but what they conceal. If "woman"
means home, love, and sex, what "woman" *doesn't* mean, in general
currency, is work, class, and politics. This is not to suggest that domestic, personal or sexual dimensions of life are not political: far from
it. It is just that questions of class power frequently hide behind the
omnipresent and indisputable gender difference, the individual fascination of which overrides political and social divisions we might
prefer to forget (or say goodbye to, like Andre Gorz[6]). In mass culture
this phenomenon appeared in, for example, the Valentine's Day headline of the *Daily Mirror*—"Mr. Britain, This is Your Wife"—with a
series of mother and child photos that were successfully non-specific
in terms of class, standing for a universal/national wife and motherhood. In academic circles the same syndrome is often equally apparent
in the stress on sexual (rather than class) interpellation, in the concern
with the construction of the (raceless, classless) gendered subject, and
above all, in the current preoccupation with "desire." Obviously these
areas are important, yet the focus on them seems to have gone hand
in hand with neglect of other issues. For example, speech and writing
have as much to do with class as with "desire." But sexuality and
"desire" are special to us *all*, and herein lies their appeal as the "hot"
topics of the moment. *C'mon Colman's, Light My Fire*!

As soon as one stops talking about "masculinity" and "femininity"
as timeless psychoanalytic universals and looks at the particular historical structures which have led up to our present culture, the idea
of a sort of "pure" signification of difference evaporates, and we can
see *what* differences are expressed by the m/f divide.[7] We live today
to a great extent in carefully divided spheres: work/leisure, public/
private, political/domestic, economic life/emotional life, and so on.
The political value of these divisions is manifest. If there is a strike
(the sphere of work/politics), then "ordinary people," "housewives,"
"consumers" (those in the domestic/individual sphere) suffer. The fact
that the same people literally straddle both spheres becomes forgotten,
as, for example, when the miners are pictured holding the tax-payers
to ransom, as if miners weren't tax-payers themselves. But it is difference that makes meaning possible, and though in reality these
spheres are *not* separate, it is their separation into sort of ideological
pairs that gives them meaning. What "home" means to a working man
is something opposite to work, though for a woman whose work-place

These two posters provide a perfect example of the division between male-work-social and female-leisure-natural. The ad for beer shows a man in a hard hat, obviously thirsty from work, consuming a pint of Harp lager. He is presented as culturally specific: it would be possible to guess his job within perhaps half a dozen guesses—construction worker, engineer, builder, oil worker: someone who works outdoors in a blue denim shirt. Firmly located in time and place, his clothes show that he could only be in the present; and he is fair-skinned, blond, obviously a white American or European.

The advertisement for Colman's mustard on the left is the flip-side of the lager ad. Despite the fact that the woman in it appears to be eating a piece of Kentucky Fried Chicken, she herself is the feast that is offered. Her pose places her not as consumer, but as up for consumption; though her remark is addressed to the product, her body is addressed to the passing viewer. Sprawled on a tiger skin in front of an ornate but historically unplaceable fireplace, she is, like it, waiting to be lit, and a leopard is bringing her the mustard from back right of frame.

We are back to jungle imagery, the tiger and leopard suggesting a wildness and sexuality that are quite outside culture (even though they are awaiting a cultural product, the Colman's mustard, to burst into flame). The woman is

fairly dark and not easy to place either historically or geographically: she has a slightly Eastern appearance, but is impossible to locate in time. Although she is surrounded by cultural accoutrements, they are ones which signify wildness and exoticism, making them appear natural and connecting her sexuality and availability with the natural instincts of the beasts. Sexual difference is suggested in that her surroundings are far from "feminine": it is unlikely that she killed the tiger whose skin she is lying on, and whoever did is presumably the masculine presence (or absence) which is required to light her fire. Femininity needs the "other" in order to function, even as it provides "otherness."

A fire to be lit, and a fire to be put out: he needs the product with a drive that comes from his own masculinity, his activity at work; while she needs the product to bring alive her universal femininity, which is represented as passive and completely separate from the social world. He is a particular man; she is Woman, femininity, all women. But her placement with the wild beasts, *outside* culture, conversely places her culture, the culture of the Colman's mustard, *within nature*. The social construct of female "sexuality" does not appear as class-specific; it offers each and every one of us a hot line back to the wild, an escape from the mundane problems of the present.

it is, it may *not* have the same meaning of "leisure." One of the reasons
mass culture is so little concerned with work or political movements
is that most people turn on the TV to forget about these things. This
obvious but important point is frequently overlooked by those of us
whose work it is to observe and write about mass culture, as the function of these artifacts in daily life tends to be overshadowed by the
process of detailed textual analysis. This rigid separation of work and
leisure *feels* necessary because, since most of working life is so ex-
ploitative and much of social and political life so oppressive, people
want to "get away from it all."

Not only are activities divided: the drive to escape into personal life
arises from the way that values are divided too, in equally schizophrenic fashion, so that all the things society claims to value in private
and family life (caring, sharing, freedom, choice, personal development)—the kind of values that every tabloid runs its human warmth
or heartbreak stories on—are regarded as entirely inappropriate in
the sphere of political, social and economic life. Their lack there can
be covered up, however, by locating these qualities in women and in
the family, as cornerstones of our culture. Women, the guardians of
"personal life," become a kind of dumping ground for all the values
society wants off its back but must be perceived to cherish: a function
rather like a zoo, or nature reserve, whereby a culture can proudly
proclaim its inclusion of precisely what it has *ex*cluded. It is as if Western capitalism can hold up an image of freedom and fulfillment and
say, "look, our system offers this!" while in fact the reason these values
are squeezed into personal life (and a tight squeeze it is, too) is that
they are exactly what the economic system fundamentally negates,
based as it is on the values of competition and profit, producing lack
of control, lack of choice and alienation. In this sea of exploitation it
does indeed appear that *Woman Is an Island*.

Thus, while we seem to have little choice over, for example, nuclear
weapons, we tend to think of ourselves as having freedom or happiness inasmuch as these qualities are manifested in our personal lives,
the part of life represented by femininity. And the sphere which is
supposedly most different from the capitalist system is crucial to it,
both economically and in producing its meanings. The family provides
the most lucrative market for modern consumer economies; in Britain
80% of all shopping is done by women. The "natural" phenomena of
the family and sexuality throw back an image of a "natural" economy,
while the economy penetrates and indeed constructs these "natural"
and "personal" areas through a mass of products—liberally offering
us our own bodies as sites of difference: *You Can Use Pond's Cream and
Cocoa Butter All Over. Here. Or There.*

It is in consuming that we appear to have choice, and in personal

Woman is an island. Fidji is her perfume.

Woman and colony become completely confused here: Fiji is an island but has been appropriated as nothing but a perfume; while the wearer of perfume, Woman, has been turned into an island, generalized, non-specific, but reeking of exoticism. The feminine and the exotic are perfectly merged, as both are colonized by The French Quarter, which wraps its red, white and blue flag round the lot. (The picture is bordered in red, white and blue, the same colors as on the tie of the "Q" around the bottom left caption.) Woman is an island because she is mysterious, distant, a place to take a holiday; but she is also an island within ideology—surrounded and isolated, as the colony is by the colonizer, held intact as the "Other" within a sea of sameness. If Fidji can be wrapped up in the chic French scarf of femininity, femininity is equally enclosed, gift-wrapped within culture, not as one of its own products but as a package tour of the natural.

You can use Pond's Cream and Cocoa Butter all over.
Here. Or there.

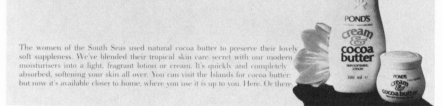

The women of the South Seas used natural cocoa butter to preserve their lovely
soft suppleness. We've blended their tropical skin care secret with our modern
moisturisers into a light, fragrant lotion or cream. It's quickly and completely
absorbed, softening your skin all over. You can visit the Islands for cocoa butter;
but now it's available closer to home, where you use it is up to you. Here. Or there.

"Here, or There"—a hint of the sexual, of forbidden places: the photo
shows us pretty much of "here," the skin that is visible; it is the "there" which
is left to be imagined, the darkest and most secret place where Pond's Cocoa
Butter might be used. The "all over" is dangerous and safe at the same time:
it points to its extremity—*even* "there"!—and "there" is the other, the furthest
place, the sexual; yet the gap between "here" and "there" is smoothed over
in the democratic application of Pond's Cocoa Butter—it knows no difference.

However, the sexual reverberation produced by the main caption and the photo is at once undercut and reinforced by the small print beneath. The voyage across the body becomes a voyage across the globe. The wonders of modern production ("We've blended their tropical skin care secret"—presumably not a secret any more—"with our modern moisturisers") can bring the mysteries of distant cultures right back home, while, of course, improving them slightly. These mysteries are at once feminine and foreign: they pose a distance to be overcome ("now it's available closer to home") and to be maintained: their "tropical skin care secret" and "natural cocoa butter" are what keep the women of the South Seas at the apex of femininity with their "lovely soft suppleness." The different has been incorporated and yet is preserved symbolically for the sake of choice: after all, if you wish, "You can visit the Islands for cocoa butter"—an entirely imaginary quest*—and "where you use it is up to you." You are free to choose: apparently, between cultures; and yet in reality the only choice you do have is between places on your body— where to put the cocoa butter once you have it. After its circuitous voyage through the sphere of global distribution, the ad returns us to the product and allows us to choose how to distribute it—on ourselves.

This brings us back to the sexual meaning of the caption. For although the longer text reveals the geographical dimension of "here or there," the image, despite appearing to illustrate this text, negates it. With its colonial backdrop of tropical plants and a white parrot on the veranda, the photo does indeed take us "there" but precisely by bringing it here—onto the page. The "here" of the picture is the "there" of the text: in the exotic setting of the photo only the sexual innuendo of "here or there" operates, as the other differences have been dissolved. Within the image, the decor of white lacquered chairs and venetian blinds suggests the colonizer rather than the colonized. The woman is culturally unplaceable. She could be a "South Seas Woman," or equally, a white appropriator of the Tropical Secret. These ambiguities turn the figure in the photo into simply "Woman": her head and shoulders are cut off, at once emphasizing the "secret" region of the body and preventing her racial or cultural identification. So the reality of colonization disappears, as cultural differences represent, and in the process are reduced to, the "differences" offered by the female body, which, in turn, both stands for the "Other" culture and provides the negation of its Otherness.

*As Lacan says, the symbolic requires difference, which the imaginary tries to leap across.

relations that we appear to have freedom. As long as women are carrying those values individually, *for* society, they do not have to be put into operation socially. Women who protest "as women" against the bomb are either engaging in a very effective use of society's own values against itself or accepting society's ideological definition of themselves as inherently more caring. Whatever their uses, the values of interpersonal relations, feeling, and caring are loaded onto women in direct proportion to their off-loading from the realities of social and economic activity.

This can be seen in everyday terms, as the "personal life" that is set up in opposition to work becomes the justification for work: men (as if only men go out to work) are exhorted to work harder, so as to earn more, so as to insure their home and family, invest for their children, enhance their leisure time, buy more exciting holidays, etc. The daily grind appears meaningful only because of the life outside it. The social structure is justified not in social but in personal and individual terms. This shows how separation and difference, the opposition between terms, produce meaning not just in theory but in day-to-day life. Similarly, the idea of "woman" and the "personal" as a repository for the values society wants to be rid of can be seen literally in current social policies in Britain—policies which have deliberately replaced social services for the handicapped and elderly with the explicit assumption that women will perform these services individually, unpaid, in the home. The government then seems to be the champion of the individual, the home, and family—which is exactly where it is dumping its unwanted burden! This illustrates in practice the separation of sign and referent: the "return to the family" *stands* for something quite different from the hardship, disguised as responsibility, which is in fact being "returned" to real families.

If this kind of "concrete semiotics" seems a little far-fetched, one might ask what other kind of semiotics could possibly be of any use politically? I see a Marxist semiotics as an enterprise that tries to understand both a structure and its content—concerned with a system of meaning, but one whose meanings function within actual historical systems. The need of our society both to engulf Others and to exploit "otherness" is not only a structural and ideological phenomenon; it has been at the root of the very development of capitalism, founded as it is on the imperialist relations described by Rosa Luxembourg in the quotation above. If woman is the great Other in the psychology of patriarchal capitalist culture, the Other on which that culture has depended for its very existence is the colony, which, as Luxembourg shows, it needed simultaneously to exploit and to destroy. Capitalism is not a system which can function alone in equilibrium. It always

Here Pond's Cream and Cocoa Butter is less coy about unveiling its tropical mystery: "For centuries, the women of the South Sea Islands have been envied for their soft skin." The Other is pictured less ambiguously, and its capture proclaimed more triumphantly. In showing an actual (albeit very "white"-looking) South Seas woman the control of difference is more complete, and we are placed not between two worlds, but in control of both: "Now your skin can have the best of both worlds." The product has brought the Other together with the known, and the timeless into modernity. "For centuries" and "for generations" the secret has been kept but now the "traditional South Seas recipe" is combined with "modern, well-tried moisturizers." In this way the tradition of a different culture appears as the modern achievement of our own.

needs some imbalance, something other than itself: riddled with contradictions, it is not internally sufficient. Our current standard of living derives in part from the incredibly cheap labor exploited by multinational companies in "developing countries," which produce many of our consumer goods on wages that would be unacceptable to us, and from the control of markets internationally. Western banks make enormous loans, at enormous interest, to impoverished Eastern Bloc countries. Economically, we need the Other, even as politically we seek to eliminate it.

So, with colonial economies as with the family, capitalism feeds on different value systems and takes control of them, while nourishing their symbolic differences from itself. The "natural" and "exotic," the mystery of foreign places and people, appear both as separate from our own culture and as its most exciting product: *Discover The Tropical Secret For Softer Skin.* Travel and holiday advertising offers us the rest of the world in commodity form, always represented as completely different from the fast pace of Western "culture," yet apparently easily packaged by it nonetheless. Rather as, in individual psychology, the repressed, instead of disappearing, is represented or replaced by a symptom or dream image, so in global terms different systems of production (colonial, feudal) which are *sup*pressed by capitalism are then incorporated into its imagery and ideological values: as "otherness," old-fashioned, charming, exotic, natural, primitive, universal.

What is taken away in reality, then, is re-presented in image and ideology so that *it stands for itself* after it has actually ceased to exist. The travel images of "colorful customs," of exotic cultures, of people apparently more "natural" than ourselves but at the same time expressing our own "naturalness" for us—all these images of "otherness" have as their referent an actual Otherness which was and is still being systematically destroyed, first by European then by American capital. Yet it is the *idea* of "natural" and "basic" cultures which seems to guarantee the permanence (and, ironically, the universality) of capitalist culture. It is the value system of our own society that we "read off" other societies; we seek to naturalize our own power structures in the mirror of "natural" life as pictured outside capitalism. Other societies can be used in the same way that the family is used to show work without revealing class; little wonder that, for example, car advertising selects so many images of women and peasants, since their labor can be presented as "natural" and autonomous.[8] But just as the commodity which expresses another's value loses its own identity in the process, so those "primitives"—women and foreigners—who are so valuable in reflecting capitalism's view of itself are robbed of their own meanings and speech, indeed are reduced to the function of

This woman-in-sea-with-garland image is the typical representation of the exotic; conversely, femininity is represented by the "woman of the islands": half-naked, dark-haired, tanned. Yet her features make her equally likely to be a white American or European woman who has *acquired* the "natural tan of the islands." It is striking that the deep-tan advertising genre, and the exotic "southern" images, never use either African-looking models or politically contentious places: in this ad "the islands" are obviously Hawaii, but in general there are many imaginary "islands" in make-up, suntan, and perfume ads which serve to represent an "other" place and culture without actually having to recognize any real other country and its culture. The "desert island" is the ideal location for the "other"; it is more easily colonized than an entire continent,* and picturing the colony as female makes it so much more conquerable and receptive.

Of course, when the caption offers its product "to all skin types for a safe, dark, natural tan" it doesn't really mean a "natural tan." If one were naturally dark, of course, one would be black—a contingency not anticipated by the ad, which clearly does *not* address "all skin types" but, like almost all public imagery, assumes its audience to be white.

*The early capitalist pioneer Robinson Crusoe did well in this respect.

Fashion is the area of social communication where the function of difference is perhaps most vividly seen. A debutante could go to a party in a pair of overalls and be regarded as highly fashionable; a plumber could not. It is currently "in" for the young and well-fed to go around in torn rags, but not for tramps to do so. In other words, the appropriation of other people's dress is fashionable provided it is perfectly clear that you are, in fact, *different* from whoever would normally wear such clothes.* Fashion photographers are very fond of re-placing models in the original locations of the styles they wear: you see glamorous, leggy women posing in denim shirts in gas stations, pouting women in boiler-suits and cloth caps perched on factory equipment (both examples from actual fashion features in British magazines), or women in khaki draped across camels or Land Rovers in deserts—the colonial safari look.

In these concoctions from Chelsea Girl, the borrowing of the exotic is very much in evidence. Yet the clothes manage to suggest both colonized and colonizer together with their mixture of sari-style wrap and military khaki— "safari dress," to quote the catalogue—blended with "punjabi trousers" and topped by a choice of army cap or turban. This proximity of army gear to the "exotic" is very revealing: the entire colonial relation can be expressed in one outfit. A recent fascination with the whole phenomenon of colonization has been seen in Britain with the popular, "high-class" TV drama, "The Jewel in the Crown"; and the nature and level of this interest are pretty much the same as the current fashion preoccupation. The *meaning* of British colonization in India is eclipsed as the two sides of a real conflict are rolled into one and come to stand for an "otherness" and "exoticism" that have no content, merely a style.

It is fine fashion to wear a turban if you are white, as these glossy photos show, even though in Britain sikhs who wear turbans for religious reasons are subject to much racist abuse. I once heard a girl with pink hair and two rings through her nose complaining about the way Indian women wear saris in this country—"It's not right for them to try and stay different once they come here, they should make an effort to fit in."

---

*A more general example of this, and of the importance of the relation clothes have to work, is the way that working class people tend to dress up to go out—if you have been wearing overalls or jeans all day you want to get out of them and demarcate your leisure time—while the "professional" middle class tends to dress down.

commodities. We are the culture that knows no "other," and yet can offer myriad others, all of which seem to reflect, as if they were merely surfaces, our own supposed natural and universal qualities. To have something "different" captive in our midst reassures us of the liberality of our own system and provides a way of re-presenting real difference in tamed form: *Keep It Dark, Keep It Safe*. We do not like real Others but need to construct safe ones out of the relics of the Others we have destroyed—like the Stepford Wives, the perfect, robotically feminine wives manufactured by the men of Stepford from selected components of their original, human wives. The real women are killed in the process.

Capitalism's constant search for new areas to colonize finds both an analogue and an expression in the processes of fashion: *Chelsea Girl Spring/Summer Collection 1984*. But by fashion I don't merely mean clothes. The bourgeois always wants to be in disguise, and the customs and habits of the oppressed seem so much more fascinating than "his" own. How many of the London middle class really want to live in a traditionally middle class area like Kensington? How much more original to move eastwards, into "poorer" (and cheaper) areas, interesting converted warehouses, narrow Dickensian streets with ornate old pubs. But where do the inheritors of this working class landscape end up, once the imaginative middle classes have moved in and knocked through the front parlor walls? In enormous and desolate tower blocks, even farther east, while the leader of the Social Democratic Party enjoys a view of the docks and the flavor of the authentic in historic Limehouse. Why is this geographical survey relevant? Because it shows how characteristics of social difference are appropriated within our culture to provide the trappings of individual difference: *Isn't it Nice to Be Brown When Everyone Else is White*. The bourgeois is obsessed with whatever it is that "he" hasn't got, whether a suntan or a sense of community. And while the former is buyable, the latter, despite the movements of the property market, is not. Yet it is a premise of capitalism that everything can be exchanged. Academics will sometimes exchange an investigation of their own "culture" for the more colorful and exotic field of other people's, and in the intricacies of these mass cultural texts it becomes possible, literally, to lose oneself. As Marie-Antoinette played dairymaid, we sometimes play "popular culture," in a way that is fashionable only because we feel, ultimately, that we can pull back and reassert our difference. It is crucially important to study "mass culture" and its specific texts, but not in order to understand "the masses"; the ideology of difference is not, in fact, different from the ideologies that imprison us all.

The fashion for tans shows most clearly of all the necessity of difference in producing meaning, and also reveals how the relation of ideological phenomena to production is frequently central to their meaning (despite the supposed outdating of this concept within contemporary Marxism). When the nature of most people's productive work, outdoors, made a suntan the norm for working people, a pale skin was much prized, a mark of luxury: not just a symbol but an indexical sign of leisure time, a measure of distance from the masses' way of life. Now, however, a deep suntan stands for exactly the same things—leisure, wealth, and distance—for it must involve *not* being at work for the majority of people, and therefore suggests having the wealth for both leisure and travel.

In fact, this ad for Ambre Solaire offers you self-tanning lotion which doesn't require hours in the sun; however, the fake tan it produces only has a meaning because it *does* suggest time in the sun, leisure, etc. It is typical within ideology that the method of the product, the self-tanning, actually denies what it means, which is "real suntan"—making the inaccessible accessible, while simultaneously boasting that it is uniquely hard to obtain. In theory, anyone and everyone could buy fake-tan lotion and get a tan, yet the tan still represents difference, as the caption shows.

There is another kind of difference which this provocative caption completely ignores. "Isn't it nice to be brown when everyone else is white?" Yes, but only if you were white to start with. The racism of a white colonial society *isn't* very nice.

## NOTES

1. Rosa Luxembourg, *The Accumulation of Capital* (London: Routledge & Kegan Paul, 1963), p. 368. I am indebted to Sheila Rowbotham in her book *Woman's Consciousness, Man's World* (London: Pelican Books, 1973) for drawing my attention to this work and in particular to the implications of the passage quoted. My own argument about colonization owes much to her.

2. Roland Barthes, *Mythologies* (London: Paladin, 1973), pp. 151–52.

3. Ferdinand de Saussure, *Course in General Linguistics* (New York: McGraw-Hill, 1966), p. 117.

4. Ernesto Laclau, *Politics and Ideology in Marxist Theory* (London: New Left Books, 1977), p. 161: "A class is hegemonic not so much to the extent that it is able to impose a uniform conception of the world on the rest of society, but to the extent that it can articulate different visions of the world in such a way that their potential antagonism is neutralized."

5. Claude Levi-Strauss, *The Savage Mind* (London: Weidenfeld and Nicolson, 1966).

6. Andre Gorz, *Farewell to the Working Class* (London: Pluto Press, 1982).

7. In her article, "Woman as Sign," in *m/f* no. 1 (1978), Elizabeth Cowie explores the place of women as bearers of meaning in societies from both a psychoanalytic and an anthropological point of view. However, in locating "woman" as a sign produced entirely through exchange, her argument becomes tautological, as women come to signify nothing but difference, and difference is signified simply through the fact that women are exchanged while men are not. "Woman is produced as a sign within exchange systems in as much as she is the signifier of a difference in relation to men, i.e., women are exchanged rather than men. . . . The position of women as sign in exchange therefore has no relation to *why* women are exchanged, in other words, it has no relation to the 'idea' of women in society" (p. 56). This particular analysis, which is important in that it was one of the first to examine women not as signified but as sign, stops short at the formal production of the sign and never looks at what that sign means, the content of the signifying system. What woman the sign means, according to this account, is the concept "woman," which in itself means simply exchangeability.

8. I have gone into this argument in more detail in "The History of Photographs Mislaid," *Photography/Politics: One* (London: Photography Workshop, 1979).

# 7

# THE INCORPORATION
# OF WOMEN
## A COMPARISON OF NORTH AMERICAN
## AND MEXICAN POPULAR NARRATIVE

## Jean Franco

There have probably never been so many techniques for telling stories as there are in this era of mass culture: cinema, television and radio soap opera, comic-strip novels, photonovels, print narrative, certain genres of popular song, and even advertisements. And, despite the obstinately high number of illiterates, there have never been so many readers and certainly never so many women readers. In the United States, about half of the paperback book market consists of mass market fiction (predominantly romance) for women. In Mexico, two popular series whose readers are mainly women sell between 800,000 and one million copies each week for each volume.[1] Since every issue is probably read by more than one woman, these figures are significant indices of the "feminine," at least as it is constructed in modern society.

The study of modern mass culture narrative for women raises several crucial questions:

• That the pluralism of mass-culture narrative (which ranges from conventional romances to "liberation" stories) does not produce "contradictions" suggests that there is no "dominant ideology" in the old sense but rather a process of constantly changing tactics and adaptations to circumstance. With respect to women, can it be said that this pluralism, together with the internationalization of mass culture, has constituted new kinds of feminine subjects that conflict with older national "femininities"?

• Since we are dealing with a transnational phenomenon, it may seem no longer to make sense to distinguish between U.S.-produced romances and Mexican photonovels, between Brazilian and U.S. tele-novels. Should we not rather disregard national boundaries and consider the position of different mass culture narratives within the international division of labor?

● The issue of women's "conservatism" seems to be at stake in many mass culture narratives addressed to women. Why have these narratives appropriated forms that seem anachronistic even by mass cultural standards?

In order to answer these questions, as well as the more general one of how the feminine is constructed in the multinational era, I intend to draw on U.S.-produced advertising, on romantic fiction—Utopian stories told to women as potential consumers—and on Mexican comic-strip novels—stories directed to women as potential members of the labor force. Since advertising is in many ways the paradigmatic form of modern mass culture, I would like to begin by considering the whiskey ad illustrated here, an ad, which, like most advertising, works on the understanding that women are incorporated differently into the dominant order than are men.

A couple sits at a table in a tropical setting with a whiskey bottle between them. The man is represented synecdochically by a hand grasping a full glass, the woman by a face reflected in an empty glass. Much of the scene (a tropical setting with palm trees, the woman's sun glasses) is reflected upside down on a glass table. The world that is beyond that couple is inverted, as are all other objects except the whiskey glasses, the man's hand, and the woman's reflected face. The crucial gender difference is underlined by the fact that the man's hand is not a reflection whilst the woman's face, though not inverted, is reflected in her own empty glass.

In an uncanny manner, the ad seems to revitalize Marx's description of ideology as a kind of *camera obscura* that inverts real relationships. But there is a characteristically modern twist, for the ad juxtaposes an inverted world of nature (reflected palm trees) and an "ideological" world which is right side up (the man's hand, the whiskey bottle, and the reflection of the woman's face), placing the illusory against the "real." In addition, the woman is radically different from the man, since the man's hand belongs to a different plane of reality than does the woman's face, which is seen only in reflection, as if drowned in the glass. The operation we perform when we look at the ad differs according to whether we are male or female—whether we look as a man and thus identify with the active hand which sums up "man" as one who possesses and acts and whose presence requires us to make the intellectual operation of associating hand with man, with holding, holding the expectant (not yet empty) glass, a man seeing a dimly reflected woman who might be made his woman; or whether we look as a woman seeing a reflection that might be hers and the hand that might hold her. But clearly the woman's relation to the advertisement

Descubre al hombre que toma Buchanan's.

is mediated differently from that of the man, since the woman sees herself not only as the reflection of herself but as the reflection of man's desire for her, a desire that is associated with a "real" (and not a reflected) hand holding a glass. Man is represented through synechdoche, woman through the synechdoche and the specular image. And though woman is apparently addressed by the ad ("Descubra al hombre que toma Buchanan's"), she is also objectified by it, since the red color of her lips is associated with the "lip" of the bottle and with the bottle top lying on the table. Thus drinking is associated with kissing the woman.

Not surprisingly, this different positioning of men and women in relation to the real has become a topic of heated debate. Some feminists have drawn on the work of Lévi-Strauss to explain how it is that woman may be at once both subject and object, as in the ad. They have emphasized that the exchange of women on which "primitive" societies build their kinship system becomes the "political unconscious" of capitalist society.[2] One of the most interesting accounts of the way this political unconscious might affect female consciousness, at least in the high noon of the bourgeoisie, is that offered by John Berger in his novel *G* wherein the split female personality (he is speaking of middle-class women in early twentieth century Europe) is associated with the fact that she is owned by a man while at the same time she is able to think like one. Berger writes:

> A woman's presence was the result of herself being split into two, and of her energy being inturned. A woman was always accompanied— except when she was quite alone—by her own image of herself. Whilst she was walking across a room or whilst she was weeping at the death of her father, she could not avoid envisaging herself walking or weeping. From earliest childhood she had been taught and persuaded to survey herself continually. And so she came to consider the surveyer and the surveyed within her as the two constituent yet always distinct elements of her identity as a woman. . . . This subjective world of the woman, this realm of her presence, guaranteed that no action undertaken within it could ever possess full integrity; in each action there was an ambiguity which corresponded to an ambiguity in the self, divided between surveyer and surveyed.
>
> When she is alone in her room and sure of being alone, a woman may look at herself in a mirror and put out her tongue. This makes her laugh and, on other occasions, cry.[3]

Unlike the accounts given of female subjectivity by Sigmund Freud and Jacques Lacan, Berger's analysis suggests that there are social underpinnings to woman's problematic self and that these have their origin in her exchange value in very specific conditions of capitalist society. Although there is nothing new in considering woman the surveyor and the surveyed, Berger's description of woman's split consciousness is very different from that of Lacan (for whom we are all split from the lost object of desire), since it suggests a chronic social anxiety of one who is evaluated on the basis of appearance alone. One part of woman (that which would parody by sticking out her tongue or would express opposition by crying) is suppressed in any social situation and can only be expressed in private in front of the mirror, which assures her of her real identity. Again, what is new is not that a class of women are evaluated for looks but rather that this class has resources which have to be censored. The mistake Berger makes seems to be in thinking that men, unlike women, have access to an authentic self. Nevertheless, male identity can be less self-consciously secured, since society connives in recognizing the intellectual and productive work of the male (the hand on the whiskey glass).

Now it is interesting that this split female personality which seems, at least in Berger's view, to be related to woman's dual role as token in exchange and as thinking person has become a primary mechanism of mass culture narrative. In at least one form of this narrative—the romance—women are invited to reenact the process of censorship by which the thinking part of themselves has to be suppressed. Women are plotted into the social as people who must be seduced and whose relation to the social is that of seductress. While the social circumstances (property relationships) which made this their strongest option have disappeared, they are still positioned in this way within society. Mass culture narrative guides women through the social labyrinth. Yet as I shall show, there are various plots which may be differentiated according to what it is that women are being asked to sacrifice. In the case of romantic fiction, women are asked to sacrifice their intelligence, whereas in the comic strip novels they often sacrifice romance. Thus women's "difference" is not always seen in the same way, even though the manner in which women are positioned usually depends on quite archaic mechanisms—a kind of anachronistic "political unconscious" which nevertheless allows the modern woman to be constituted. This anachronism is deployed in mass culture narrative addressed both to relatively affluent women (the mass of women in the metropolitan countries and selected groups of privileged consumers in the third world) and to women who are integrated or about to be integrated into the lower levels of the work force. Thus the ancient form of romance is deployed to represent the utopian side of modernization, the utopia in which there can be unlimited gratification without guilt or social disapproval. The dystopia that corresponds to it is the world of oppressive work in which the very commodities that promise gratification are produced. The (utopian) romance provides women with a dream of an ideal reconciliation between their individual desire for love and their desire for social approval, a reconciliation which will be achieved by a process of self-censorship. On the other hand, in the popular literature addressed to those women who are positioned differently within the international division of labor, romance is shown to be deceptive.

Though both romance and exemplary literature are archaic in form, they incorporate women very differently into the social. In the romance, the prime element is woman's adaptability to rules that she has not made and over which she has no control. This adaptability, as Warren Sussman has recently shown, was widely canvassed in the United States at a moment when the old style puritan ethic was fast disappearing and a culture of abundance was taking its place.[4] Thus the "modern" side of romance is its emphasis on unquestioning adaptation to a situation of abundance, while the Mexican comic strips I shall examine—the *libros semanales*—both support a work ethic and display their modernity in rather different fashion from the romance—by attacking machismo and even promoting, at times, sexual liberation. It is only by comparing narratives which correspond to different levels of the international division of labor that we can appreciate the fact that different narrative strategies are deployed when women are addressed as consumers than are deployed when they are addressed as potential members of the work force. While romance forgets the world of work, the Mexican *libros semanales* offer work and emancipation from the extended family as forms of escape from violent and bitter family situations.

Though there are many kinds of women's romantic fiction, the Harlequin romances can be taken as paradigmatic. They are distributed not only in North America but also in Latin America, although the Hispanic world had generated its own particular form of romantic literature for women—the Corín Tellado romance whose popularity antedates the Harlequin romances. The Corín Tellado novels were widely read in the sixties and early seventies and have been adapted to the photonovel format. They are similar to the Harlequin in many ways, although if anything there is an even stronger emphasis on luxury items, expensive clothes, and jewelry.[5] In Latin America, however, there are now many other sub-genres of narrative for women, many of which—the *libro semanal*, the television soap opera, and the type of photonovel known as *novelas rojas*—can no longer be classified as romance. Indeed, because they present such a violent contrast to romance, I shall concentrate on this type of fiction, and especially on the comic-strip version of the *libro semanal*.

Before discussing this comic-book literature, however, we need to examine a question that has long puzzled feminists—namely, why in countries like the United States and in some sectors of Latin America this anachronistic formula literature should be so attractive. The very genre of romance, as Fredric Jameson has shown, is a leftover from a long-vanished world of knighthood. These "magical narratives," with their sharply opposing yet ultimately fused sets of characters, have enjoyed a remarkably long life, so much so that Northrop Frye saw them as archetypical of "the search of the libido or desiring self for a fulfillment that will deliver it from the anxieties of reality but will still contain that reality."[6] As Jameson notes, "the problem raised by the persistence of romance as a mode is that of substitutions, adaptations, and appropriations, and raises the question of what, under wholly altered historical circumstances, can have been found to replace the raw materials of magic and Otherness which mediaeval romance found ready to hand in its socioeconomic environment."[7] Though Jameson briefly mentions the resurfacing of romance in modern mass culture, it has been left to feminist critics to attempt to explain the deployment of this anachronistic form in the era of mass culture— an attempt that was stimulated by recognition of its overwhelming popularity.

Many of these critics, however, were caught in a dilemma, neither wanting to adopt an elitist position of condemning romance readers as passive nor wanting altogether to endorse this literature. Ann Snitow, for instance, comes to the conclusion that romances feed "certain regressive elements in female experience," but refuses to dismiss them out of hand: "to observe that they express primary structures of our social relations is not to claim either a cathartic usefulness for them or a dangerous power to keep women in their place."[8] Rosalind Coward believes that women's romantic fiction "restores the childhood world of sexual relations and suppresses criticism of the inadequacy of men, the suffocation of the family, or the damage inflicted by patriarchal power. Yet it simultaneously manages to avoid the guilt and fear which might come from that childhood world. Sexuality is defined firmly as the father's responsibility and fear of suffocation is overcome because women achieve a sort of power in the romantic fiction."[9] And in an illuminating analysis that owes much to recent Freudian criticism, Tania Modleski suggests that the very tightness of the Harlequin plot is proof of the degree of control needed to cope with women's resentment, which can only be "managed" by making the heroine perform a "disappearing act," by making her sacrifice "her aggressive instincts, her pride and—nearly—her life." Readers, according to Modleski, are thus forced into a kind of schizoid reaction, having to cope with both the heroine's self-surrender and their own revenge fantasies directed against the proud male. Far from achieving undiluted escape, they experience a compulsion to repeat the reading because there is no real life solution to these contradictory feelings.[10]

Though Janice Radway criticizes literary and psychoanalytical analyses of this type, her own study, *Reading the Romance*, bears out these very conclusions. Radway interviewed a group of readers who claimed that the romances enabled them to escape from family and everyday routines and to enter a private world. The readers also affirmed their preference for romances in which heroes and heroines fulfilled certain requirements in a way that allowed the plot to be resolved without raising tension to the point where it caused pain. These romance readers seemed to share the Freudian view that the subject seeks to avoid painful tensions and if a direct satisfaction of desire is not available then a more circuitous route to satisfaction will be taken. Radway also concludes that the repetitive style of the romances, their use of familiar syntax and language and of a trustworthy narrator means that they function as cultural myths even though the readers remember them as distinct stories.[11]

Radway's study of the modern development of this "category literature" shows that despite its reliance on formulae, a trait it shares with orally transmitted tales, it is a relatively new phenomenon. Oral tradition persists within communities that hand down stories through verbal communication, whereas modern formula literature has been devised on the basis of market studies and has been targeted to particular sectors of the population in order to meet well-tested needs. But despite the fact that the formulae are made necessary by mass production, Radway stresses that they provide readers with a considerable amount of reading pleasure—a pleasure which she, in common with other feminist critics, recognizes as utopian—that is, promising to fulfill desires that come from society itself.[12] Certainly the producers of Harlequin romances show some awareness of the relation of their product to a "private self," for their television commercials play on women's desire for privacy. For example, one of them shows a young girl coming in from a cold and stormy night and settling down to her cup of tea and a Harlequin. The storm stands for all that women want to shut out: a turbulent and uncontrollable world, whether of work or of family relations. It presents them not precisely with escape, but with a world in which the rules, once learned, bring about a magic resolution.

Of course, the Harlequin is not the only contemporary genre to use archaic forms. The Western offers a parallel on the masculine side, and even advertisements often show a hankering after the pomp and glory of the Tsars (vodka ads) or the manor house. But the Harlequins' use of the archaic evokes more than a manorial setting; it also slips in, as if they were a fact of nature, gender relationships in which men have both power and knowledge, and in which women have to be tutored. Manorial space and time (the preferred "chronotope" of Harlequins) allows the narrative to be read as a quest whose successful outcome can be anticipated and repeated an infinite number of times, a quest, moreover, which shows the conditions under which women can attain social power—that is, through seduction of the powerful and adaptation to unwritten rules. Their reward for successful apprenticeship is not only marriage, but comfort and abundance.

Since there have been so many discussions of the Harlequin romance, and since its basic plot structure is well known, I will not reiterate the main features. While there is an obvious risk in laying too much emphasis on a single example, I am now going to do precisely that, partly because the novel I have chosen for analysis, the widely read *Moonwitch* by Ann Mather, explicitly reveals the corporate wolf in sheep's clothing. Though the "deep structure" of the plot is like that of all other Harlequins, the surface narrative offers us a convenient example of the fable of woman's incorporation into the social order. In *Moonwitch*, an orphan named Sara is literally bequeathed by her grandfather on his deathbed to the Kyle Textile Corporation. Thus Sara is already incorporated from the outset of the novel, which will show how in romances woman's desire to be her true self is really the desire to be so incorporated. It is true that the grandfather believed that the corporation was controlled by his old friend J.K. What complicates the plot is that, unknown to the grandfather, J.K. has retired, leaving the corporation in the hands of his hard-headed, unsympathetic son, Jarrod, who does not want to be burdened with a schoolgirl ward. Rather than contesting the will, however, he hands Sara over to J.K., who whiles away his retirement by "educating" her into the social demands of corporate life even though she has hitherto been preparing for a career as an artist. As in most Harlequin novels, mothers do not socialize their daughters, and social programming of a serious kind is left to the male.

J.K. lives in a manor house, the euphemistic setting for corporate society in which Sara now has to school herself by learning about fashion, good taste, and proper social behavior. As Pierre Bourdieu shows, euphemism is necessary in order for the dominant groups to secure the adherence of the dominated to their social program, for it glosses over the underlying exploitation and oppression.[13] In *Moonwitch*, the euphemistic figure of the manor house suggests that the corporation now occupies the place of the older aristocracy, whose right to rule it has inherited. The corporation is the natural successor to the aristocracy.

After this initial step into the corporate zone, Sara's trajectory follows the familiar Harlequin pattern in which the hero and heroine misrecognize each other's intentions. She believes Jarrod to be hard and cold and clings to the fatherly J.K. Jarrod, for his part, believes her to be a social climber, although he is sexually attracted to her. Jarrod's hard unpleasantness thus seems to conflict with the benevolent protectiveness of J.K. The details of the plot are not relevant here except to note that by making Sara the ward of a corporation, the author underlines the fact that the final marriage is to a particular social order. The heroine's misrecognition of the hero's character tells the reader that though he appears on the surface to be harsh, selfish, and ego-centered, he is in reality a bounteous, generous father-substitute. The marriage contract which ends the novel recognizes that the heroine is worthy of her true place in society while showing that recognition of this right is bestowed on her by the patriarchal

order—only after she has learned its rules of postponement of gratification and obedience. And part of this obedience involves reassessing what initially appears to be disagreeable, and even unnatural,
so that it becomes desirable.

If we now return to Jameson's discussion of modern romance, it
will have become obvious that the male and female are opposing positions whose differences will achieve resolution in the harmony of
marriage, though without this implying any equality between them.
As feminist critics of romance have shown, women enjoy traversing
the familiar plot terrain not only because it is familiar but also because
it ends satisfactorily, ends moreover by giving them an unequivocal
place in the world as adored and valued objects. The Harlequin plot
responds directly to the devaluation of women by showing one way
in which they can negotiate a satisfactory contract with corporate society: that is, by postponing gratification, by accepting that their power
stems from their ability to seduce successfully, and by showing that
legitimate seduction (which implies the exercise of self-control) will
eventually allow them full membership in society as women and consumers. The success of Harlequins may in fact be due to their ac-
knowledgement of women's desire for recognition, and also of their
desire to be valued, which is a direct consequence of their devalued
position in society as a whole.

There are parallels to Harlequins in Latin America—in particular,
the Corín Tellado novels that I have already mentioned. Like the
Harlequins, Corín Tellado offers a felicitous solution to the "female"
problem. However, the proliferation of other types of literature for
women in Latin America—particularly in Brazil and in Mexico—suggests that the difficulty of plotting the course of women as consumers
might be greater in those societies where women are incorporated
first of all into the work force, a process that might require a radical
change in their attitude to the family.[14] Moreover, the euphemism,
which is a feature of Harlequins, only works when it is possible to put
a benign face on corporate society—something that becomes difficult
when society is breaking down, when there is physical violence and
torture. Thus it is interesting to contrast the Harlequin with certain
forms of Mexican popular literature for women, particularly the *libro
semanal*—a comic-strip novel in which women's socialization is shown
from a radically different perspective.[15]

First, however, it is important to situate this literature within the
general development of the culture industry. In Mexico, mass production was introduced in a way that has no parallel in the U.S., since
it was in part a state-directed operation initiated with Vasconcelos'
attempt to publish and distribute classical texts throughout Mexico in
the years immediately following the revolution. Mass book production

and the manufacture of cheap books designed to improve and educate the public have been a consistent feature of the Mexican publishing scene. The Sepsetenta paperbooks published during the presidency of Luis Echeverría also made scholarly writing in popularized form accessible to a large public. Publication of literary works for mass audiences continued under López Portillo, and presently there are reeditions of classical Mexican texts available at the kiosks for a mere six pesos.

Throughout the fifties, commercial publishing in Mexico was dominated by Fondo de Cultura Económica, which developed a system of door-to-door sales, and by "family" publishers such as Era and Joaquín Mortíz. However, by the mid-sixties a new phenomenon had established itself: the intensive distribution, in supermarkets and by subscription, of American-owned magazines such as *Reader's Digest* and *Cosmopolitan*. Until the early sixties, the major publication for women had been *La familia*. In the sixties and seventies, ten new women's magazines appeared, all of them controlled by big publishing conglomerates such as Provenemex (associated with the television monopoly, Televisa), Publicaciones Continentales (linked to the Hearst corporation), and Mex-Ameris (controlled by the powerful Mexican group headed by O'Farrill, with strong connections to the Monterey industrial group). Many of these magazines—*Vanidades, Claudia, Buenhogar*—are expensive to produce, are directed to a middle or upper class public, use a great deal of North American material, and link their articles to the sale of consumer products.[16] At the same time, to meet the needs of people with elementary reading knowledge and slight buying power, new genres began to appear, particularly the photonovel and the comic-strip novel.

The alternative meanings that were increasingly available in mass culture productions, together with the criticism of the intelligentsia seeking to widen the democratic basis of society, have severely challenged the power of the state to monopolize the production of meaning. Hitherto, of course, the Mexican Revolution had constituted the semantic axis around which social meanings were transmitted and understood, and in relation to which sexual, racial, and class categories had been defined. Though the government was able to control films (even censoring government-subsidized films like *Las abandonadas* when sectors like the military were offended) and was able to exert indirect pressure on publishers, there was plainly a growing gulf between the ideal image of Mexico and the reality of the people's everyday life, culture, and practices. This became painfully apparent in the sixties, not only in the growing political opposition which culminated in the 1968 massacre of students at Tlatelolco but also in the defensive reactions of the state itself—in its use of force as well as in seemingly minor incidents such as the banning of the Spanish version of *The Children of Sánchez*, which is a tape-recorded account of a family living on the margins of poverty in Mexico City. Though the methods and conclusion of its compiler, the U.S. anthropologist Oscar Lewis, are open to criticism, the government's attempted censorship was an index of how wide a gulf had been revealed between the image of the Mexican and the urban reality. Lewis, in fact, shows us a family some of whose members aspire to individual self-realization and who, far from being spurred by revolutionary idealism, are torn by jealousy and rivalry, and are dominated by a stern and emotionally remote father.[17]

As we shall see, the gulf between past and present, the older generation and the younger generation, is reflected in the comic-strip novels I have chosen to analyze. But the novels also function in a more overtly propagandistic way. The trend away from the reformist state (el estado de compromiso) to a deregulated society which makes scarcity the major incentive of the work force has generally been presented under the euphemistic label of "modernization." And because women have been a major factor in the development of new industries, women too have to be modernized. Though magazines and television not only display commodities but carry with them the connotations of modernity, unlimited consumption (or desire for consumption) in a society of scarcity has its dangers. Hence, as I have said, along with the new magazines there appeared different kinds of popular literature—some of them specifically designed to encourage a work ethic.

In a study of photonovels, Cornelia and Jan Butler Flora showed that mass culture literature was an instrument for integrating the population into the labor force, as well as into consumer culture: "Seen as an evolutionary process, these stories separate a woman from her actual environment and prepare her to accept the necessity of marginal participation as consumption is added to her function of reproduction of household labor."[18] In contrast to the glossy and often glamorous photonovels, however, the *libros semanales*, or comic-strip novels, have attracted little critical attention. Unlike the photonovels, comic-strips are usually printed on cheap paper, sell for very little money, and reach a vast public in the lower strata of society. They use formulaic plots, though these have not been developed on the basis of careful market research of readers' tastes, as has been carried out in the United States. Rather, they gauge these tastes from already existing literature, particularly from the crime sections in the popular press; thus they include violent and often sexually explicit material.[19] The novels are, moreover, crudely drawn and frequently use short hand indexes of emotion, which are common in U.S. comics but which are left untranslated into Spanish (for instance, "Snif Snif" indicates weeping). The color is a monotonous sepia tone and the covers are often unattractive; they thus lack the slick appeal of the photonovel as well as the escapist fantasy provided by Corín Tellado. Precisely because the *libros semanales* are so unglamorous and are so clearly intended for women who are integrated or are about to be integrated into the work place, they need a different kind of modernization plot— one that cannot simply hold out the carrot of consumption.

It is interesting that this modernization plot bears a striking resemblance to the religious story in which the random persecutions and events of a holy person's life are shown to have a transcendental meaning once they are seen from God's perspective. However, when this kind of utterance is deployed in a secular society, it produces a narrative problem. The plot tells only part of the story, for there is no universal system of belief which can be taken for granted. Thus the meaning of the events is obscure unless it is interpreted for us by the extra-narrative voice, whose authority is deliberately vague. This voice strives toward the status of an aphorism or doxa, but its support cannot be religion, nor does it necessarily conform to state ideology. For this overt message not only is frequently out of line with the events of the story but also introduces values which have little in common with the nationalist ideology that had for so long dominated the discourses of post-revolutionary Mexico.

Here an example is necessary; in *Los nuevos ricos* (año xxxii, 9 de marzo de 1984), the plot appears to focus on adultery. The wife of Luis Felipe, who has married her husband for his money, seduces his more attractive brother, Luciano. The novel opens with the dramatic moment of Luciano's seduction and suicide. The family and Luis Felipe know nothing of the adulterous affair and thus find the suicide inexplicable. At this point, the plot needs an explanatory flashback which appears to have little to do with the adultery story. Luis Felipe's father is a "nuevo rico" who had begun life as a peasant. Returning from the fields one day with an aunt, he finds his home burned down and his family killed. A Mexican reader might be expected to connect this happening with the Revolution or the Cristero war, but in fact it is the state which has perpetrated the crime. Soldiers in search of a fugitive have wantonly destroyed the family. Thus the novel is able both to recall Mexico's violent past and to attribute the violence to the state which is careless of individuals. The "accident" drives the father and his aunt from the village to the city where, starting from humble origins, they make a fortune in fruit dealing. The father marries, has two sons, and appears to be at the pinnacle of success when the suicide occurs. The adulteress is now summarily punished. Haunted by Luciano's ghost, she dies after confessing the crime. This sequence of events—seduction, suicide, remorse and repentance are, obviously, the stuff of which traditional Catholic literature in defense of the

family was made. But there is a surprise. At the end of the *libro semanal*,
Luis Felipe comes to the conclusion that he must leave home and start
afresh, in other words, that he must repeat his father's separation
from roots in order truly to become a person. The explicit moral
unexpectedly places the blame on the parents, for not taking more
care of their children, rather than on the adulteress. "Money and social
position kill even the most sincere feeling. Luciano and Luis Felipe's
parents forgot that they owed their children love and instead amassed
a large fortune which, as the novel shows, was of no use to them."
What is interesting here is not so much that the moral tries to guide
the reading of the stories as that there is no narrative logic which
could possibly make this conclusion appear to follow naturally from
the events.

One might argue that this is just a sign of bad writing, if it were
not for the fact that similar morals encourage these "counter-factual"
readings in many of the *libros semanales* and they all add up to the
same modernization story: the family is a drag and has to be left
behind. This seems a curious message for a country like Mexico in
which the family has, at least in theory, always provided a network of
support. *Los nuevos ricos* also stands in contrast to the classical nineteenth century treatment of aberrant sexual behavior, which was punished in order to cement the family. Nana and the lady of the Camelias
were sick members of society; as such they were put to death in order
to invigorate the family institution. In the Mexican *libro semanal*, the
family is usually an obstacle to the individual, and adultery is one of
the consequences of many members of the same family sharing a
single house. The ideal is either a nuclear family distanced from the
parental home or single men and women making it on their own. This
crucial moment of separation does not come about in childhood;
rather, it is played out between a rising younger generation and a
corrupt older generation. The official ideology of post-revolutionary
Mexico which had been based in theory on the desirability of state-
directed (paternalistic) reform, with each generation building on the
contribution of prior generations, is here confronted with a different
story—one in which progress can be achieved only by sacrificing close
ties with the "sick members of society."

What is the nature of this sickness? It is usually the older generation
which is guilty of violence, rape, drunkenness, and greed (though
occasionally the blame is placed on younger males). If the Harlequins
seem to have their roots in romance, the *libros semanales* have their
roots in naturalism, in which evil is passed on from one generation
to another. In *Las abandonadas* (año xxxii, 1 de febrero de 1984),
Amapola gives birth to a child after being raped in the presence of
her drunken father. The rapist, a storekeeper, marries her and she

has a second child by him before starting on her inevitable downward career to prostitution. But the story of Amapola is only a digression; the rest of the novel centers on Cecilia, the child born of rape and destined to be brutalized by the father and her step-mother. Cecilia makes an effort to be accepted first by the father and then by Amapola, whom she seeks out. But having realized the futility of this, she leaves for the city, takes a job in an office, and invites her younger sister to join her there. "Children are soft wax and must be molded. Unhappy children become unhappy adults but happy children will grow up to have homes that are filled with peace and love."

Clearly this moral does not follow from the logic of the plot; if it did, Cecilia would be as evil as her parents. Once again the conclusion we might "naturally draw" from the life story is thwarted, though this time by the story's ending, which seems to contradict the moral that supports a culture of poverty thesis in which generations are trapped in the same unproductive cycle as their parents. Only by drawing the conclusion that the girls should leave the family and go to the city to work can we square the moral with the story.

In both of the examples I have discussed, the focus is not so much on women as on the family as an institution. Mexican post-revolutionary ideology had permitted a high degree of secularization in public life, while leaving the traditional patriarchal family untouched and absorbing machismo into its national image. The Mexican family is thus an extremely complex institution—the source not only of considerable tensions, especially among the poor, but of support and of daily communication which the state and its institutions cannot replace. Yet unlike the Harlequin, the *libro semanal* does not show romance as a possible or even likely "escape." It is true that some *libros semanales* end with marriage, but often the weight of the moral is placed not on the romantic side of marriage but on marriage as a working partnership. This is true in *Lo que no quiso recordar* (año xxii, 29 de junio de 1984), in which the heroine Chelo marries a friendly architect after some misadventures with an unscrupulous brother-in-law who has tried to blackmail her into a relationship. The moral declares that "true love has faith and confidence in the partner knowing that despite hardship, troubles and economic problems, their mutual love will make them confident that all will be right in the end." Though in this case the reader might be expected to arrive at the conclusion without prompting, the suggestion that marriages face economic hardship is not reflected in the plot. Yet it is not a totally gratuitous observation, for it serves as a warning that the romantic element should not blind the reader to the fact that marriage is a working relationship. It underlines the fact that, unlike in Harlequins, romance is not the issue.

One explanation of the disjunction between plots and explicit moral messages may lie in the source of the stories—daily life as told in readers' letters or the sensational press. These provide the violence and sensationalism which the Mexican readers obviously seek.[20] Why such subject matter should be more attractive than euphemistic romance is not altogether clear, unless it has to do with a desire to dramatize lives that might otherwise seem pointless. At the same time, since the violence is most often attributed to a regressive mentality, it clearly belongs to the past and not to the modernity toward which the *libro semanal* points its readers. In the modernization tale, the ingrained habits of the "typical Mexican"—violence, machismo, and drunkenness—have to be repudiated, and since the older generation of men do not appear likely to reform themselves, then women must simply cut out of the traditional family and embrace the work ethic.

In Mexico, the overlapping of old and new discursive formations, of old and new plots, and of old and new proverbial wisdom gives rise to a great many contradictions which surface in popular narrative. Loyalty to the neighborhood network, to one's place of origin (*Viva Jalisco*), or to the extended family had been key themes in popular song, in mythology, and in film. While much nationalist and regional sentiment, especially feelings associated with place of origin and the family, is still conveyed on film and television and in popular culture, there is also a systematic parody of "tradition" in the media and a devaluing of many residues of more archaic ways of life—machismo, superstition, veneration of the older generation. In order to persuade people of the need to separate from the past, the novels imitate exemplary literature in showing the evils of machismo and in portraying the hard-drinking male who assesses his virility through violence, especially violence against women, as a barbarian. The ideal male in the *libro semanal* is a young professional or young worker who can be trusted to form a nuclear family in which the wife will also go out to work. As for the women, they are invited to see themselves as potential victims of a plot—the plot of the old Mexico that has passed on its tradition of machismo and thus has harmed them. If instead of reading themselves into the plot as helpless victims they turn their resentment against the older generation of males and separate themselves from this influence, then they can expect to succeed. The determinism of one generation transmitting its defects to the next can be transcended and women may start life anew as members of the work force.

It is therefore not surprising to find an explicitly "feminist" ideology in some of the *libros semanales*. The heroine of *Una mujer insatisfecha* (año xxxii, 7 de diciembre de 1984) is married to a boring and impotent business man who believes in patriarchy and the traditional values of family life. Luisa is repelled by his puritanical attitude toward marital relations and quarrels with her Italian mother-in-law, whose ideas on marriage are strictly traditional. She sets up her own consultancy as a designer and meets another man, but refuses to enter into a relationship with him because it promises to be as oppressive as the one with her husband. Back in her mother's house, she hangs up the telephone when her new lover calls making demands on her, feeling "free, happy and without ties." More surprising is the plot of *Desprestigiada* (año xxxii, 12 de octubre de 1984), in which the heroine, Luisa, a flirt who likes to pick up male visitors to the Pyramids, is raped by a "foreigner" (probably a Central American) who works in the post office. When she discovers that she is pregnant, she has an abortion, thanks to the help of a traditional curandera and a woman doctor. But the foreigner rapes her a second time, since he wants a child he can adopt and take back to his own country. The rape (which is somewhat unusual as an adoption procedure) is, however, less germane to the conclusion than the birth of the illegitimate child. The foreigner's plan to seize the baby is thwarted when he is picked up as an illegal immigrant, and it is Luisa who takes care of the baby—until the child is weaned. The reader might expect this to be the ending, but this is not a story about a girl's redemption through motherhood. Rather, as soon as the child is old enough to be left with another person, she is handed over to Luisa's mother and Luisa goes back to her old life, picking up men at the Pyramids. The only moral lesson is that in the future Luisa must be more careful.

There is considerable irony in this attack on machismo in the guise of liberation. It plays on the sentiments of 1968, on the difference between the modernity of the young and the blind conformity of the old. And it does so thanks to the anachronistic form in which random acts of violence are interpreted for the reader by the moral or by a surprise ending. Often this moral and ending are so arbitrary in relation to the sequence of events that they highlight the arbitrary nature of all narratives, including the master narrative of nationalism with its appeal to rootedness, to place, and to community.

In older forms of social narrative, the "story" tended to be woven out of lived "experience." This term, now rightly treated with suspicion because of its empirical bias, has nevertheless to be introduced, since the process of a human life ("the logic of mortality") cannot help but be the most powerful of paradigms. We fell in love and married and had children and all this seemed to happen naturally. Of course, we were still woven into a social plot in which marriage and the family not only satisfied needs for affection and recognition but also contributed to social reproduction. Nevertheless, this plot was built on events—childhood, adolescence, maturation—which appeared to be natural. But the modernization plot works against this formerly "natural" state of affairs, showing that life-stories are not what they seem. In Harlequins, romance is a prize available only to those who are able to learn the conditions under which female power can be exercised. In the *libros semanales*, the family is not seen as the inevitable source of satisfaction for a woman.

What is particularly intriguing about this is that there are photo-novels now being produced in California which use real life material in order to persuade Mexican males to stay in Mexico. The series, *Los mojados*, is based on the tragedies of Mexicans who emigrated to the United States in search of the "accursed dollar" and who found only disaster and death.[21] Thus certain real life stories can be used to persuade one sector of the population—women—that the family and the province are not their only destiny, while other stories can persuade men to stay at home and not swell the immigrant population of the United States. Mass culture narrative thus deals with problems that go far beyond entertainment. By addressing itself to serialized readers, it can appeal to private feelings and private lives. Yet this literature commutes private sentiments into stories which map out (plot) the way that different sectors of the population can be incorporated into the international division of labor. Whereas the Harlequin can use the powerful parallel between the stages of socialization and the ritual of passage from adolescence to womanhood, the *libros semanales* often depict a violent break between women as workers and women as family members. On the other hand, the plots of both seem to depend on the fact that women experience considerable anxiety and uncertainty as to where they stand in relation to society. What the *libros semanales* reveal is that there is not a single model for the sex/gender system under capitalism, but multiple options. Further, when these options fly in the face of women's daily life practices or beliefs, they have to be plotted as a simulation of real life in order to persuade the readership to change its attitudes. The *libro semanal* thus bears some resemblance to the CIA guerrilla manual which, since it could not appeal to the real life situations of Nicaraguans, had to resort to instructions on simulating events (an execution, for instance) in order to provide such "experience." Far from being peculiarly post-modern, this kind of plotting belongs to the hallowed tradition of the church, with its staging of miracles and marvels. The "literary resources" printed at the end of the contra manual could quite well have come from a Jesuit manual. But the Church, whatever its capacity for manipulation, had both its transcendental signified and its moral code which went hand in hand with belief in an after-life. The *libro semanal*, on the other hand, offers travail without Utopia, and self-reliance without any moral standpoint to help deal with human relations other than that offered by the disembodied corporate voice.

Women, then, are plotted in different ways according to their positions in the international division of labor. Curiously, it is women in the most affluent sectors (or those who can aspire to that affluence) who are invited most vigorously to give up their cultural capital (they must suppress the thinking part of themselves) and to find security in their own narcissistic image. No wonder the romance almost never portrays a woman in her thirties or forties—experience is dangerous. In the lower strata of the international division of labor, work or individual emancipation takes the place of romance. These novels suggest that "love" is a luxury, a fantasy not of all women but of middle and upper class women seeking the complementary male who will heal the split in their personalities. Both the romance and the *libro semanal* plot the incorporation of women into society, though the *libro semanal* may ultimately be more insidious, since it sanctions economic exploitation in the guise of emancipation from the violence and oppression of working class males. In any case, what is crucially missing from mass literature is any form of female solidarity; the plots of both types of narrative reinforce the serialization of women—the very factor that makes their exploitation, both as reproducers of the labor force and as cheap labor, so viable even in corporate society.

## NOTES

1. These are *Risas, lágrimas, amor* and the *Libros Semanales*, the latter published by Novedades editoras.

2. See Gayle Rubin, "The Traffic in Women," *Towards an Anthropology of Women*, ed. Rayna Reiter (New York: Monthly Review Press, 1975).

3. John Berger, *G* (New York: Pantheon, 1980), pp. 149–51.

4. Warren I. Sussman, *Culture as History: The Transformation of American Society in the Twentieth Century* (New York: Pantheon, 1984), pp. 115–17.

5. For a brief discussion of the Corín Tellado romance, see Carola Garcia Calderon's *Revistas Femininas, La mujer como objeto de consumo* 2nd edition, (Mexico: El Caballito, 1980) and Virginia Erhart's "Amor, Ideologiá y Enmascaramiento en Corín Tellado," in *Casa de las Américas* (La Habana) no. 77:93–101.

6. Northrop Frye, *Anatomy of Criticism* (Princeton, NJ: Princeton University Press, 1957), p. 73. Quoted in Fredric Jameson, *The Political Unconscious* (Ithaca, NY: Cornell University Press, 1981), p. 110.

7. Fredric Jameson, "Magical Narratives," *The Political Unconscious*, pp. 130–31.

8. Ann Barr Snitow, "Mass Market Romance: Pornography for Women is Different," *Powers of Desire: The Politics of Sexuality*, ed. Ann Snitow, Christine

Stansell and Sharon Thompson (New York: Monthly Review Press, 1983), p. 246.

9. Rosalind Coward, *Female Desire: Women's Sexuality Today* (New York: Paladin, 1984), p. 196.

10. Tania Modleski, *Loving With a Vengeance: Mass Produced Fantasies for Women* (New York: Methuen, 1984), p. 37.

11. Janice A. Radway, *Reading the Romance: Women, Patriarchy and Popular Literature* (Durham, NC: University of North Carolina Press, 1984), p. 25.

12. Ibid., p. 207.

13. Pierre Bourdieu, *Ce que parler veut dire* (Paris: Fayard, 1982).

14. The issue of the relation of women's magazines to modernization has been discussed by Michèle Mattelart in her article, "Notes on Modernity: A Way of Reading Women's Magazines," in *Communication and Class Struggle*, ed. Armand Mattelart and Seth Siegelaub (New York: International General, 1979), pp. 158–70.

15. Some of the information on the *libros semanales* comes from an interview by Tununa Mercado of the general editor of the *libros semanales*, Alicia Ibañez Parkman, conducted in the summer of 1984. For a discussion of *Risas, lágrimas, amor*, see Charles Tatum and Harold E. Hinds, "Mexican and American Comic Books in a Comparative Perspective," in *Mexico and the United States: Intercultural Relations and the Humanities*, ed. Juanita Luna Lawhn, Juan Bruce-Novoa, Guillermo Campos, and Ramón Saldívar (Texas: San Antonio College, 1984).

16. See Carola Garciá Calderón, *Revistas Femininas. La mujer como objeto de consumo*.

17. Oscar Lewis, *The Children of Sánchez* (New York: Random House, 1964). On the transformation of everyday life under the impact of the new media, see Raul Cremona, "El poder de la cultura de la televisión," in *Political Cultural del Estado Mexicano*, ed. Moises Ladrón de Guevara (Mexico: Secretaría de la Educación Pública, 1983), pp. 201–26.

18. Cornelia Butler Flora and Jan Flora, "The Photonovel as a Tool for Class and Cultural Domination," *Latin American Perspectives* V, no. 1 (Winter 1978):33.

19. See Cornelia Butler Flora, "Images of Women in Latin America Fotonovelas: From Cinderella to Mata Hari," paper presented at the Latin American Studies Association Annual Conference, Pittsburgh, April 5, 1979.

20. Several critics have noted that Mexican popular culture seems to favor melodramatic representation. Carlos Monsivais first commented on this in an article, "Cultura urbana y creación intelectual," in *Casa de las Américas* No. 116 (1979). It has also been mentioned in various articles by Jesús Martín Barbero. See, for instance "Cultura popular y comunicación de masas, *"Materiales para la comunicación popular* 3 (Lima, 1984).

21. These comics, available on the Mexican border, are published in San Isidro, California.

# 8
# FRAGMENTS OF A FASHIONABLE DISCOURSE

## Kaja Silverman

The image of a woman in front of the mirror, playing to both the male look and her own, has become a familiar metaphor of sexual oppression.[1] Despite this cautionary emblem, I would like to reopen the case on self-display via a brief consideration of dress and adornment, which, as I will attempt to demonstrate, turns upon a much more complex circuit of visual exchange than might at first appear.

The history of Western fashion poses a serious challenge both to the automatic equation of spectacular display with female subjectivity, and to the assumption that exhibitionism always implies woman's subjugation to a controlling male gaze. As a number of fashion critics have already observed, ornate dress was primarily a class rather than a gender prerogative during the fifteenth, sixteenth and seventeenth centuries, a prerogative which was protected by law.[2] In other words, sartorial extravagance was a mark of aristocratic power and privilege, and as such a mechanism for tyrannizing over rather than surrendering to the gaze of the (class) other. Moreover, the elegance and richness of male dress equalled and often surpassed that of female dress during this period, so that in so far as clothing was marked by gender, it defined visibility as a male rather than a female attribute.

It was not until the eighteenth century that the male subject retreated from the limelight, handing on his mantle to the female subject. During the second half of that century, the voluminous clothing and elaborate wigs of the nobleman slowly dwindled into what would eventually become the respectable suit and *coiffure à la naturelle* of the gentleman, while female dress and headpieces reached epic proportions.

Quentin Bell attributes the new modesty in male dress to the rise of the middle class, and the premium it placed upon industry. He argues that whereas in earlier centuries wealth was associated with leisure and with lavish dress, it came in the eighteenth century to be associated with top-management work, and thus with sartorial sobriety. However, because leisure was still a way of life for the middle class woman, it became her "responsibility" to display her husband's wealth through her clothing:

> The nobleman, like the lady, was a creature incapable of useful work; war and sport were the only outlets for his energy, and a high degree of conspicuous leisure was expected of him. Equally, it was important that he should in his own person be a consumer.... But now ... idleness was no longer the usual sign of wealth. The man who worked was not infrequently in receipt of a larger income than the men who drew rents off him; an industrious life no longer implied a poor or laborious existence, and therefore ceased to be dishonorable. It was sufficient, therefore, that a man should demonstrate by means of his black coat, cylindrical hat, spotless linen, carefully rolled umbrella, and general air of refined discomfort that he was not actually engaged in the production of goods, but only in some more genteel employment concerned with management or distribution....
>
> But the demands of conspicuous consumption remain. Men might escape them, but woman could not.... [On] all public and social occasions it was [woman's] task to demonstrate [man's] ability to pay and thus to carry on the battle, both for herself and her husband.[3]

Bell offers a plausible explanation of the economic and social determinants responsible for the elimination of sumptuousness in male dress, and its intensification in female dress, but he fails to address the psychic consequences of these changes, or their implications for sexual difference. He accounts for the greater lavishness of female clothing exclusively in terms of class, reading it as the obligatory demonstration of the bourgeois woman's financial dependence upon her husband—as a mark, that is, of her subordinate monetary status. (However, at one point earlier in the same book Bell describes the sartorial transformation quite differently, at least hinting at the possibility that it inflicted greater losses upon the male than upon the female subject: "It was as though the men were sacrificing their hair, and indeed all their finery, for the benefit of women."[4] I am more than a little intrigued by this fleeting avowal of male castration, particularly when it is further elaborated with respect to baldness: "ever since the days of Elisha men have been deeply sensitive to the crowning injustice of nature; the wig gave them a century and a half of immunity. Dignified, not too unpractical in its later stages, above all discreet, it was one of the most flattering contrivances ever invented, and yet it went").[5]

In his classic study, *The Psychology of Clothes*, J.C. Flugel also attributes the changes in male dress during the eighteenth century to a shift in class relations. As a result of that shift, he suggests, masculine clothing ceased to proclaim hierarchical distinction and became a harmonizing and homogenizing uniform, serving to integrate not only male members of the same class, but male members of different classes. However, Flugel is ultimately much more concerned with the psychoanalytic than with the social ramifications of what he calls "The Great Masculine Renunciation," arguing that it worked to inhibit the narcissistic and exhibitionistic desires which were so flamboyantly expressed through aristocratic sumptuousness in preceding centuries. He concludes that since the eighteenth century these desires have been obliged to seek out alternate routes of gratification, and have consequently undergone the following vicissitudes: 1) sublimation into professional "showing off"; 2) reversal into scopophilia; and 3) male identification with woman-as-spectacle.[6]

The exhibitionistic bases of the first of these vicissitudes, professional "showing off," are perhaps most evident in the case of spectator sports, where expertise is virtually synonymous with corporeal display, and where viewing pleasure tends to be vicarious rather than overtly erotic. However, the frequency with which the word "performance" is used to designate masculine success in a wide range of other professional fields indicates that it serves a compensatory function there as well.

The second of these vicissitudes, scopophilia, has of course been closely interrogated by feminists, but they have considered it to be primarily a defense against castration anxiety, and a means of mastering the female subject. Flugel's model indicates that scopophilia may also betray desires that are incompatible with the phallic function—that it may attest to a shared psychic space over and against which sexual difference is constructed. It thus maps out an important area for further feminist work.

The last of these vicissitudes, male identification with woman-as-spectacle, has not received the same amount of critical attention, although it would seem the most potentially destabilizing, at least in so far as gender is concerned. Flugel remarks that this identification may take the culturally acceptable form of associating with a beautiful and well-dressed woman, or the much more extreme and "deviant" form of actually adopting female mannerisms and dress (i.e., of transvestism). I would maintain that it also coexists with other classically male "perversions," helping to determine the choice of a fetish, and structuring even the most conventionally heterosexual of voyeuristic transactions.

One thinks perhaps most immediately in this context of the figure of Scotty (Jimmy Stewart) in *Vertigo*, who manifests such an extraordinary attachment to the particularities of Madeleine's grey suit, black dress and blonde hairdo. This is by no means an isolated example. From *Some Like it Hot* and *Jezebel* to *Death in Venice*, *Diva*, and *The Bitter Tears of Petra Von Kant*, cinema has given complex expression to the male fascination with female dress, a fascination which is always inflected in some way by identification.

More surprisingly, so has the novel. Perhaps because it arose out of the same historical moment as the Great Masculine Renunciation, that textual system has from its inception taken a passionate interest in women's clothing. In novels like *Pamela*, *Madame Bovary*, *Sister Carrie*, *Remembrance of Things Past*, and *Lolita*, what purports to be a voyeuristic preoccupation with a female figure often becomes the pretext for endlessly rummaging through her closets and drawers. I cannot help but wonder, for instance, for whom he is really shopping when Humbert Humbert spends a whole afternoon buying dresses with "check weaves, bright cottons, frills, puffed-out short sleeves, soft pleats, snug-fitting bodices and generously full skirts" for Lolita[7]—or when Marcel decides after prolonged deliberation to order not one, but four priceless Fortuny gowns for Albertine. What Angela Carter observes about *Women in Love* holds true for dozens of other French, English and American novels:

> If we do not trust the teller but the tale, then the tale positively revels in lace and feathers, bags, beads, blouses and hats. It is always touching to see a man quite as seduced by the cultural apparatus of femininity as Lawrence was, the whole gamut. . . .[8]

By characterizing the sartorial transformation that occurred at the end of the eighteenth century as a "Great Masculine Renunciation," Flugel seems to imply that exhibitionism plays as fundamental a part within the constitution of the male subject as it does within that of the female subject—that voyeurism, which is much more fully associated with male subjectivity than is exhibitionism, is only a secondary formation, or alternative avenue of libidinal gratification. Lacan suggests the same in *Four Fundamental Concepts of Psycho-Analysis*.

What tends to be most widely remembered about the Lacanian account of subjectivity is the emphasis it places upon primary narcissism (i.e., upon the decisive role of the mirror stage, which aligns the child's image with the first of the countless images around which its identity will coalesce). However, what is equally important, although less frequently remarked, is the function performed by the gaze of the Other, both at this founding moment and upon the occasion of all subsequent self-recognitions. The mirror stage is inconceivable without the presence of an other (most classically the mother) to provide scopic as well as "orthopedic" support, and to "stand in" for the Other. Her look articulates the mirror image, and facilitates the child's alignment with it. In order for the child to continue to "see" itself, it must continue to be (culturally) "seen." Lacan compares this visual mediation to photography:

> . . . in the scopic field, the gaze is outside, I am looked at, that is to say, I am a picture.
>
> This is the function that is found at the heart of the institution of the subject in the visible. What determines me, at the most profound level, in the visible, is the gaze that is outside. It is through the gaze that I enter life and it is from the gaze that I receive its effects. Hence it comes about that the gaze is the instrument through which light is embodied and through which . . . I am *photo-graphed*.[9]

At issue here is what Lacan calls the "inside-out structure of the gaze," whereby the subject comes to regard itself from a vantage external to itself—from the field of the Other.[10] The naive subject—the subject trapped within the illusions of Cartesian consciousness—imagines that it is seeing itself see itself, an experience which testifies to the involuted structure of the gaze, if not to the gaze's ultimate exteriority. In fact, the subject sees itself being seen, and that visual transaction is always ideologically organized.

If we accept this formulation, then it necessarily follows that the male subject is as dependent upon the gaze of the Other as is the female subject, and as solicitous of it—in other words, that he is as fundamentally exhibitionistic. The Great Masculine Renunciation must consequently be understood not as the complete aphanisis of male specularity, but as its disavowal. In mainstream fashion, as in dominant cinema, this disavowal is most frequently effected by identifying male subjectivity with a network of looks, including those of the designer, the photographer, the admirer, and the "connoisseur." However, the paradox upon which such an identification turns, as the visual fascination that accumulates around the figure of the fashion photographer in Antonioni's *Blow Up* or Berry Gordy's *Mahogany* would suggest, is that it can only be negotiated through spectacle. It requires the male subject to see himself (and thus to be seen) as "the one who looks at women."

I think in this respect of a 1947 photograph by Richard Avedon which shows two men admiring a woman wearing an example of Dior's New Look, while the eyes of a third are involuntarily drawn to the camera, hidden from our view (see illustration). Our vision is thus pulled in two radically different directions by the photograph. On the one hand, we are caught up in the circulation of the New Look between the designer (Dior), the fashion photographer (Avedon), and the two passing admirers—a three-way exchange that works to dis-

Renee
The New Look of Dior
Place de la Concorde, Paris
August 1947

Photographed by Richard Avedon
(copyright © 1947 by Richard Avedon Inc.
All Rights Reserved)

avow male exhibitionism. On the other hand, our attention is riveted by the look that falls outside this phallic exchange, the look that acknowledges that it is also being watched, and that in so doing foregrounds the specular bases of male subjectivity. Avedon's snapshot literalizes the metaphor of the gaze as "the instrument through which light is embodied and through which [the subject] is photographed."

Having thus firmly evacuated all three passers-by from the position of the gaze, the interpreter might well be tempted to substitute for them either the figure of the absent designer, or that of the invisible photographer, both of whom seem definitively "outside" the picture. This would be a mistake. Although the gaze is constantly anthropomorphized and individualized in this way, it proceeds from the place of the Other, and is an effect of the symbolic order rather than of human vision. Moreover, although certain subjects, machines, and institutions are always "standing in" for the gaze, it is finally unlocalizable. All this is another way of saying that despite their own visual productivity, the designer and photographer are still obliged, like the female model and the male passers-by, to see themselves from the place of the Other. And since the male subject, like the female subject, has no visual status apart from dress and/or adornment, what they see is at least in part a vestimentary "package."

Clothing and other kinds of ornamentation make the human body culturally visible. As Eugenie Lemoine-Luccioni suggests, clothing draws the body so that it can be culturally seen, and articulates it as a meaningful form.[11] Lemoine-Luccioni's point may be supported by examples from both literature and film. The eponymous heroine of Theodore Dreiser's novel, *Sister Carrie*, is presented as the quintessence of desirability, yet her physical features are never described. Her body is evoked exclusively through her meticulously described wardrobe, which, like the cut-out clothes of a paper doll, imply in advance a certain shape and stance. Similarly, the body of Charlotte (Bette Davis) in Irving Rapper's *Now, Voyager* conforms so closely to the outlines of her clothing that she can be transformed from an unsightly spinster into a beautiful sophisticate simply by substituting a fashionable suit, hairdo, and pair of high-heeled shoes for the horn-rimmed spectacles, shapeless housedress, and oxford shoes she previously wore.

Even our visual access to the *undressed* body is mediated by the prevailing vestimentary codes. In *Seeing Through Clothes*, Ann Hollander argues that throughout the history of Western art, the (female) nude has always assumed the form dictated by contemporary fashion:

> The placement, size, and shape of the breasts, the set of the neck and shoulders, the relative girth and length of the rib cage, the exact disposition of its fleshy upholstery, front and back—all these, along with

styles of posture both seated and upright, are continually shifting according to the way clothes have been variously designed in history to help the female body look beautiful (and natural) *on their terms*. Nude art, unavoidably committed to Eros, accepts these terms.[12]

Clothing exercises as profoundly determining an influence upon living, breathing bodies as it does upon their literary and cinematic counterparts, affecting contour, weight, muscle development, posture, movement, and libidinal circulation. Dress is one of the most important cultural implements for articulating and territorializing human corporeality—for mapping its erotogenic zones and for affixing a sexual identity.

Proust's *Remembrance of Things Past* offers a brilliant account of the corporeal transformations that took place as the consequence of one major change in fashionable female clothing—the demise of the bustle. The passage in question also dramatizes the semiotic shift that occurs during any such change, i.e., the relegation of the now-superseded look to the wastebasket of artificiality and absurdity, and the enshrinement of the new look as natural and free. At the same time, through its emphasis upon the occasional unruliness and super-fluity of Odette's flesh, it shows the current fashion to be as fully constructed as the outdated one. It is finally not Odette's body, but her cambric and silk that are "liberated" by the passing of the bustle:

> Odette's body seemed now to be cut out in a single silhouette wholly confined within a "line" which, following the contours of the woman, had abandoned the ups and downs, the ins and outs, the reticulations, the elaborate dispersions of the fashions of former days, but also, where it was her anatomy that went wrong by making unnecessary digressions within or without the ideal form traced by it, was able to rectify, by a bold stroke, the errors of nature, to make good, along a whole section of its course, the lapses of the flesh as well as of the material. The pads, the preposterous "bustle" had disappeared, as well as those tailed bodices which, overlapping the skirt and stiffened by rods of whalebone, had so long amplified Odette with an artificial stomach and had given her the appearance of being composed of several disparate pieces which there was no individuality to bind together. The vertical fall of the fringes, the curve of the ruches had made way for the inflexion of a body which made silk palpitate as a siren stirs the waves and gave to cambric a human expression, now that it had been liberated, like an organic and living form, from the long chaos and nebulous envelopment of fashions at last dethroned.[13]

In thus stressing the coerciveness and constraints of clothing, I do not mean to argue for the return to "prelapsarian nakedness," as Flugel ultimately does, or for a "rationalization" of dress that would permit more "natural" and "uninhibited" corporeal movement and development. Even if my sympathies were not fully on the side of extravagant sartorial display, I would feel impelled to stress as strongly as possible that clothing is a necessary condition of subjectivity—that in articulating the body, it simultaneously articulates the psyche. As Freud tells us, the ego is "a mental projection of the surface of the body,"[14] and that surface is largely defined through dress. Laplanche makes a similar point when he insists upon the need for an "envelope" or "sack" to contain both body and ego, and to make possible even the most rudimentary distinctions between self and other, inside and outside.[15] In effect, clothing is that envelope.

Before commenting upon some of the different vestimentary envelopes currently available to us, I would like to make a few final remarks about normative male dress since the Great Masculine Renunciation, and about its implications for male sexuality. To begin with, class distinctions have "softened" and gender distinctions have "hardened" since the end of the eighteenth century. In other words, sexual difference has become the primary marker of power, privilege and authority, closing the specular gap between men of different classes, and placing men and women on opposite sides of the great visual divide.

Second, whereas in earlier centuries dominant male dress gave a certain play to fancy, it has subsequently settled into sobriety and rectitude. Since the sartorial revolution, male dress has also given a very small margin to variation, remaining largely unchanged for two centuries. These last two features define male sexuality as stable and constant, and so align it with the symbolic order. In other words, they help to conflate the penis with the phallus.

Last, but by no means least, conventional male dress since the end of the Great Masculine Renunciation has effaced everything about the male body but the genital zone, which is itself metaphorically rather than metonymically evoked (i.e., which is represented more through a general effect of verticality than through anything in the style or cut of a garment that might articulate an organ beneath). This "sublimation" is another important mechanism for identifying the male subject with the phallus.

Female dress, on the other hand, has undergone frequent and often dramatic changes, accentuating the breasts at one moment, the waist at another, and the legs at another. These abrupt libidinal displacements, which constantly shift the center of erotic gravity, make the female body far less stable and localized than its male counterpart. I would also argue that fashion creates the free-floating quality of female sexuality, a quality which Flugel was one of the first to note:

[A]mong the most important of [sexual] differences is the tendency for
the sexual libido to be more diffuse in women than in men; in women
the whole body is sexualized, in men the libido is more definitely concentrated upon the genital zone; and this is true . . . both for showing
the female body and for looking at it. Hence exposure of *any* part of
the female body works more erotically than exposure of the corresponding part of the male, save only in the case of the genitals themselves.[16]

The endless transformations within female clothing construct female
sexuality and subjectivity in ways that are at least potentially disruptive,
both of gender and of the symbolic order, which is predicated upon
continuity and coherence. However, by freezing the male body into
phallic rigidity, the uniform of orthodox male dress makes it a rock
against which the waves of female fashion crash in vain.

In arguing that gender has replaced class as the primary distinguishing marker within clothing over the past two centuries, I do not
mean to suggest that economic and social differences no longer figure
centrally there. Although fashion constructs a "new" female body
every year, and thereby challenges the assumption of a fixed identity,
it does so at the behest of capital, and in the interests of surplus value
(fashionable time "clocks over" long before any garment can be worn
out or used up). Moreover, although the fashion industry operates
through replication and mass production, making variants of the same
garments available to every class, a temporal lag always separates the
moment at which such a garment is available to a select few from the
moment at which it is generally disseminated. This temporal lag guarantees that by the time most people have access to a given "look," it
will no longer be "really" fashionable, and so asserts class difference
even in the face of the most far-reaching sartorial homogenization.

I would also agree with Bell that "the history of fashionable dress
is tied to the competition between classes, in the first case the emulation
of the aristocracy by the bourgeoisie, and then the more extended
competition that results from the ability of the proletariat to compete
with the middle class."[17] However, this competition is not always a
matter of the middle class aspiring to dress like the upper class, or of
the proletariat trying to dress like the middle class. Fashionable change
is often the result of creative pressure from "below"—from the middle
class in the case of the Great Masculine Renunciation, and from the
working class in the case of skinheads and punks.

Increasingly, in the second half of the twentieth century, imaginative dress has become a form of contestation—a way of challenging
not only dominant values, but traditional class and gender demar-
cations. Clothing may function as a subcultural flag, as the zoot-suit
did for the latinos; it may assert personal style in the face of sartorial

hegemony, as it did for Baudelaire's dandy;[18] it may become the banner of a whole youth movement, as beads, jeans, and T-shirts did for the hippies; it may become the mechanism for forcing a culture to confront the negativity upon which it is based, as it is for punk; or it may grow out of the desire to reclaim spectacle for the male subject, as is manifestly the case with rock music and MTV.

These oppositional gestures are never absolute. As Dick Hebdige remarks, they "in part contest and in part agree with the dominant definitions of who and what [their wearers] are, and there is a substantial amount of shared ideological ground . . . between them and the fashion industry."[19] Deviant dress is also quickly absorbed by the fashion industry. However, I think it is too easily assumed that the absorption means recuperation, in the sense of completely neutralizing what is politically, socially, or sexually significant about a particular vestimentary mode. If a given "look" is appropriated by the fashion industry from a subculture or subordinate class, that is because its ideological force and formal bravura can no longer be ignored—because it has won not only a style war, but a pitched cultural battle. It is, moreover, no small thing to effect a change in mainstream fashion. If, as I suggested earlier, clothing not only draws the body so that it can be seen, but also maps out the shape of the ego, then every transformation within a society's vestimentary code implies some kind of shift within its ways of articulating subjectivity.

Feminism has not demonstrated the sartorial audacity and imaginativeness of some recent subcultures, nor has it evolved a single, identifying form of dress. This obviously has something to do with the heterogeneous nature of feminism itself—with its strategic refusal to toe any one party line, or to concentrate its energies on a single common front. However, I would argue that the sartorial reticence of North American feminism is also part of a larger reaction against everything that has been traditionally associated with female narcissism and exhibitionism, that it is the symptom of what might almost be called "The Great Feminine Renunciation." As I look about me in the mid-eighties, I am forcibly struck by the fact that every current vestimentary code that insists upon women's social and political equality also tends either toward the muted imitation of male dress (jeans and shirts, slacks and jackets, the "business suit"), or its bold parody (leather jackets and pants, the tuxedo "look," sequined ties). Feminism would seem to be in the process of repeating male vestimentary history.

I would like to conclude this essay with the defense of a rather different sartorial system, one which is not at present the uniform of any subcultural group (although it sprang out of the black and hippie subcultures of the 1960s'), but one which, because of its capacity for including the past by reconceiving it, would seem able to provide the female subject with a more flexible and capacious "envelope"—that style of dress which is commonly known as "vintage clothing" or "retro."

In an essay published in the *New York Times* in 1975, Kennedy Fraser proposed that retro "represents the desire to find style, but obliquely, and splendor, but tackily, and so to put an ironic distance between the wearers and the fashionableness of their clothes."[20] The phrase "ironic distance" coincides theoretically with what others have called "masquerade,"[21] and it underscores several important features of thrift-shop dressing: its affection for objects which were once culturally cherished, but which have since been abandoned; its predilection for a tarnished and "stagey" elegance; and its desire to convert clothing into costume or "fancy dress." However, Fraser is oblivious to the ideological implications of what she notes; for her, retro is simply a way of "saying something quite intense but only in a footnote."[22] She is also much too quick to characterize it as another of fashion's wiles, rather than—as I would argue—as a sartorial strategy which works to denaturalize its wearer's specular identity, and one which is fundamentally irreconcilable with fashion.

In *Système de la Mode*, Roland Barthes describes fashion as a discourse which vehemently denies the possibility of any relation with its own recent past—as a discourse predicated upon the disavowal of its own historical construction:

> As soon as the signified *Fashion* encounters a signifier (such and such a garment), the sign becomes the year's Fashion, but thereby this Fashion dogmatically rejects the Fashion which preceded it, its own past; every new Fashion is a refusal to inherit, a subversion against the oppression of the preceding Fashion; Fashion experiences itself as a Right, the natural right of the present over the past. . . .[23]

A critical aspect of this disavowal is the binary logic through which fashion distinguishes "this year's look" from "last year's look," a logic which turns upon the opposition between "the new" and "the old" and works to transform one season's treasures into the next season's trash.

Retro refuses this antithesis. Because its elements connote not only a generalized "oldness," but a specific moment both in the (social) history of clothing, and in that of a cluster of closely allied discourses (painting, photography, cinema, the theater, the novel), it inserts its wearer into a complex network of cultural and historical references. At the same time, it avoids the pitfalls of a naive referentiality; by putting quotation marks around the garments it revitalizes, it makes clear that the past is available to us only in a textual form, and through the mediation of the present.

By recontextualizing objects from earlier periods within the frame of the present, retro is able to "reread" them in ways that maximize their radical and transformative potential—to chart the affinities, for instance, between fashions of the forties and femininism in the eighties, or between fashions of the twenties and the "unisex look" of the late sixties. Vintage clothing is also a mechanism for crossing vestimentary, sexual, and historical boundaries. It can combine jeans with sawed-off flapper dresses or tuxedo jackets, art deco with "pop art" jewelry, silk underwear from the thirties with a tailored suit from the fifties and a body that has been "sculpted" into androgyny through eighties-style weight lifting.

Thrift-shop dressing recycles fashion's waste, exploiting the use value that remains in discarded but often scarcely-worn clothing. Because it establishes a dialogue between the present-day wearers of that clothing and its original wearers, retro also provides a means of salvaging the images that have traditionally sustained female subjectivity, images that have been consigned to the waste-basket not only by fashion, but by "orthodox" feminism. In other words, vintage clothing makes it possible for certain of those images to "live on" in a different form, much as postmodern architecture does with earlier architectural styles or even with the material fragments of extinct buildings. It is thus a highly visible way of acknowledging that its wearer's identity has been shaped by decades of representational activity, and that no cultural project can ever "start from zero."

## NOTES

1. The most influential feminist critique of female spectacle is Laura Mulvey's "Visual Pleasure and Narrative Cinema," *Screen* 16, no. 3 (1975):6–18.

2. See René Konig, *The Restless Image*, trans. F. Bradley (London: Allen & Unwin, 1973), pp. 11, 139; and Quentin Bell, *On Human Finery* (London: Hogarth, 1976), pp. 23–24.

3. Bell, p. 141.

4. Ibid., p. 126.

5. Ibid., p. 123 f.

6. J.C. Flugel, *The Psychology of Clothes* (London: Hogarth, 1930), pp. 117–19.

7. Vladimir Nabokov, *Lolita* (Greenwich, CT: Fawcett, 1955), p. 99.

8. Angela Carter, *Nothing Sacred* (London: Virago, 1982), pp. 162–63.

9. Jacques Lacan, *The Four Fundamental Concepts of Psycho-Analysis*, trans. Alan Sheridan (New York: Norton, 1978), p. 106.

10. Ibid., p. 82.

11. Eugenie Lemoine-Luccioni, *La Robe* (Paris: Seuil, 1983), p. 147.

12. Ann Hollander, *Seeing Through Clothes* (New York: Viking, 1975), p. 91.

13. Marcel Proust, *Remembrance of Things Past*, trans. C.K. Scott Moncrieff and Terence Kilmartin (New York: Random House, 1982), Vol. I, p. 665.

14. This is the approved editorial gloss of the following line from *The Ego and the Id*: "the ego is first and foremost a body-ego; it is not merely a surface entity, but is itself the projection of a surface" (*The Standard Edition of the Complete Psychological Works of Sigmund Freud*, trans. James Strachey [London: Hogarth, 1953–1966], Vol. IX, p. 26).

15. Jean Laplanche, *Life and Death in Psychoanalysis*, trans. Jeffrey Mehlman (Baltimore: Johns Hopkins University Press, 1976), pp. 80–81.

16. Flugel, p. 107.

17. Bell, p. 155.

18. Baudelaire describes dandyism as "the burning desire to create a personal form of originality," a "cult of the ego" which "can even survive what are called illusions" (*Selected Writings on Art and Artists*, trans. P.E. Chavet [Cambridge, England: Cambridge University Press, 1972], p. 420).

19. Dick Hebdige, *Subculture: The Meaning of Style* (London: Methuen, 1979), p. 86.

20. Reprinted in Kennedy Fraser, *The Fashionable Mind: Reflections on Fashion, 1970–1982* (Boston: David R. Godine, 1985), p. 125.

21. See, for instance, Mary Ann Doane, "Film and the Masquerade: Theorising the Female Spectator," *Screen* 23, nos. 3 and 4 (1982):74–87.

22. Fraser, p. 125.

23. I quote from the English translation of this book, *The Fashion System*, trans. Matthew Ward and Richard Howard (New York: Hill and Wang, 1983), p. 273.

# IV.
# REDRAWING THE BOUNDARIES BETWEEN ART AND ENTERTAINMENT

# 9

# THE TERROR OF PLEASURE

## *THE CONTEMPORARY HORROR FILM AND POSTMODERN THEORY*

## Tania Modleski

In the *Grundrisse,* Karl Marx's description of the capitalist as a werewolf turns into an enthusiastic endorsement of that creature's activities. Marx tells us that the capitalist's "werewolf hunger," which drives him continually to replace "living labor" with "dead labor" (that is, human beings with machines), will lead to a mode of production in which "labour time is no longer the sole measure and source of wealth."[1] Thus, in the words of one commentator, "capitalism furnishes the material basis for the eventual realization of an age-old dream of humankind: the liberation from burdensome toil."[2] Marx's critics have tended to place him in the role of mad scientist, with his vision of the miracles to be wrought by feeding the werewolf's insatiable appetite. Writers from Jacques Ellul to Isaac Balbus have argued (to mix narratives here) that allowing the capitalist his unhindered experimentation in the "workshops of filthy creation"—his accumulation of more and more specimens of dead labor—cannot possibly provide a blessing to humankind.

These critics claim that rather than truly liberating humanity by freeing it from burdensome toil, the proliferation of dead labor—of technology—has resulted in the invasion of people's mental, moral, and emotional lives, and thus has rendered them incapable of desiring social change. To quote Jacques Ellul, who has traced the intrusion of technique into all aspects of human existence, "as big city life became for the most part intolerable, techniques of amusement were developed. It became indispensable to make urban suffering acceptable by furnishing amusements, a necessity which was to assure the rise, for example, of a monstrous motion picture industry."[3] In advanced capitalism, the narrative shifts, though the genre remains the same: physical freedom—that is, increased leisure time—is bought at the price of spiritual zombieism. The masses, it is said, are offered various forms of easy, false pleasure as a way of keeping them unaware of their own desperate vacuity. And so, apparently, we are caught in the toils of the great monster, mass culture, which certain critics, including some of the members of the Frankfurt School and their followers, have equated with ideology. For the Frankfurt School, in fact, mass culture effected a major transformation in the nature of ideology from Marx's time: once "socially necessary illusion," it has now become "manipulative contrivance," and its power is such that, in the sinister view of T. W. Adorno, "conformity has replaced consciousness."[4]

Today many people tend to believe that other, more sophisticated approaches to the issue have superseded the Frankfurt School's conception of mass culture as a monstrous and monolithic ideological machine. The work of Roland Barthes is often cited as an example of such an advance. But when Barthes offers the converse of the proposition that mass culture (for example, the cinema) is ideology and contends rather that "ideology is the Cinema of society," we are entitled, I think, to question just how far this removes us from many of the premises we think we have rejected.[5] Isn't Barthes here implying that both cinema and ideology, being seamless and without gaps or contradictions, create what the Frankfurt School called the "spurious harmony" of a conformist mass society?

According to many of the members of the Frankfurt School, high art was a subversive force capable of opposing spurious harmony. On this point especially, certain contemporary theorists have disagreed. In *The Anti-Aesthetic*, a recent collection of essays on postmodern culture, the editor, Hal Foster, suggests the need to go beyond the idea of the aesthetic as a negative category, claiming that the critical importance of the notion of the aesthetic as subversive is now "largely illusory."[6] However, despite such pronouncements, which are common enough in the literature of postmodernism, I believe it can be shown that many postmodernists do in fact engage in the same kind of oppositional thinking about mass culture that characterized the work of the Frankfurt School. Take, for example, Barthes' writings on pleasure. Although it is inaccurate to maintain, as critics sometimes do, that Barthes always draws a sharp distinction between pleasure and jouissance (since in *The Pleasure of the Text* Barthes straightaway denies any such strenuous opposition), whenever Barthes touches on the subject of mass culture, he is apt to draw a fairly strict line— placing pleasure on the side of the consumer, and jouissance in contrast to pleasure. Here is a remarkable passage from *The Pleasure of the Text*, in which Barthes begins by discussing the superiority of a textual reading based on disavowal and ends by casually condemning mass culture:

> Many readings are perverse, implying a split, a cleavage. Just as the child knows its mother has no penis and simultaneously believes she has one . . . so the reader can keep saying: *I know these are only words, but all the same.* . . . Of all readings that of tragedy is the most perverse: I take pleasure in hearing myself tell a story *whose end I know*: I know and I don't know, I act toward myself as though I did not know: I know perfectly well Oedipus will be unmasked, that Danton will be guillotined, *but all the same.* . . . Compared to a dramatic story, which is one whose outcome is unknown, there is here an effacement of pleasure and a progression of *jouissance* (today, in mass culture, there is an enormous consumption of "dramatics" and little *jouissance*).[7]

Anyone who has read Christian Metz's persuasive argument that disavowal is *constitutive* of the spectator's pleasure at the cinema will find it difficult to give ready assent to Barthes' contention that mass culture deprives the consumer of this "perverse" experience.[8] And anyone who is acquainted with the standardized art products—the genre and formula stories—which proliferate in a mass society will have to admit that their import depends precisely upon our suspending our certain knowledge of their outcome—for example, the knowledge that, as the critics say, the gangster "will eventually lie dead in the streets." Barthes' remarks are illuminating, then, not for any direct light they shed on the high/mass culture debate, but because they vividly exemplify the tendency of critics and theorists to make mass culture into the "other" of whatever, at any given moment, they happen to be championing— and, moreover, to denigrate that other primarily because it allegedly provides pleasure to the consumer.

While Barthes' *The Pleasure of the Text* has become one of the canonical works of postmodernism, in this respect it remains caught up in older modernist ideas about art. In an essay entitled "The Fate of Pleasure," written in 1963, the modernist critic Lionel Trilling speculated that high art had dedicated itself to an attack on pleasure in part because pleasure was the province of mass art: "we are repelled by the idea of an art that is consumer-oriented and comfortable, let alone luxurious."[9] He went on to argue that, for the modernist, pleasure is associated with the "specious good"—with bourgeois habits, manners, and morals—and he noted, "the destruction of what is considered to be specious good is surely one of the chief literary enterprises of our age."[10] Hence, Trilling has famously declared, aesthetic modernity is primarily adversarial in impulse.

The "specious good," or "bourgeois taste," remains an important target of contemporary thinkers, and postmodernism continues to be theorized as its adversary. Indeed, it might be argued that postmodernism is valued by many of its proponents insofar as it is considered *more* adversarial than modernism, and is seen to wage war on a greatly expanded category of the "specious good," which presently includes meaning (Barthes speaks of the "regime of meaning") and even form.[11] For example, in an essay entitled "Answering the Question: What is Postmodernism?" Jean-François Lyotard explicitly contrasts postmodernism to modernism in terms of their relation to "pleasure." For Lyotard, modernism's preoccupation with form meant that it was still capable of affording the reader or viewer "matter for solace and pleasure, [whereas the postmodern is] that which denies itself the solace of good forms, the consensus of a taste which would make it possible to share collectively the nostalgia for the unattainable."[12] It is important to recognize the extent to which Lyotard shares the same animus as the Frankfurt School, although his concern is not merely to denounce *spurious* harmony, but to attack *all* harmony—consensus, collectivity—as spurious, that is, on the side of "cultural policy," the aim of which is to offer the public "well-made" and "comforting" works of art.[13]

Although Lyotard has elsewhere informed us that "thinking by means of oppositions does not correspond to the liveliest modes of postmodern knowledge," he does not seem to have extricated himself entirely from this mode.[14] Pleasure (or "comfort" or "solace") remains the enemy for the postmodernist thinker because it is judged to be the means by which the consumer is reconciled to the prevailing cultural policy, or the "dominant ideology." While this view may well provide the critic with "matter for solace and pleasure," it is at least debatable that mass culture today is on the side of the specious good, that it offers, in the words of Matei Calinescu, "an ideologically manipulated illusion of taste," that it lures its audience to a false complacency with the promise of equally false and insipid pleasures.[15] Indeed, the contemporary horror film—the so-called exploitation film or slasher film—provides an interesting counterexample to such theses. Many of these films are engaged in an unprecedented assault on all that bourgeois culture is supposed to cherish—like the ideological apparatuses of the family and the school. Consider Leonard Maltin's capsule summary of an exemplary film in the genre, *The Brood*, directed by David Cronenberg and starring Samantha Eggar: "Eggar eats her own afterbirth while midget clones beat grandparents and lovely young school teachers to death with mallets."[16] A few of the films, like *The Texas Chainsaw Massacre*, have actually been celebrated for their adversarial relation to contemporary culture and society. In this film, a family of men, driven out of the slaughterhouse business by advanced technology, turns to cannibalism. The film deals with the slaughter of a group of young people travelling in a van and dwells at great length on the pursuit of the last survivor of the group, Sally, by the man named Leatherface, who hacks his victims to death with a chainsaw. Robin Wood has analyzed the film as embodying a critique of capitalism, since the film shows the horror both of people quite literally living off other people, and of the institution of the family, since it implies that the monster is the family.[17]

In some of the films the attack on contemporary life strikingly recapitulates the very terms adopted by many culture critics. In George Romero's *Dawn of the Dead*, the plot involves zombies taking over a shopping center, a scenario depicting the worst fears of the culture critics who have long envisioned the will-less, soul-less masses as zombie-like beings possessed by the alienating imperative to consume. And in David Cronenberg's *Videodrome*, video itself becomes the monster. The film concerns a plot, emanating from Pittsburgh, to subject human beings to massive doses of a video signal which renders its victims incapable of distinguishing hallucination from reality. One of the effects of this signal on the film's hero is to cause a gaping, vagina-like wound to open in the middle of his stomach, so that the villains can program him by inserting a video cassette into his body. The hero's situation becomes that of the new schizophrenic described by Jean Baudrillard in his discussion of the effects of mass communication:

> No more hysteria, no more projective paranoia, properly speaking, but this state of terror proper to the schizophrenic: too great a proximity of everything, the unclean promiscuity of everything which touches, invests, and penetrates without resistance, with no halo of private protection, not even his own body, to protect him anymore. . . . The schizo is bereft of every scene, open to everything in spite of himself, living in the greatest confusion.[18]

"You must open yourself completely to us," says one of *Videodrome's* villains, as he plunges the cassette into the gaping wound. It would seem that we are here very far from the realm of what is traditionally called "pleasure" and much nearer to so-called *jouissance*, discussions of which privilege terms like "gaps," "wounds," "fissures," "splits," "cleavages," and so forth.

Moreover, if the text is "an anagram for our body," as Roland Barthes maintains, the contemporary text of horror could aptly be considered an anagram for the schizophrenic's body, which is so vividly imaged in Cronenberg's film.[19] It is a ruptured body, lacking the kind of integrity commonly attributed to popular narrative cinema. For just as Baudrillard makes us aware that terms like "paranoia" and "hysteria," which film critics have used to analyze both film characters and textual mechanisms, are no longer as applicable in mass culture today as they once were, so the much more global term "narrative pleasure" is similarly becoming outmoded.

What is always at stake in discussions of "narrative pleasure" is what many think of as the ultimate "spurious harmony," the supreme ideological construct—the "bourgeois ego." Contemporary film theorists insist that pleasure is "ego-reinforcing" and that narrative is the primary means by which mass culture supplies and regulates this pleasure. For Stephen Heath, Hollywood narratives are versions of the nineteenth-century "novelistic," or "family romance," and their function is to "remember the history of the individual subject" through processes of identification, through narrative continuity, and through the mechanism of closure.[20] Julia Kristeva condemns popular cinema in similar terms in her essay on terror in film, "Ellipsis on Dread and the Specular Seduction":

> [The] terror/seduction node . . . becomes, through cinematic commerce, a kind of cut-rate seduction. One quickly pulls the veil over the terror, and only the cathartic relief remains; in mediocre potboilers, for example, in order to remain within the range of petty bourgeois taste, film plays up to narcissistic identification, and the viewer is satisfied with "three-buck seduction."[21]

But just as the individual and the family are *dis*-membered in the most gruesomely literal way in many of these films, so the novelistic as family romance is also in the process of being dismantled.

First, not only do the films tend to be increasingly open-ended in order to allow for the possibility of countless sequels, but they also often delight in thwarting the audiences' expectations of closure. The most famous examples of this tendency are the surprise codas of Brian de Palma's films—for instance, the hand reaching out from the grave in *Carrie*. And in *The Evil Dead*, *Halloween*, and *Friday the Thirteenth*, the monsters and slashers rise and attempt to kill over and over again each time they are presumed dead. At the end of *The Evil Dead*, the monsters, after defying myriad attempts to destroy them, appear finally to be annihilated as they are burned to death in an amazing lengthy sequence. But in the last shot of the film, when the hero steps outside into the light of day, the camera rushes toward him, and he turns and faces it with an expression of horror. In the final sequence of *Halloween*, the babysitter looks at the spot where the killer was apparently slain and, finding it vacant, says, "It really was the bogey man."

Secondly—and this is the aspect most commonly discussed and deplored by popular journalists—these films tend to dispense with or drastically minimize the plot and character development that is thought to be essential to the construction of the novelistic. In Cronenberg's *Rabid*, the porn star Marilyn Chambers plays a woman who receives a skin transplant and begins to infect everyone around her with a kind of rabies. The symptom of her disease is a vagina-like wound in her armpit out of which a phallic-shaped weapon springs to slash and mutilate its victims. While the film does have some semblance of a plot, most of it comprises disparate scenes showing Marilyn, or her victims, or her victims' victims, on the attack. Interestingly, although metonymy has been considered to be the principle by which narrative is constructed, metonymy in this film (the contagion signified by the title) becomes the means by which narrative is *disordered*, revealing a view of a world in which the center no longer holds. Films like *Maniac* and *Friday the Thirteenth* and its sequels go even further in the reduction of plot and character. In *Friday the Thirteenth*, a group of young people are brought together to staff a summer camp and are randomly murdered whenever they go off to make love. The people in the film are practically interchangeable, since we learn nothing about them as individuals, and there is virtually no building of a climax—only variations on the theme of slashing, creating a pattern that is more or less reversible.

Finally, it should scarcely need pointing out that when villains and victims are such shadowy, undeveloped characters and are portrayed equally unsympathetically, narcissistic identification on the part of the audience becomes increasingly difficult. Indeed, it could be said that some of the films elicit a kind of *anti*-narcissistic identification, which the audience delights in indulging just as it delights in having its expectations of closure frustrated. Of *The Texas Chainsaw Massacre*, Robin Wood writes, "Watching it recently with a large, half-stoned youth audience who cheered and applauded every one of Leatherface's outrages against their representatives on the screen was a terrifying experience."[22] The same might be said of films like *Halloween* and *Friday the Thirteenth*, which adopt the point of view of the slasher, placing the spectator in the position of an unseen nameless presence which, to the audiences' great glee, annihilates one by one their screen surrogates. This kind of joyful self-destructiveness on the part of the masses has been discussed by Jean Baudrillard in another context— in his analysis of the Georges Pompidou Center in Paris to which tourists flock by the millions, ostensibly to consume culture, but also to hasten the collapse of the structurally flawed building.[23] There is a similar paradox in the fact that *Dawn of the Dead*, the film about zombies taking over a shopping center, has become a midnight favorite at shopping malls all over the United States. In both cases the masses are revelling in the demise of the very culture they appear most enthusiastically to support. Here, it would seem, we have another variant of the split, "perverse" response favored by Roland Barthes.

The contemporary horror film thus comes very close to being "the other film" that Thierry Kuntzel says the classic narrative film must always work to conceal: "a film in which the initial figure would not find a place in the flow of a narrative, in which the configuration of events contained in the formal matrix would not form a progressive order, in which the spectator/subject would never be reassured . . . within the dominant system of production and consumption, this would be a film of sustained *terror*."[24] Both in form and in content, the genre confounds the theories of those critics who adopt an adversarial attitude toward mass culture. The type of mass art I have been discussing—the kind of films which play at drive-ins and shabby downtown theaters, and are discussed on the pages of newsletters named *Trashola* and *Sleazoid Express*—is as apocalyptic and nihilistic, as hostile to meaning, form, pleasure, and the specious good as many types of high art. This is surely not accidental. Since Jean-François Lyotard insists that postmodernism is an "aesthetic of the sublime," as Immanuel Kant theorized the concept, it is interesting to note that Kant saw an intimate connection between the literature of the sublime and the literature of terror, and moreover saw the difference as in part a matter of audience education: "In fact, without the development of moral ideas, that which, thanks to preparatory culture, we call sublime, merely strikes the untutored man as terrifying."[25] And there is certainly evidence to suggest that the converse of Kant's statement has some truth as well, since a film like *The Texas Chainsaw Massacre*, which might seem designed principally to terrify the untutored man, strikes a critic like Robin Wood as sublime—or at least as "authentic art." Wood writes, "*The Texas Chainsaw Massacre* . . . achieves the force of authentic art. . . . As a 'collective nightmare,' it brings to a focus a spirit of negativity, an undifferentiated lust for destruction that seems to lie not far below the surface of the modern collective consciousness."[26] It is indeed possible for the tutored critic versed in preparatory film culture to make a convincing case for the artistic merit of a film like *The Texas Chainsaw Massacre*, as long as art continues to be theorized in terms of negation, as long as we demand that it be uncompromisingly oppositional.

However, instead of endorsing Wood's view, we might wish to consider what these films have to teach us about the *limits* of an adversarial position which makes a virtue of "sustained terror." Certainly women have important reasons for doing so. In Trilling's essay, "The Fate of Pleasure," he notes almost parenthetically that, according to the *Oxford English Dictionary*, "Pleasure in the pejorative sense is sometimes personified as a female deity."[27] Now, when pleasure has become an almost wholly pejorative term, we might expect to see an increasing tendency to incarnate it as a woman. And, indeed, in the contemporary horror film it is personified as a lovely young school teacher beaten to death by midget clones (*The Brood*), as a pretty blond teenager threatened by a maniac wielding a chainsaw (*The Texas Chainsaw Massacre*), or as a pleasant and attractive babysitter terrorized throughout the film *Halloween* by a grown-up version of the little boy killer revealed in the opening sequence. Importantly, in many of the films the female is attacked not only because, as has often been claimed, she embodies sexual pleasure, but also because she represents a great many aspects of the specious good—just as the babysitter, for example, quite literally represents familial authority. The point needs to be stressed, since feminism has occasionally made common cause with the adversarial critics on the grounds that we too have been oppressed by the specious good. But this is to overlook the fact that in some profound sense we have also been historically and psychically identified with it.

Further, just as Linda Williams has argued that in the horror film woman is usually placed on the side of the monster even when she is its pre-eminent victim, so too in the scenario I outlined at the beginning woman is frequently associated with the monster mass culture.[28] This is hardly surprising since, as we have seen, mass culture has typically been theorized as the realm of cheap and easy pleasure—"pleasure in the pejorative sense." Thus, in Ann Douglas's account, the "feminization of American culture" is synonymous with the rise of mass culture.[29] And in David Cronenberg's view, mass culture—at least the video portion of it—is terrifying because of the way it feminizes its audience. In *Videodrome*, the openness and vulnerability of the media recipient are made to seem loathsome and fearful through the use of feminine imagery (the vaginal wound in the stomach) and feminine positioning: the hero is raped with a video cassette. As Baudrillard puts it, "no halo of private protection, not even his own body . . . protect[s] him anymore." Baudrillard himself describes mass-mediated experience in terms of rape, as when he speaks of "the unclean promiscuity of everything which touches, invests and penetrates without resistance." No resistance, no protection, no mastery. Or so it might seem. And yet the mastery that these popular texts no longer permit through effecting closure or eliciting narcissistic identification is often reasserted through projecting the experience of submission and defenselessness onto the female body. In this way the texts enable the male spectator to distance himself somewhat from the terror. And, as usual, it is the female spectator who is *truly* deprived of "solace and pleasure." Having been denied access to pleasure, while simultaneously being scapegoated for seeming to represent it, women are perhaps in the best position to call into question an aesthetics wholly opposed to it. At the very least, we might like to experience more of it before deciding to denounce it.

Beyond this, it remains for the postmodernist to ponder the irony of the fact that when critics condemn a "monstrous motion picture industry" they are to a certain extent repeating the gestures of texts they repudiate. And the question then becomes: How can an adversarial attitude be maintained toward an art that is itself increasingly adversarial? In *The Anti-Aesthetic*, Hal Foster considers modernism to be postmodernism's other, and he pointedly asks, "how can we exceed the modern? How can we break with a program that makes a value of crisis . . . or progress beyond the era of Progress . . . or *transgress the ideology of the transgressive?*"[30] Foster does not acknowledge the extent to which mass culture has also served as postmodernism's other, but his question is pertinent here too.

Part of the answer may lie in the fact that for many artists, transgression is not as important a value as it is for many theorists. A host of contemporary artistic endeavors may be cited as proof of this, despite the efforts of some critics to make these works conform to an oppositional practice. In literature, the most famous and current example of the changed, friendly attitude toward popular art is Umberto Eco's *The Name of the Rose*, which draws on the Sherlock Holmes mystery tale. Manuel Puig's novels (his *Kiss of the Spider Woman*, for example) have consistently explored the pleasures of popular movies. In the visual arts, Cindy Sherman's self-portraiture involves the artist's masquerading as figures from old Hollywood films. The "Still Life" exhibition organized by Marvin Heiferman and Diane Keaton consists of publicity stills from the files of Hollywood movie studios. In film, Rainer Werner Fassbinder continually paid homage to Hollywood melodramas; Wim Wenders and Betty Gordon return to *film noir*; Mulvey and Wollen to the fantastic; Valie Export to science fiction; and so on.

A few theorists have begun to acknowledge these developments, but usually only to denounce them. In a recent article entitled "Postmodernism and Consumer Society," Fredric Jameson concludes by deploring the fact that art is no longer "explosive and subversive," no longer "critical, negative, contestatory, . . . oppositional, and the like."[31] Instead, says Jameson, much recent art appears to incorporate images and stereotypes garnered from our pop cultural past. However, instead of sharing Jameson's pessimistic view of this tendency, I would like to end on a small note of comfort and solace. Perhaps the contemporary artist continues to be subversive by being nonadversarial in the modernist sense, and has returned to our pop cultural past partly in order to explore the site where pleasure was last observed, before it was stoned by the gentry and the mob alike, and recreated as a monster.

## NOTES

I would like to thank the Graduate School at the University of Wisconsin-Milwaukee for funding this project by generously awarding me a summer research grant in 1984.

1. Karl Marx, *Grundrisse: Foundations of the Critique of Political Economy* (Middlesex, England: Penguin, 1973), p. 706.

2. Isaac Balbus, *Marxism and Domination* (Princeton, NJ: Princeton University Press, 1982), p. 41.

3. Jacques Ellul, *The Technological Society*, trans. John Wilkinson (New York: Vintage, 1964), pp. 113–14.

4. Theodor W. Adorno, "Culture Industry Reconsidered," trans. Anson G. Rabinbach, *New German Critique* 6 (Fall 1975):17.

5. Roland Barthes, "Upon Leaving the Movie Theater," trans. Bertrand Augst and Susan White, *University Publishing* 6 (Winter 1979):3.

6. Hal Foster, "Postmodernism: A Preface," *The Anti-Aesthetic: Essays on Postmodern Culture*, ed. Hal Foster (Port Townsend, WA: Bay Press, 1983), p. xv.

7. Roland Barthes, *The Pleasure of the Text*, trans. Richard Miller (New York: Hill and Wang, 1975), pp. 47–48. Earlier Barthes remarks that "no significance (no *jouissance*) can occur, I am convinced, in a mass culture . . . for the model of this culture is petit bourgeois" (p. 38).

8. Christian Metz, *The Imaginary Signifier: Psychoanalysis and the Cinema*, trans. Celia Britton, Annwyl Williams, Ben Brewster, and Alfred Guzzetti (Bloomington: Indiana University Press, 1982), pp. 99–148.

9. Lionel Trilling, "The Fate of Pleasure: Wordsworth to Dostoevsky," *Partisan Review* (Summer 1963):178.

10. Ibid., p. 182.

11. Roland Barthes, *Image, Music, Text*, trans. Stephen Heath (New York: Hill and Wang, 1977), p. 167.

12. Jean-François Lyotard, "Answering the Question: What is Postmodernism?" trans. Régis Durand, *Innovation/Renovation: New Perspectives on the Humanities*, ed. Ihab Hassan and Sally Hassan (Madison: The University of Wisconsin Press, 1983), p. 340.

13. Ibid., p. 335.

14. Jean-François Lyotard, *La Condition postmoderne* (Paris: Minuit, 1979), p. 29.

15. Matei Calinescu, *Faces of Modernity: Avant-Garde, Decadence, Kitsch* (Bloomington: Indiana University Press, 1977), p. 240.

16. Leonard Maltin, *T.V. Movies*, revised edition (New York: Signet, 1981–82), p. 95.

17. Robin Wood, *American Nightmare: Essays on the Horror Film* (Toronto: Festival of Festivals, 1979), pp. 20–22.

18. Jean Baudrillard, "The Ecstasy of Communication," trans. John Johnston, *The Anti-Aesthetic*, pp. 132–33.

19. Barthes, *The Pleasure of the Text*, p. 17. Barthes, however, specifies the "erotic body."

20. Stephen Heath, *Questions of Cinema* (Bloomington: Indiana University Press, 1981), p. 157.

21. Julia Kristeva, "Ellipsis on Dread and the Specular Seduction," trans. Dolores Burdick, *Wide Angle* 3, no. 3 (1979):46.

22. Wood, p. 22.

23. Jean Baudrillard, *L'Effet beaubourg: implosion et dissuasion* (Paris: Galilée, 1977), pp. 23–25.

24. Thierry Kuntzel, "The Film Work 2," trans. Nancy Huston, *Camera Obscura* 5 (1980):24–25.

25. Immanuel Kant, *Critique of Judgment*, trans. James Creed (Oxford: Clarendon, 1952), p. 115, quoted in Franco Moretti, *Signs Taken for Wonders* (London: Verso, 1983), p. 253 n. See his chapter on "The Dialectic of Fear" for a very different reading of the vampire image in Marx.

26. Wood, p. 22.

27. Trilling, p. 168.

28. Linda Williams, "When the Woman Looks," *Re-vision: Essays in Feminist Film Criticism*, ed. Mary Ann Doane, Patricia Mellencamp, and Linda Williams, The American Film Institute Monograph Series, Vol. III (Frederick, MD: University Publications of America, 1984), pp. 85–88.

29. Ann Douglas, *The Feminization of American Culture* (New York: Avon, 1977).

30. Foster, p. ix. My emphasis.

31. Fredric Jameson, "Postmodernism and Consumer Society," *The Anti-Aesthetic*, p. 125.

# 10
## BRIEF ENCOUNTERS
### *MASS CULTURE AND THE EVACUATION OF SENSE*

## Dana Polan

To set the scene, two seemingly exclusive interpretations of the same mass cultural phenomenon. . . . In one moment of the revised edition of his *American Film Genres*, Stuart Kaminsky sets out to analyze thematically the mythic import of one of the most sociologically significant film genres: the Hong Kong kung fu movie.[1] Kaminsky suggests that the emotional appeal of the movies for their primarily male audience derives not from any simple attraction of the kinetic thrill of balletic bodies and dramatically amplified sounds; rather, Kaminsky finds the import of the kung fu films to lie in the ways that their narratives become parables of contemporary social dynamics. For Kaminsky, there is a formula to the kung fu film—a formula in which a man from the lower classes shows how physical skill and a violent prowess can enable the oppressed to triumph over the rulers of society. The kung fu film is an allegory of a class revenge (and indeed, many of the films explicitly use revenge for the death of the hero's friend or lover as a device to get the plot going), and this allegory finds an emotional resonance in the genre's audience, which is generally composed of men in the same economic and social situation as the hero.

Against this, we might contrast the analysis of a Derridean film-maker and theorist, Claudine Eizykman, in her book, *La jouissance-cinéma*.[2] Eizykman begins by asserting the weighty, oppressive presence of a dominant, uniform mass culture, devoted to the regime of N.R.I. (that is, narrative, representation, and industrial or institutional standardization). But as a Derridean (and as an avant-garde filmmaker who is turning to contemporary critical theory for a support for her own experimental practice), Eizykman argues that the regime of the

N.R.I. is only a restricted, restrained economy of signs that, no matter how hard it tries to naturalize itself as the necessary totality of culture today, can only take its place within a larger general economy of free-floating signifiers where virtually anything is possible—where the uniformity of mass culture can find itself relativized by endless *différance*, an undoing of all narrative and representational fixities. Significantly, Eizykman sees the kung fu film as one of the cinematic forces that exceeds the realm of the N.R.I.; avoiding any consideration of the regularities of the genre's *narrative* line, Eizykman finds an avant-gardist's pleasure in the kung fu battle as pure visual and aural spectacle. To her, it is a display of movements and sounds that ceases to be about anything but its own kinesis. Narrative here becomes at most what the Russian Formalists called a *device*, a mechanism whose only function is to provide as many excuses as possible for the scenes of spectacle; thus, Eizykman's ideal kung fu film would seem to be one in which no story is told and in which one simply witnesses battle after battle after battle. But, at the extreme, even this might not be enough; suggesting that the presence of any recognizably human shape on screen can throw an experimental cinema back into the restricted and restricting realm of representation, Eizykman argues the importance of seeing representational films literally out of focus—of watching anthropomorphic forms become pure form, with no content behind them.

I find the juxtaposition of these two essays intriguing in a number of ways. Most immediately, there is the seeming paradox of two so evidently exclusive readings of the same cultural form. To be sure, both analyses have a mythic dimension to them: Kaminsky falls for a myth of art as social commentary—in this case, a kind of nineteenth century naturalist form that represents characters working to escape from the environment that constrains them—while, for all her avant-gardism, Eizykman returns to the great classic myth of art as purposive non-purposiveness (to use Kant's term), a transcendental offer of escape from the all-too-purposive cares of an ordinary, mass, industrialized, and institutionalized world. Significant in this respect is the fact that the two authors are completely at odds about where to situate the Hong Kong genre. For Kaminsky, the kung fu film, as a genre of rigorously mythic narrativity, belongs so naturally in a book that announces itself to be about *American* film genres that he provides no explanation for the inclusion of this non-Hollywood form in his book. In contrast, for Eizykman, the non-Hollywood situation of kung fu seems automatically (or easily) to allow the genre to escape the dominant regime.

Yet what is most striking is the way in which these seemingly divergent interpretations can finally seem to rely on a single, insistent mythology, taking on the form of a duality in which each term supposes and necessitates the other. Despite their differences of interpretation, both Kaminsky and Eizykman share in the ideological binary opposition of mass culture and avant-garde culture. Ultimately, they merely disagree about the assignation of this or that cultural form—for example, the kung fu film—to one side or the other of this dichotomy. For both analysts, mass culture is essentially the regime of content, theme, the formulaic regularity of simple explanatory myths, an art tied to the givens of an everyday world. Modernist culture is the escape from all this, the promise of a realm in which the world is not talked about, the promise of an activity that makes no claims on worldly activity. Indeed, not that far from Eizykman, Kaminsky offers special praise to *Once Upon a Time in America* for the ways in which its complex temporal structure operates modernist variations on the mythic regularity of the Hollywood gangster genre.

Nothing, we might say, has been simpler than criticism's ability to define mass culture as a *simple* cultural form. Indeed, in the way that some cultural anthropologists have shown how much the constitution of a society depends on that society's ability to construct some sort of Other on which to focus its disapprobation so that its own mainstream social relations may seem normal, mass culture has become one of culture studies' most recurrent Others—a repository and a stereotypic cause of all the social ills of life under capitalism.[3] The most obvious kind of exception—the euphoric sort of celebration of popular culture to be found in *The Journal of Popular Culture* (published by the Popular Culture Association)—really does no more than reiterate the same scapegoating mechanism, exalting cases of popular culture only when the mythic, spiritual, transcendental values usually attributed to high culture can also be projected onto them.

Notwithstanding the self-acclaimed modernity of so much critical work, this work still can remain tributary to some of the oldest philosophic frameworks. Take for example the throwaway discussion of mass culture that suddenly pops up with all the air of expressing an obvious truth in J. M. Bernstein's *The Philosophy of the Novel: Lukács, Modernism, and the Dialectics of Form.* An extended contrast of Lukács's classicism with Adorno's modernism suddenly finds itself resolved by the arrival of mass culture, which Bernstein takes to be the really intrusive form as opposed to both the Lukácsian novel and Adorno's art of negation:

> Autonomous literature . . . represents the culmination of a social process by which realism's ambivalent critical and collusive relation to our practical ideology was broken in two, one half of which . . . preserves its critical dimension by creating a world apart, while the other half, the world of popular fiction, which inundates itself in the raw facts of

power, money, success, middle-class sexual fantasies, airports, and automobiles, has lost all ability to write against our time.[4]

Bernstein's binary opposition of "a world apart" and "raw facts" is
finally little removed from Book 10 of the *Republic*: an "inundation"
in everyday concerns removes art's critical edge and makes it inappropriate as a critically redemptive force for a split society. That mass
art may be a potentially contradictory cultural form, blending progressive and regressive elements, is never considered, and Bernstein
instead assembles a series of cliches whose very lack of self-interro-
gation is one of the strategies used to encourage assent. And yet,
certain close analyses of precisely the sorts of mass cultural forms that
Bernstein seems to have in mind—for example, night-time soap operas of "power, money, success, middle-class sexual fantasies, airports,
and automobiles" like *Dynasty* or *Dallas*—suggest how hard it is to fit
such forms into simple models. For instance, Jane Feuer reveals how
frequently these shows employ the nonrealist, nonnarrative rhetoric
that a discourse of formal deconstruction attributed to certain works
outside the mainstream of dominant culture.[5] Not that the presence
of such deconstructive technique within the mass cultural work makes
it necessarily a subversive form; part of the impetus of Feuer's analysis
is to point out the paradox of this highly mainstream artform bearing
the very same formal traits which are often taken to constitute a challenge to the mainstream. Rather than understanding formal innovation to be a deconstruction of dominant ideology, we might want
to deconstruct the whole underlying philosophy of a critical practice
that places innovation and dominance in opposition, that understands
mass culture to be an ideological form that is most effective when it
is formally and thematically most simple.

I would suggest that much of our contemporary critical theory has
been blocked in its analysis of cultural politics today by its reliance on
a belief in the stable existence of a whole series of reductive dichoto-
mies; on the univocal valorization of one term in the dichotomy over
the other; and on the assumption that a number of different dicho-
tomies are parallel, equivalent, or even interchangeable (as in the
process by which an opposition of "simple" and "complex" is mapped
onto oppositions of "mass culture" and "high culture" or, in recent
work, onto oppositions of "hegemonic" [or ideological] and "counter-
hegemonic" [or subversive]).

Probably no assumption has been more prevalent in recent critical
theory than that which equates narrative and ideology. At the extreme,
narrative becomes not *one of the forms* through which ideology works,
but *the only form* that ideology ever assumes.[6] Such an equation necessitates two conclusions that have constrained much of our ability

to analyze culture today: on the one hand, that anything narrative in form must support the work of ideology; and on the other hand, that anything non-narrative must necessarily challenge the operations of ideology.

If one looks at narrative as a formal model—a logic of controlled temporal transformations within a structure of causality—it is certainly possible to imagine that narrative could serve an ideologically constraining end. In Pierre Sorlin's words, "to envision time in the form of a linear unfolding along which events take place is to privilege a certain form of evolution; points of resistance, elements which don't integrate into a continuous line, the inexplicable, the complex all disappear."[7] A. J. Greimas goes so far as to maintain that the structure of narrative is really nothing more than the structure of all language— the enunciation of a problem followed by a solution, the necessary conjunction of a subject with a temporalizing prediction. This premise can imply that narrative is fundamentally constitutive of our everyday cognitive frameworks.[8] But this may so enlarge the province of narrative that we can imagine nothing that would not be included in it. One way out of this dilemma has been proposed by Fredric Jameson, who uses Greimas' model while rejecting its assumption that finding *a* structure of social logic is the same as finding *the* structure underlying all social logics.[9] Agreeing with Greimas that "narrative is the central function or instance of the human mind,"[10] Jameson allows narrative an ambivalence and ideological openness that Greimas' emphasis on single-strand narrative lines appears to close off. Specifically, Jameson argues that Greimas's use of the semiotic rectangle—a fixed set of initial semantic terms out of which a narrative's unfolding will be generated—in no way *necessitates* one, and only one, unfolding. Each manifest narrative is, for Jameson, a "strategy of containment" which works to gloss over other narrative possibilities but out of which these other narrative possibilities can always be read, can always be reconstructed. Every narrative, then, is an allegory which, even when it gives an explicit single answer to its initiating problem, can always give a glimpse of other answers—no matter how fleeting a glimpse, or utopian an answer.

Jameson's open model suggests a way to understand narrative as more than the expression of a single mythology (even if Jameson's own reading practice doesn't always adhere to this openness). Whereas the notion of a narrative logic constructs narrative as a form that channels all multiplicities toward the singularity of a necessary, univocal, and inevitable Sense of an Ending—as, for example, in film theorist Raymond Bellour's conception of American classic cinema as a logic that endlessly retells a story in which two people, man and woman, become a single unit, a marital couple[11]—the notion of nar-

rative as an allegorical interplay of alternative narrative lines offers a
way to detect progressive as well as regressive elements, to understand
narrative as no simple rendition of a simple ideology.

But Jameson's understanding of the way narrative's essential multiplicity takes place through the presence of *latent* narratives *beneath*
a single, *manifest* narrative line may be no more than one historically
specific way to understand narrative as an interplay of multiple logics.
Indeed, the very fact that Jameson's decision about what constitutes
the allegory within a manifest narrative is a highly subjective one—
in other words, the very fact that his readings may be unreproducible
by anyone other than Jameson—suggests a critical limitation to the
notion of a "political unconscious." The presence of the allegorical
level finally becomes something imputed to a text by the creative
reader (like Jameson), so any notion that the political unconscious
might have a real, historical existence outside of a reading—in the
text or in its historical conditions of production—becomes difficult to
maintain.[12] Despite the implicit critique of American deconstruction
that runs through *The Political Unconscious*, Jameson's theory comes
precariously close to the ahistorical method of the deconstructionists,
for whom every message is already multiplied, exceeded, by a fundamental and irreducible duality. Finding a double-strand allegory
everywhere may be as historically limited as Greimas' finding a single-
strand logic everywhere.

Even if every narrative is inevitably a blend of latent and manifest
logics, it is necessary to complement this initial insight with a historical
analysis that points out the varying ways in which the multiplicity of
narrative logics is, in different situations, sometimes enabled, sometimes repressed, sometimes transfigured. Rather than adopt Jameson's view that multiplicity takes the form of a duality of manifest and
latent, we might find at certain moments several narrative possibilities,
all equally manifest. Thus, in my work on American film narrative in
the 1940s, I argue that the moment of the war presents two very
different value systems—the value of commitment to a fighting cause
and the value of romantic attachment to a member of the opposite
sex—which frequently split narrative into irreconcilable strands.[13] For
example, the very title of the 1944 film *Uncertain Glory* indicates a
certain doubt in the heart of an American supposedly devoted whole-
heartedly to the war effort: what is the glory of war commitment, the
film seems to ask, if it means leaving behind the woman you love, a
woman who has herself discovered love for the first time? Although
some films suggest a way to resolve uncertainty—in *Man-Hunt*, the
woman is killed and the man becomes a one-man war-machine to
avenge her death—the fact of uncertainty remains, often showing up
directly as a question about engagement that the characters must face,

knowing all the while that there may be no single logic large enough, synoptic enough, to include all contingencies, all multiplicities.

But the understanding of narrative as a historically variable form also points to a need to reflect back on the second of the two problems that I suggested can come from the equation of narrative with ideology: namely, that such an equation assumes that the non-narrative will somehow constitute a challenge to the hegemonic workings of ideology. We can see such an equation at work in one of the most important studies in narrative theory and analysis, Roland Barthes' *S/Z*. It is useful to look carefully at this text to pinpoint some of the historical problems of contemporary narrative theory for the study of mass culture.[14] In *S/Z*, Barthes tries to outline some of the contours of what he refers to as "limit-works," artistic texts that engage in a certain reversing of the codes of narrative representation. Echoing the argument of his early study, *Writing Degree Zero*, in which he had posited a breakup (occurring around 1850) of the conditions and forms of traditional modes of representation, Barthes now finds the paradigmatic staging of such a breakup in an 1830 story by Balzac, "Sarrasine." Some of Barthes' analysis is purely formal—for example, he shows that the narrative figures a certain disruptive contagion of frame-story and framed-story—but for the most part it suggests ways in which the narrative's breakup is finally a breakup of the whole political-psychical economy of the early nineteenth century social order. Most importantly, when Barthes speaks of the story's reversing of the stabilities of the *Symbolic* code, he is not referring to a story's play with literary symbols; rather, as Rosalind Coward and Jack Ellis's analysis of *S/Z* within a tradition of ideology-critique makes clear, Barthes' notion of the Symbolic refers back to Lacan's theorization of a Symbolic level of language as the level in which the human subject takes his/her place in a whole network of social meanings, values, and precepts organized around the evident strength of a dominant power.[15] The Symbolic is the social dimension, and Lacan specifically enables a theorization of the Social that ties together psychical and political economies around the emergence of a phallic power.

If the Symbolic is normally in place, "Sarrasine" would dramatize and render a situation in which the Symbolic order underlying the whole of social and psychical relations has begun to unravel. Specifically, the centering of the narrative's enigma on a castrato—that is, on a figure in a complicated relation to the phallus—becomes ultimately a kind of de-centering in which identity becomes unstable; in which a contagious force blurs boundaries, transgresses frontiers, and disrupts the divisions, fixities, and fetishes that the Symbolic order requires for its steady, secure operation.

As if to underscore further the ties of a psychoanalytic analysis of narrative to a historical and ideological analysis, Barthes suggests that the breakup of what we can metaphorically call a "psychical *economy*" actually has ties to a dismantling of the literal economy of the early nineteenth century order. What "Sarrasine" presents early on as the enigma of the origin and force of the mysterious family's wealth is an enigma that has both a specifically biographical answer—the wealth comes from the scandalous success of the castrato as an opera singer under the patronage of a Cardinal—and a broader financial one— modern wealth is no longer a wealth that has been passed down from generation to generation, a wealth that signifies stability and that centers itself on the fixity of gold as a monetary standard. Where gold would seem quite obviously and naturally to signal its own meaning, the emergence of paper money, of a specifically bourgeois wealth as opposed to an aristocratic one, creates the potential for a free-floating situation of endless simulacra, a meaning cut off from all bases:

> The difference that opposes feudal society to bourgeois society, the index to the sign, is this: the index has an origin, the sign has none; to move from the index to the sign is to abolish the last (or the first) limit, the origin, the foundation, the end-all, is to enter into the unlimited process of equivalences, of representations that nothing can any longer stop, orient, fix, consecrate. . . . [S]igns (monetary, sexual) are crazy since, contrary to indices (the regime of sense for the older society), they are not founded on an original, irreducible, incorruptible, unmovable alterity of their elements. . . . [In] the sign . . . the two *parts* interchange, signified and signifer turning around each other in an endless process. . . . Following after the feudal index, the bourgeois sign is a metonymic trouble (p. 47).

But already, this notion of the troubling of a signifying order suggests a certain limitation to Barthes' analysis in a historical sense. Not only does Barthes want to argue a split between representation before the middle of the nineteenth century and subsequent representation; he also wants to argue a split within the bourgeois moment—what he will develop as the conflict of readerly and writerly texts—and this sense of a split internal to the bourgeois economy can only fit ambiguously within the totalizing economic determinism of an argument based on the emergence of a new monetary standard. That is, there is little analysis in Barthes' argument of the conditions that would allow the possibility of a split—why, for example, would a crisis of the sign not lead to only the writerly? Why would the bourgeoisie not be so drawn to writerly texts that these would become the readerly form for a free-floating bourgeois consciousness? Ultimately, any hopes of what we might call a Barthesian *sociology* of writing disappear under Barthes' adherence to the mass/high split within cultural criticism.

Indeed, it would be rather easy to read many works from popular

culture as limit-texts in Barthes' sense and find in them a troubling
of both the orders of narrative and the orders of a Symbolic economy.
Again, such a reading might tell us less that such works fall outside
the sway of dominant ideology than that the terms in which we theorize the relations of mass culture to dominance need to be expanded.
Perhaps mass culture is at the limits of simple, univocal representation,
rather than firmly and fully immersed in it (or inundated by it, as
Bernstein would have it).

For example, one recurrent aspect of popular culture is its self-
reflexive dimension—its pointed commentary on, and even pastiche
or parody of, its own status as cultural item. Hence, the intrigue (a
word that can refer both to the workings of plot and to the emotional
involvement built out of suspense) of a 1981 "Blondie" comic strip
illustrated here. The strip is about the psychological grip that highly
conventionalized narrative forms have on our lives (all we need to
know is that Dagwood's story involves an heiress getting killed to know
what kind of story he is reading); but beyond that, the form of Dagwood's story is not that different from the story we read: while one
appears in a magazine and the other in a newspaper, both seem dominated by the sense of an ending, and both share the vulnerability of
ephemeral media open to a cutting up, a dispersion. But it is the very
evanescent quality of the story—a cartoon we read quickly and don't
even waste any thought over—that enables the cartoon to take on
some of the most writerly qualities of experimental art. There is a
certain non-obviousness to the cartoon—what, exactly, is its point?
What precisely is its humor? What ultimately is its end, and what is

the sense of that ending? There is a certain non-sense of the cartoon's sense that hovers around our consumerist reading and leaves somewhat ambiguous what it is that we have consumed.

To be sure, one could read mythic meanings into the cartoon and find in it an expression of a social thematics. For example, substitute the recipe taken away to another house for the children or princesses spirited away in magic tales, and one would easily have a modern-day version of the Proppian folk tale, with Dagwood as the adventurous hero who wanders out into an alien territory to restore things to their proper place.[16]

But it would be as possible to read the strip as figuring an impossibility of heroic narrative. Indeed, if Propp's allegory gives us the image of the Symbolic order in the prowess of a hero working under the sureness of authority figures (such as the king who will bless the union of hero and rescued princess),[17] the "Blondie" comic can seem to be on the other side of the Symbolic, a limit-text edging into a world where the phallus is in doubt, rendered unstable by a contagious insufficiency of value and authority. Indeed, the "Blondie" series literally begins as a rejection of the Non/Nom of the Father, as Blondie refuses to follow her rich father's demands that she marry an equally rich man and instead runs off with good-for-nothing Dagwood.[18] Away from the father, "Blondie's" world can only be one in which masculinity slips from its sure position, and where the boundaries and divisions that Barthes finds so central to the maintenance of the Symbolic come undone. We might even go so far as to find an uncannily Sarrasinian moment in this particular strip, when the discovery of the cutting is rendered visually by Dagwood sitting under a sharp, downward-pointing mark of exclamation while Blondie lies next to him, emitting what for Barthes is the ultimate sign of castration: a Z, "the letter of mutilation . . . stinging like a punishing whip . . . an oblique and illegal cutting edge . . . the letter of deviance . . . initial of castration . . . lack's wound" (p. 113). Symbolic castration here is the threat of a full loss of control, the threat of a world of sexual difference where women cut out strudel recipes and invest narrative with a dangerous contingency. Against the security of his suburban bedroom, against his mastery of narrative through the position of consuming reader, Dagwood must venture out into a malevolent world governed by contingency rather than logic (why, for example, does Herb consider reading a detective story more inconsiderate than asking for a strudel recipe at 2:30 in the morning?). Significantly perhaps, Dagwood's first sign of a reassumption of mastery—the smile that breaks across his face in panel 9 as Tootsie successfully digs out the recipe—occurs simultaneously with a second "Z" in a position not far from Blondie's. Dagwood's mastery is a temporary and purely fictive one;

power for the suburban man is grounded in little if any sustaining value. Hence, a certain irony in the last frame: Dagwood as the man who is happy with the little that he can pull from a crazy situation, luxuriating in a sense of an ending that he got wrong and that left him with a black eye.

Admittedly, this is a deliberately fanciful reading of the "Blondie" strip, but it still seems certain that Dagwood is a version of masculinity after the break-up of a "feudal" order of phallic power. As a comic strip of suburban America, "Blondie" participates in that dethroning of fathers that radical conservatives so bemoan—and that leads them in a Reaganite moment to wish for a Friendly Fascist return to a world governed by strong men. This is not to say that "Blondie" is a subversive text, for its figuration of the powerless male depends on a figuration of a very different sort of powerlessness in the female; it is, however, to suggest that for all its *feuilleton* simplicity, "Blondie" is no simple mythic representation of "raw facts of power, money, success, middle-class sexual fantasies," etc. If it has a fantasy, it is more the postmodernist one in which all wishes for a world beyond have been rendered impossible and in which one encounters nothing but endlessly cyclical bursts of absurdity (as with all the vendors of weird gadgets who continually come to Dagwood's door).

For his analysis of the breakdown of an economy of representation, Barthes seems to have relied most immediately on the work of Jean-Joseph Goux, who, in a number of articles published in *Tel Quel* around the time of Barthes' investigations (and later collected into a book, *Economie et symbolique*), argues the simultaneous, interdependent, equivalent, and interchangeable historical emergence of gold and of a phallic power of the Symbolic father.[19] But Goux's most recent work—for example, his 1984 book, *Les Monnayeurs de langage*—suggests a historical limit to the kind of ideological critique that Barthes finds in the breakdown of feudal representation.[20]

In *Les Monnayeurs de langage*, Goux continues to argue the tie of phallic power to the power of gold and, like Barthes, even suggests how a nineteenth (and early twentieth) century literary modernism announces and represents a crisis of representation, a troubling of phallic power. But, contrary to Barthes, Goux now suggests that the breakdown of a form of power can easily imply its replacement by other newly-emergent forms of power. Power doesn't always take shape as the power of the Symbolic Father, and the overthrow of a centered, authoritative Symbolic may simply mean that other forms of power-relations—often more subtle than the model of a feudal power focused on a lordly figure—have come into dominance. Thus, for Goux, the overthrow of the Law of the Father in the overthrow of gold not only brings about the emergence of a free-floating eco-

nomic sign, but also ties this emergence to the parallel emergence of
a new law that finds its force in the transnational monopoly—the new
corporation whose micropolitical channels of control are so widespread and dispersed that no single authoritative father-figure is necessary to put the machine into operation. What sociologists have seen
as the death of the nuclear family and the loss of the father's control
in that family, Goux sees as a necessary complement of a late capitalism, in which the family is no longer the site of productive relations,
but an outmoded holdover from earlier days.

To take an example (mine, not Goux's), while an older capitalism
emphasized a psychical, financial frugality centered on the father as
the principal productive force—as in the feudalism of the Victorian
family, where "to spend" was to waste both money and sperm—the
late capitalism of what we now refer to as post-industrial society—a
society of services and information, of a flow of desire—is a capitalism
that encourages excessive expenditure, that desires a desire that is not
sublimated or organized within the frame of the Oedipalized family.
Thus in California's Silicon Valley, the hi-tech white-collar workers
are encouraged to reject notions of a centered authority, the Nom-
de-pere that, for Lacan, is also the Non-de-pere. Everyone dresses
casually; higher-ups are to be addressed by their first names; subcultural eccentricities (for example, office door graffitti) are invited
(and so are rendered systematic and no longer eccentric); non-familial
relationships are encouraged (at one Silicon Valley company, the en-
gineers come to work in snazzily painted vans in which they can meet
other workers for not-so-furtive trysts during the lunch hour). The
moment of late capitalism may work not so much by a repression as
by a positive incitation, an invitation to individuals to exceed previous
boundaries, to be in excess of an analytic, literally conservative control
of productivity. As Stephen Heath suggests in his study of odes to
orgasmic energy in recent mainstream popular fiction, the valorization
of sexuality can work hand in hand with a valorization of free-floating
capitalism as the site where such sexuality can most readily find its
space, a productive field.[21]

The transition to late capitalism has immense implications for the
study of mass culture; it may well be that such capitalism implies new
forms of mass culture that older analytic models—like narrative analysis, centered on logic, coherence, and stability—can no longer explain.
For example, the Oedipal trajectory that film theorist Raymond Bellour sees as central to American film narrative may cease to be appropriate for Hollywood narrative in the moment of late capitalism.
Where Bellour suggests a historical tie of Oedipalism to the effects of
the French Revolution in a new ideology of property possession and
the centrality of the bourgeois home in everyday life, many films stage

the irrelevance or impossibility of such an ideology in the new space of late capitalism.[22] For example, in films of the forties—a period that many sociologists take to be pivotal for the development of a society focused on modes of information, rather than on modes of production[23]—we can see a certain disavowal of Oedipus, of the formation of a domestic unit as the psychoanalytically necessary answer to initial narrative problems. For example, the 1945 film noir *Detour* maintains the Oedipal configuration only as an impossible memory that is forever closed off to the errant hero.[24] Outside the classic logic, the hero, Al Roberts, finds an illogic of contingency, loss, and non-progressing repetition. In a kind of parody of the old American pioneer dream, Al sets off to the West to find his symbolically golden-haired girl, only to discover the brute fact of a non-mythic world—a Los Angeles that seems to be nothing but cheap hotel rooms and one used car lot after another. Entering the postmodern moment and its culture, Al discovers a world beyond myths beyond the security of stable logics and stable meanings. The detour of the film's title is finally not only the detour of its specific narrative but also the detour of the whole American mythology of quest and conquest as that mythology finds itself undercut by the ambiguities of an age that is increasingly giving itself over to unbridled productivity and especially to the production of information as the ultimate commodity.

Similarly, many postwar musicals seem to participate directly in a situation where notions of family, domesticity, and sublimation of energies, are no longer to be the exclusive end of narrative drives. Instead, the musicals frequently figure narrative as a device for spectacle—that is, for a kind of showing off of form, a rejection of themes and meaningful mythologies for a new, non-signifying notion of art as endless, meaningless display. If narrative remains from time to time in such art, it frequently does so either as a mark of the kind of anachronism that an art of spectacle will transcend or as a force that will ironically engage in its own dissolution and supercession by spectacular form.

Hence, to take one example, the 1950 musical, *Summer Stock*, can seem like nothing so much as a commentary on the irrelevance of narrative to an art that wishes to celebrate an endless, de-sublimated spectacle cut off from all narrative ends. In its initial premise of a young farm woman, Jane Falbury (Judy Garland), resolving to keep her farm going at all costs, *Summer Stock* adheres for a while to an appearance of narrativity; we are here in the presence of one of the oldest American narrative myths: the productive conquest of the land through the application of a resolute will.

But it is all this American classicism that the film will work to disavow, substituting for the older American dream of earthy conquest a new dream of America as an endless performance, what Dennis Giles calls "the permanent show."[25] When theater performer Joe Ross (Gene Kelly) shows up on the farm, the pioneer narrative gets de-routed, even forgotten (after a while, there is no longer any reference to the running of Jane's farm). The only goal is that of a good show and, as if to further the sense of spectacle as a rejection of all narrative sense, the show (entitled *Summer Stock*, just like the film) that Joe stages has no narrative logic, but is just a series of disconnected sketches (despite his early description of it as the story of a guy and a girl falling in love). Not coincidentally perhaps, Jane's two numbers in this show only reveal the degree to which she has left behind the American pioneer narrative: on the one hand, "Shout hallelujah, come on, get happy" figures the musical itself as a new source of spiritual redemption, while the end-song ("Howdy neighbor, happy harvest") shows the ultimate enframement of pioneer myths within a new framework of spectacle, as the song that Jane sang earlier when she had managed to buy a tractor now becomes a song for the show's cast to sing on stage as the film ends. Even more, the ending of the film in a per-manent show effects a certain displacement of romance; within the narrative, Joe and Jane may kiss, may seal their love for each other, but the end of the narrative and the end of the film don't coincide. They kiss, but the show must go on. What is important for the new world of show is not the ending in romance, but the more spectacular "ending" in song-and-dance—Jane and Joe on stage, part of a group, playing to us and not to each other.

In another postwar musical, *Easter Parade* (1948), the heroine, Han-nah Brown (Judy Garland), has as her life goal to walk down Fifth Avenue on Easter decked out in spectacular finery. In a film that posited Hannah from the start as a sort of object of spectacle, arbi-trarily picked to be in a show by a showman, Don Hewes (Fred Astaire), who contended that he could make any girl a star, the end only further represents the loss of self in the world of spectacle. After their dec-larations of love, Hannah and Don begin a walk down Fifth Avenue as the camera pulls back, and they are lost in the crowd. What some writers only a few years later will bemoan as the fate of the "man in the crowd," "the man in the gray flannel suit," is in the musical a source of celebration, the virtue of a complete merging of self into the vastness of a mass spectacle.

A number of theorists have portrayed as dismal the fate of the bourgeois subject in confrontation with the new situation of a post-modern age where meaning floats, where signs proliferate in a non-sensical progression—as in the attempt (described by Fredric Jame-son) by the bourgeois subject to negotiate the deliberate confusion of such postmodern experiences as Los Angeles's Hotel Bonaventura.[26]

Intimately tied to the increasing irrelevance of the individual productive monad within the modern world system, postmodernism
would be a culture of loss, of alienation, of endless confusion. Yet
what the theorists have seen as a negative situation ironically becomes
a source of pleasure for much of the art itself. Hence, for example,
the finding of humor in bad taste or even deliberate non-humor in a
show like *Saturday Night Live*; hence, too, the carnivalesque joy that
film critic Robin Wood witnessed in an urban audience's paroxysms
of delight at the chainsaw-toting, poor-white-trash Leatherface of *The
Texas Chainsaw Massacre*, who cuts up urbanites to compensate for the
effects of late capitalism (the film suggests that Leatherface goes about
his work to keep the family sausage company in business);[27] hence,
too, the strangeness for me of watching, in an urban shopping mall,
*The Blues Brothers Movie*, in which one scene, cheered to a virtually
orgiastic degree by the audience, shows the Blues Brothers driving
through a mall exactly like the one we were sitting in and wreaking
destruction at every turn as shoppers (looking exactly like the members of the audience) scramble for their lives.[28]

In a series of articles on postmodernist culture, Jameson suggests
that this culture is characterized by pastiche, collage, and schizophrenia.[29] I would suggest that we add to this list *incoherence*, in the literal
sense of the inability or unwillingness of culture to cohere, to follow
an evident logic. This is not to say that we couldn't find a logic of the
incoherent by tying the individual cultural text—as Jameson does—
to the broader transformations of late capitalism. But it does seem
that the experience of individual works (and even this notion of the
singular, isolated work is coming to seem an incoherent anachronism)
is one that older logical models can't explain. For example, what notion of narrative's transparent construction of a diegetic universe
could match the strangeness of the fact that the television show *Mork
and Mindy*, which is about an extraterrestrial, originated as a spin-off
of *Happy Days*, a quaint show about everyday life in the American
fifties? Perhaps there is the slightest glimpse of a logic—after all, part
of our conception today of the fifties is tied to all the fifties movies
about *It, The Terror From Beyond Space* and other menacing aliens—
but the incoherence comes from the very vagueness of the logic; rational explanation becomes only one more element in a spectacular
combination which no one element's presence is enough to explain.
Similarly, what notion of the television dramatic series as inheritor of
the ostensible narrative and representational goals of the nineteenth
century novel could really account for the conceit by which the television show *Dallas*, can substitute one actress (Donna Reed) for another
(Barbara Bel Geddes) in the role of a central character (Miss Ellie)?
To be sure, one could always run, as the producers themselves did,

to a notion of the television audience as a passive, accepting entity, but this would be to block analysis with cliches of the mass that are little different from notions of a rabble or a mindless horde. Rather, I would suggest that such specific incoherences become acceptable because culture and everyday life in general has made incoherence part of the norm. Even though this may seem the vaguest, most non-analyzable of terms I would say that there is a fundamental *weirdness* in contemporary mass culture that we need to confront and theorize.

Notions of spectacle, of play, and indeed of the post-structuralist conception of play as a floating of signifiers apart from all signifying intentions might well aid us in this task. For example, Claudine Eizykman's conception of the kung fu film as a visual spectacle may help us more than Kaminsky's reading of the genre within a narrative logic, but at the same time we would have to deconstruct Eizykman's distinction between the avant-garde and the realm of the N.R.I. and acknowledge that mass culture today takes on the form generally attributed to experimental art. This art works through an interplay, a kind of montage, of moments that vaguely hint at meaning and moments that disavow posited meanings, engage in contradiction, undercut every sense by a subsequent or coincident non-sense. For example, an interview show like *The Tonight Show* is in many ways little different from a modernist montage. Each individual bit—each interview—may have a certain sense, a message (as in those moments when a star enounces some moralizing platitude that the audience enthusiastically applauds), but the whole effect of the show comes from the incongruous confrontation of each bit with the other, the ongoing flow that forces each scene to give way to the next.

If, in Althusserian terms, we understand the ideological to involve an attempt at reproducing the conditions for the production of a society's fundamental operations,[30] then postmodern mass culture is no less a part of the ideological than was the mass culture imagined by older, thematic cultural theories. But where the older theories frequently understand the ideological work of culture to lie in its creation of effective social subjects—so that, in Kaminsky's analysis, the kung fu movie offers meaningful models of behavior to its audience members—the new mass culture may operate by offering no models whatsoever, preferring instead a situation in which there are no stable values, in which there are no effective roles that one could follow through from beginning to end. In an age where a certain level of unemployment has become structurally obligatory for the workings of the system—the age of what some sociologists have referred to as "The Deindustrialization of America"—it may no longer be necessary for capitalism to produce a ready-and-waiting pool of interpellated subjects. If the older mass culture works by offering the stability of singular myths—for example, the skillful triumph over the upper classes in the Kaminsky version of the kung fu film—that allow the individual the dream of a society that centers around that individual's own will and subjectivity, the new culture presents a situation in which will ceases to matter, in which one can come to luxuriate in one's own loss of will. More than ever, mass culture can come to encourage a powerlessness; but whereas the powerlessness of culture according to the role-model theory of culture comes from its offering of an identity that is simplistic in the face of power's real force—as in the simplicity of the kung fu film, in which it is imagined that the defeat of one evil rich man is the same as the defeat of all evil, all class prerogative—powerlessness in postmodern mass culture now comes from a situation in which the montage of elements calls into question each and every role that one might care to adopt. There is no position except that of an alienated cynicism. Indeed, as Marcia Landy and Lucy Fischer suggest in an analysis of the postmodern mass culture film *The Eyes of Laura Mars*, some of the new works of mass culture even anticipate and include as part of their system the very sorts of criticisms that one might direct against them.[31] *The Eyes of Laura Mars*, for example, works to preempt criticism by including images of critics and intellectuals who voice the very sorts of criticisms that one might feel encouraged to make of a film that so deliberately plays on blends of sexuality and violence.

Thus, as much as we still wish to continue the close, textual analysis of individual works of mass culture, two other analytic operations become necessary for the study of mass culture in the age of the Society of the Spectacle. On the one hand, we need to understand how each text, and each moment in a text, is part of a larger *intertextuality* pieces in a montage that robs each piece of any enduring sense or value. In this perspective, each part of mass culture needs to be studied as part of that flow that Raymond Williams suggested was part of the specific operation of commercial television.[32] Flow involves the transcendence of meaningful units by a system whose only meaning is the fact of its global non-meaning.

On the other hand, then, it is necessary to understand the whole of this montagist social text within the overall operations of capitalism today. Otherwise, we are left in a position of bewildered estrangement before what I have referred to as the "weirdness" of contemporary mass culture. If the notion of flow can suggest how each work of culture becomes part of a vast spectacle, it is equally important to suggest how spectacle becomes the source of a *Society* of the Spectacle—that is, how spectacle intertwines with the construction of contemporary social relations. For example, we might suggest that the limitations of Eizykman's post-structuralist avant-gardism come from her stopping her analysis at the first stage; she shows perfectly well how the kung fu film transcends narrative for the sake of a gripping but meaningless spectacle, but she doesn't examine how such spectacle might function within late capitalism, and so is left with the inevitable, modernist conclusion that spectacle and late capitalism are antagonistic forces.

But even if one accepts the idea of a late capitalist culture that would be a mixture of mass and postmodern culture, I must note some major limitations about the omnipresence and omnipotence of a society of the spectacle as I have outlined it here. First, spectacle doesn't exclude or prohibit the presence of older, more meaningful thematic forms of mass culture within the broader display of spectacle. As I have already suggested, the montage of spectacle even seems to require thematic elements whose supersession gives the montage its particular power; while watching music videos, for example, one can have the sense of seeing specific images and references that might have an explanatory power but that ultimately add up to nothing particularly helpful to an interpretation. As part of that process of pastiche that Jameson attributes to postmodern culture, contemporary mass culture overflows with all sorts of allusions to earlier, more stable cultural forms; these allusions vaguely seem to offer interpretive clues (for example, it seems vaguely meaningful that Donna Reed—ideal mom of the late 1950s—became Miss Ellie), but they finally only re-emphasize the impossibility of interpretation, of finding a univocal path through the incoherence of the new art.

Given the status of the mass culture of spectacle as a specifically historical form, we would also want to keep in mind that the future of spectacle would be dependent on historical constraints. Indeed, while I may have seemed to present spectacle as the necessary effect of late capitalism, we might also want to take note of ways in which late capitalism maintains older myths of individual initiative, of pioneer conquest, as part of its operation. For example, in the Reaganite moment, there seems to be a reinvestment in narratives of the most mythic sort; even the assassination attempt will be narrativized as the strong hero's triumph over brute materiality—the president who can joke on the way to the hospital and who can ride a horse and chop wood only weeks later. The Reagan mythology works by appeal to the oldest images of family, of patriarchy, and of homestead, and it is not surprising to see a return to narratives that try to celebrate these values. Thus, if postmodern mass culture seemed to reject Oedipalism for a free-floating situation of endless desublimation, a strong narrative like *An Officer and a Gentleman* will return us to the oldest versions of the Proppian magic tale—the hero as gentleman who rescues a Cinderella from a banal existence of trouble and travail (all to the music of ex-6os rad Joe Cocker, who now tells us that "Love lifts you up where you belong").

Furthermore, the Reagan moment seems to encourage certain mediations of myth and spectacle in narrative devoted to systematically functional excess. That is, we get a whole slew of narratives which suggest that one should run wild, be excessive, get crazy (as the title of one film puts it), but only as long as the best way to do all this is within the constraints of an American productivity; hence, films like *Porky's*, *Police Academy* and especially *Stripes* (which was made before the Reaganite moment, but which anticipated it), where zaniness, disobedience, and egoism all can find their greatest welcome in the new space of the modern army—where membership in a fighting force literally allows the most extreme of misfits to be all that he can be.

We might even go so far as to argue that certain historical situations require the mixture of stable myths with a free-floating liberation from other myths. Above all, I want to suggest that the power of spectacle is inextricably linked to the functions of sexual difference in late capitalist society; that is, the offer of a freedom from logics, from rational controls, is often held out to a male at the price of the reification of woman.[33] Hence, as I mentioned earlier, the rejection of the Father in "Blondie" is matched by a stabilization of woman as force of domesticity. Regularly, spectacle figures a woman as the anachronism that blocks frivolity, a figure that can only subsist in the new world either as a fetishized reminder of traditional stereotypes (for example, music video, where the freedom of men to reject values like school and middle-class propriety goes hand-in-hand with a virtually Victorian iconography of women wearing garter belts, leather, black lace, etc.) or as a conservative individuality that must be converted to a new way of life against her own will; hence a film like the postwar musical, *The Pirate*, where the young woman, Manuela, who disdains the world of entertainment, will be hypnotized by the clown, Serafin (Gene Kelly), to reveal her inner core of performance, and will finish the film singing to us, "Be a clown, be a clown."

All this is to suggest that we can't simply replace our older theories of mass culture with a new one of spectacle. Rather, we need to build toward a totalizing method, one that combines systems of knowledge to deal with a social system that itself engages in a spectacular combining, or merging, of all sorts of residual and emergent forms. It is toward an analysis of our complicated contemporaneity that I direct the thoughts of this essay.

## NOTES

1. Stuart Kaminsky, *American Film Genres*, revised edition (Chicago: Nelson-Hall, 1984).

2. Claudine Eizykman, *La Jouissance-cinéma* (Paris: Union Generale d'Editions, 1976).

3. On the constitution of mass culture as the avant-garde's Other, see Loren Shumway, "On the Intelligibility of the Avant-Garde Manifesto," *French Literary Series* v. 7 (1980):54–62.

4. J. M. Bernstein, *The Philosophy of the Novel: Lukács, Modernism and the Dialectics of Form* (Minneapolis: University of Minnesota Press, 1984), p. 252ff.

5. Jane Feuer, "Melodrama, Serial Form, and Television Today," *Screen* 25 (January-February 1984):4–16.

6. See, for example, Terry Eagleton, "Ideology, Fiction, Narrative," *Social Text* 2 (Summer 1979):62–80.

7. Pierre Sorlin, *Sociologie du cinéma* (Paris: Aubier Montaigne, 1977), p. 20.

8. See A. J. Greimas, *Semantique structurale* (Paris: Larousse, 1966).

9. See Fredric Jameson, *The Political Unconscious: Narrative as a Socially Symbolic Act* (Ithaca: Cornell University Press, 1981); and applications of the Greimasian model in such studies of his as *Fables of Aggression: Wyndham Lewis, the Modernist as Fascist* (Berkeley: University of California Press, 1979); and "After Armageddon: Character Systems in Dr. Bloodmoney," *Science-Fiction Studies* 2, no. 1 (March 1975):31–42.

10. Jameson, *The Political Unconscious*, p. 13.

11. See "Alternation, Segmentation, Hypnosis: An Interview with Raymond Bellour," *Camera Obscura* 3–4 (Summer 1979):71–103.

12. Hence, the limitations of Jameson's *Fables of Aggression* where Jameson's theoretical need to privilege Wyndham Lewis's writing practice leads Jameson to posit realism and mass culture—the forms that Lewis wrote against —as simple, univocal forms. *Fables of Aggression* reinstitutes the mass/avant-garde hierarchy that a notion of the political unconscious promised to overcome.

13. See my *Power and Paranoia: History, Narrative, and the American Cinema, 1940–1950* (New York: Columbia University Press, 1986).

14. Roland Barthes, *S/Z* (Paris: Seuil, 1972).

15. Rosalind Coward and Jack Ellis, *Language and Materialism: Developments in Semiology and the Theory of the Subject* (London: Routledge and Kegan Paul, 1977).

16. A number of critics have tried to use Propp in a similar way to analyze the role of myths in contemporary American culture. See, for example, Dennis Porter's Proppian analysis of baseball in "The Perilous Quest: Baseball as Folk Drama," *Critical Inquiry* 4, no. 1 (Autumn 1977):143–57.

17. On the parallels of Propp and the Lacanian representation of the Symbolic, see Teresa de Lauretis, *Alice Doesn't: Feminism, Semiotics, Cinema* (Bloomington: Indiana University Press, 1984), pp. 103–57.

18. See Maurice Horn, *Women in the Comics* (New York: Chelsea House, 1981).

19. Jean-Joseph Goux, *Economie et symbolique: Freud/Marx* (Paris: Seuil, 1973).

20. Jean-Joseph Goux, *Les Monnayeurs de langage* (Paris: Galilée, 1984).

21. Stephen Heath, *The Sexual Fix* (New York: Schocken, 1984).

22. Raymond Bellour, "Un jour, la castration," *L'Arc* 71 (1978):9–23.

23. See, for example, Marvin Harris, *America Now: The Anthropology of a Changing Culture* (New York: Simon and Schuster, 1981).

24. See Tania Modleski, "Film Theory's Detour," *Screen* 23, no. 5 (November-December 1982):72–79.

25. Dennis Giles, "Show-Making," *Movie* 24 (Spring 1977):14–25.

26. Frederic Jameson, "Postmodernism, or the Cultural Logic of Late Capitalism," *New Left Review* 146 (July-August 1984):53–93.

27. Robin Wood, "The Return of the Repressed," in Wood et al., *The American Nightmare: Essays on the Horror Film* (Toronto: Festival of Festivals, 1979), p. 22.

28. For a similar analysis of this phenomenon in relation to George Romero's film *Dawn of the Dead*, see Tania Modleski's "The Terror of Pleasure: The Contemporary Horror Film and Postmodern Theory," in this volume.

29. See especially "Postmodernism and Consumer Society," in *The Anti-Aesthetic: Essays on Postmodern culture*, ed. Hal Foster (Port Townsend, WA: Bay Press, 1983), pp. 111–25.

30. Louis Althusser, "Ideology and Ideological State Apparati," *Lenin and Philosophy and Other Essays*, trans. Ben Brewster (New York: Monthly Review Press, 1971).

31. See Marcia Landy and Lucy Fischer, "*The Eyes of Laura Mars:* A Binocular Critique," *Screen* 23, no. 3 (September–October 1983):4–19.

32. Raymond Williams, *Television: Technology and Cultural Form* (New York: Schocken Books, 1975).

33. Even more, the equation of femininity with all the forces that supposedly block spectacle and free-play can lead to a violent aggression against the woman, an attempt to remove her from the scene. As Tania Modleski notes in her essay on the horror film in this volume, the horror genre may be postmodernist in every way but its image of woman as a blockage to a full outpouring of energy.

Similarly, other writers have begun to examine what Elaine Showalter refers to as the new genres of masculine cross-dressing—fictional and non-fictional discourses that promote a sexual transformation of men while either fetishizing women or removing them from attention altogether. See Showalter, "Critical Cross-Dressing: Male Feminists and the Woman of the Year," *Raritan* 3, no. 2 (Fall 1983):130–49. Most recently, Alice Jardine has suggested how even the most seemingly avant garde of critical theories—in her example, the work of Deleuze and Guattari with their invocation of subversion as a "becoming-woman"—limits the possibilities for struggle to men, making women nothing more than the spiritual engenderers of male transfiguration. See Jardine, "Woman in Limbo: Deleuze and His Br(others)," *SubStance* 44/45 (1984):46–60.

# 11

# MASS CULTURE AS WOMAN
## *MODERNISM'S OTHER*

## Andreas Huyssen

I.

One of the founding texts of modernism, if there ever was one, is Flaubert's *Madame Bovary*. Emma Bovary, whose temperament was, in the narrator's words, "more sentimental than artistic," loved to read romances.[1] In his detached, ironic style, Flaubert describes Emma's reading matter: "They [the novels] were full of love and lovers, persecuted damsels swooning in deserted pavilions, postillions slaughtered at every turn, horses ridden to death on every page, gloomy forests, romantic intrigue, vows, sobs, embraces and tears, moonlit crossings, nightingales in woodland groves, noblemen brave as lions, gentle as lambs, impossibly virtuous, always well dressed, and who wept like fountains on all occasions."[2] Of course, it is well known that Flaubert himself was caught by the craze for romantic novels during his student days in the Collège at Rouen, and Emma Bovary's readings at the convent have to be read against this backdrop of Flaubert's life history—a point which critics rarely fail to make. However, there is ample reason to wonder if the adolescent Flaubert read these novels in the same way Emma Bovary would have, had she actually lived—or, for that matter, as real women at the time read them.

Perhaps the answer to such a query will have to remain speculative. What is beyond speculation, however, is the fact that Emma Bovary became known, among other things, as the female reader caught between the delusions of the trivial romantic narrative and the realities of French provincial life during the July monarchy, a woman who tried to live the illusions of aristocratic sensual romance and was shipwrecked on the banality of bourgeois everyday life. Flaubert, on the other hand, came to be known as one of the fathers of modernism, one of the paradigmatic master voices of an aesthetic based on the uncompromising repudiation of what Emma Bovary loved to read.

As to Flaubert's famous claim: "Madame Bovary, c'est moi," we can assume that he knew what he was saying, and critics have gone to great lengths to show what Flaubert had in common with Emma Bovary—mostly in order to show how he transcended aesthetically the dilemma on which she foundered in "real life." In such arguments the question of gender usually remains submerged, thereby asserting itself all the more powerfully. Sartre, however, in his monumental *L'Idiot de la Famille*, has analyzed the social and familial conditions of Flaubert's "objective neurosis" underlying his fantasy of himself as woman. Sartre has indeed succeeded in showing how Flaubert fetishized his own imaginary femininity while simultaneously sharing his period's hostility toward real women, participating in a pattern of the imagination and of behavior all too common in the history of modernism.[3]

That such masculine identification with woman, such imaginary femininity in the male writer, is itself historically determined is clear enough. Apart from the subjective conditions of neurosis in Flaubert's case, the phenomenon has a lot to do with the increasingly marginal position of literature and the arts in a society in which masculinity is identified with action, enterprise, and progress—with the realms of business, industry, science, and law. At the same time, it has also become clear that the imaginary femininity of male authors, which often grounds their oppositional stance vis-à-vis bourgeois society, can easily go hand in hand with the exclusion of real women from the literary enterprise and with the misogyny of bourgeois patriarchy itself. Against the paradigmatic "Madame Bovary, c'est moi," we therefore have to insist that there is a difference. Christa Wolf, in her critical and fictional reflections on the question "who was Cassandra before anyone wrote about her?" put it this way:

> We have admired this remark [Flaubert's 'Madame Bovary, c'est moi'] for more than a hundred years. We also admire the tears Flaubert shed when he had to let Madame Bovary die, and the crystal-clear calculation of his wonderful novel, which he was able to write despite his tears; and we should not and will not stop admiring him. But Flaubert was *not* Madame Bovary; we cannot completely ignore that fact in the end, despite all our good will and what we know of the secret relationship between an author and a figure created by art.[4]

One aspect of the difference that is important to my argument about the gender inscriptions in the mass culture debate is that woman (Madame Bovary) is positioned as reader of inferior literature—subjective, emotional and passive—while man (Flaubert) emerges as writer of genuine, authentic literature—objective, ironic, and in control of his aesthetic means. Of course, such positioning of woman as avid consumer of pulp, which I take to be paradigmatic, also affects the woman writer who has the same kind of ambition as the "great (male) modernist." Wolf cites Ingeborg Bachmann's tortured novel trilogy *Todesarten* (Ways of Dying) as a counter-example to Flaubert: "Ingeborg Bachmann *is* that nameless woman in *Malina*, she *is* the woman Franza in the novel fragment *The Franza Case* who simply cannot get a grip on her life, cannot give it a form; who simply cannot manage to make her experience into a presentable story, cannot produce it out of herself as an artistic product."[5]

In one of her own novels, *The Quest for Christa T*, Wolf herself foregrounded the "difficulty of saying I" for the woman who writes. The problematic nature of saying "I" in the literary text—more often than not held to be a lapse into subjectivity or kitsch—is of course one of the central difficulties of the post-romantic, modernist writer. Having first created the determining conditions for a certain historically specific type of subjectivity (the Cartesian cogito and the epistemological subject in Kant, as well as the bourgeois entrepreneur and the modern scientist), modernity itself has increasingly hollowed out such subjectivity and rendered its articulation highly problematic. Most modern artists, male or female, know that. But we only need to think of the striking contrast between Flaubert's confident personal confession, "Madame Bovary, c'est moi," and the famed "impassibilité" of the novel's style to know that there is a difference. Given the fundamentally differing social and psychological constitution and validation of male and female subjectivity in modern bourgeois society, the difficulty of saying "I" must of necessity be different for a woman writer, who may not find "impassibilité" and the concomitant reification of self in the aesthetic product quite as attractive and compelling an ideal as the male writer. The male, after all, can easily deny his own subjectivity for the benefit of a higher aesthetic goal, as long as he can take it for granted on an experiential level in everyday life. Thus Christa Wolf concludes, with some hesitation and yet forcefully enough: "Aesthetics, I say, like philosophy and science, is invented not so much to enable us to get closer to reality as for the purpose of warding it off, of protecting against it."[6] Warding something off, protecting against something out there seems indeed to be a basic gesture of the modernist aesthetic, from Flaubert to Roland Barthes and other poststructuralists. What Christa Wolf calls reality would certainly have to include Emma Bovary's romances (the books *and* the love affairs), for the repudiation of *Trivialliteratur* has always been one of the constitutive features of a modernist aesthetic intent on distancing itself and its products from the trivialities and banalities of everyday life.

Contrary to the claims of champions of the autonomy of art, contrary also to the ideologists of textuality, the realities of modern life and the ominous expansion of mass culture throughout the social realm are always already inscribed into the articulation of aesthetic modernism. Mass culture has always been the hidden subtext of the modernist project.

## II.

What especially interests me here is the notion which gained ground during the nineteenth century that mass culture is somehow associated with woman while real, authentic culture remains the prerogative of men. The tradition of women's exclusion from the realm of "high art" does not of course originate in the nineteenth century, but it does take on new connotations in the age of the industrial revolution and cultural modernization. Stuart Hall is perfectly right to point out that the hidden subject of the mass culture debate is precisely "the masses"—their political and cultural aspirations, their struggles, and their pacification via cultural institutions.[7] But when the nineteenth and early twentieth centuries conjured up the threat of the masses "rattling at the gate," to quote Hall, and lamented the concomitant decline of culture and civilization (which mass culture was invariably accused of causing), there was yet another hidden subject. In the age of nascent socialism *and* the first major women's movement in Europe, the masses knocking at the gate were also women, knocking at the gate of a male dominated culture. It is indeed striking to observe how the political, psychological, and aesthetic discourse around the turn of the century consistently and obsessively genders mass culture and the masses as feminine, while high culture, whether traditional or modern, clearly remains the privileged realm of male activities.

To be sure, a number of critics have since abandoned the notion of *mass* culture in order to "exclude from the outset the interpretation agreeable to its advocates: that it is a matter of something like a culture that arises spontaneously from the masses themselves, the contemporary form of popular art."[8] Thus Adorno and Horkheimer coined the term culture industry; Enzensberger gave it another twist by calling it the consciousness industry; in the U.S., Herbert Schiller speaks of mind managers, and Michael Real uses the term mass-mediated culture. The critical intention behind these changes in terminology is clear: they all mean to suggest that modern mass culture is administered and imposed from above and that the threat it represents resides not in the masses but in those who run the industry. While such an interpretation may serve as a welcome corrective to the naive notion that mass culture is identical with traditional forms of popular art, rising spontaneously from the masses, it nevertheless erases a whole web of gender connotations which, as I shall show, the older terminology "mass culture" carried with it—i.e., connotations of mass culture as essentially feminine, which were clearly also "imposed from above," in a gender-specific sense, and which remain central to understanding the historical and rhetorical determinations of the modernism/mass culture dichotomy.

It might be argued that the terminological shift away from the term "mass culture" actually reflects changes in critical thinking about "the masses." Indeed, mass culture theories since the 1920s—for instance, those of the Frankfurt School—have by and large abandoned the explicit gendering of mass culture as feminine. Instead they emphasize features of mass culture such as streamlining, technological reproduction, administration, and Sachlichkeit—features which popular psychology would ascribe to the realm of masculinity rather than femininity. Yet the older mode of thinking surfaces time and again in the language, if not in the argument. Thus Adorno and Horkheimer argue that mass culture "cannot renounce the threat of castration,"[9] and they feminize it explicitly, as the evil queen of the fairy tale, when they claim that "mass culture, in her mirror, is always the most beautiful in the land."[10] Similarly, Siegfried Kracauer, in his seminal essay on the mass ornament, begins his discussion by bringing the legs of the Tiller Girls into the reader's view, even though the argument then focuses primarily on aspects of rationalization and standardization.[11] Examples such as these show that the inscription of the feminine on the notion of mass culture, which seems to have its primary place in the late nineteenth century, did not relinquish its hold, even among those critics who did much to overcome the nineteenth century mystification of mass culture as woman.

The recovery of such gender stereotypes in the theorizing of mass culture may also have some bearing on the current debate about the alleged femininity of modernist/avant-gardist writing. Thus the observation that, in some basic register, the traditional mass culture/modernism dichotomy has been gendered since the mid–nineteenth century as female/male would seem to make recent attempts by French critics to claim the space of modernist and avant-garde writing as predominantly feminine highly questionable. Of course this approach, which is perhaps best embodied in Kristeva's work, focuses on the Mallarmé-Lautréamont-Joyce axis of modernism rather than, say, on the Flaubert-Thomas Mann-Eliot axis which I emphasize in my argument here. Nevertheless, its claims remain problematic even there. Apart from the fact that such a view would threaten to render invisible a whole tradition of women's writing, its main theoretical assumption—"that 'the feminine' is what cannot be inscribed in common

language"[12]—remains problematically close to that whole history of
an imaginary male femininity which has become prominent in literature since the late eighteenth century.[13] This view becomes possible
only if Madame Bovary's "natural" association with pulp—i.e., the
discourse that persistently associated women with mass culture—is
simply ignored, and if a paragon of male misogyny like Nietzsche is
said to be speaking from the position of woman. Teresa de Lauretis
has recently criticized this Derridean appropriation of the feminine
by arguing that the position of woman from which Nietzsche and
Derrida speak is vacant in the first place, and cannot be claimed by
women.[14] Indeed, more than a hundred years after Flaubert and
Nietzsche, we are facing yet another version of an imaginary male
femininity, and it is no coincidence that the advocates of such theories
(who also include major women theoreticians) take great pains to distance themselves from any form of political feminism. Even though
the French readings of modernism's "feminine" side have opened up
fascinating questions about gender and sexuality which can be turned
critically against more dominant accounts of modernism, it seems
fairly obvious that the wholesale theorization of modernist writing as
feminine simply ignores the powerful masculinist and misogynist current within the trajectory of modernism, a current which time and
again openly states its contempt for women and for the masses and
which had Nietzsche as its most eloquent and influential representative.

Here, then, some remarks about the history of the perception of
mass culture as feminine. Time and again documents from the late
nineteenth century ascribe pejorative feminine characteristics to mass
culture—and by mass culture here I mean serialized feuilleton novels,
popular and family magazines, the stuff of lending libraries, fictional
bestsellers, and the like—not, however, working-class culture or
residual forms of older popular or folk cultures. A few examples will
have to suffice. In the preface to their novel *Germinie Lacerteux* (1865),
which is usually regarded as the first naturalist manifesto, the Goncourt brothers attack what they call the false novel. They describe it
as those "spicy little works, memoirs of street-walkers, bedroom
confessions, erotic smuttiness, scandals that hitch up their skirts in
pictures in bookshop windows." The true novel (*le roman vrai*) by contrast is called "severe and pure." It is said to be characterized by its
scientificity, and rather than sentiment it offers what the authors call
"a clinical picture of love" (*une clinique de l'amour*).[15] Twenty years later,
in the editorial of the first issue of Michael Georg Conrad's journal
*Die Gesellschaft* (1885), which marks the beginning of "die Moderne"
in Germany, the editor states his intention to emancipate literature
and criticism from the "tyranny of well-bred debutantes and old wives

of both sexes," and from the empty and pompous rhetoric of "old wives criticism." And he goes on to polemicize against the then popular literary family magazines: "The literary and artistic kitchen personnel has achieved absolute mastery in the art of economizing and imitating the famous potato banquet. . . . It consists of twelve courses each of which offers the potato in a different guise."[16] Once the kitchen has been described metaphorically as the site of mass cultural production, we are not surprised to hear Conrad call for the reestablishment of an "*arg gefährdete Mannhaftigkeit*" (seriously threatened manliness) and for the restoration of bravery and courage (*Tapferkeit*) in thought, poetry, and criticism.

It is easy to see how such statements rely on the traditional notion that women's aesthetic and artistic abilities are inferior to those of men. Women as providers of inspiration for the artist, yes, but otherwise *Berufsverbot* for the muses,[17] unless of course they content themselves with the lower genres (painting flowers and animals) and the decorative arts. At any rate, the gendering of an inferior mass culture as feminine goes hand in hand with the emergence of a male mystique in modernism (especially in painting), which has been documented thoroughly by feminist scholarship.[18] What is interesting in the second half of the nineteenth century, however, is a certain chain effect of signification: from the obsessively argued inferiority of woman as artist (classically argued by Karl Scheffler in *Die Frau und die Kunst*, 1908) to the association of woman with mass culture (witness Hawthorne's "the damned mob of scribbling women") to the identification of woman with the masses as political threat.

This line of argument invariably leads back to Nietzsche. Significantly, Nietzsche's ascription of feminine characteristics to the masses is always tied to his aesthetic vision of the artist-philosopher-hero, the suffering loner who stands in irreconcilable opposition to modern democracy and its inauthentic culture. Fairly typical examples of this nexus can be found in Nietzsche's polemic against Wagner, who becomes for him the paradigm of the decline of genuine culture in the dawning age of the masses and the feminization of culture: "The danger for artists, for geniuses . . . is woman: adoring women confront them with corruption. Hardly any of them have character enough not to be corrupted—or 'redeemed'—when they find themselves treated like gods: soon they condescend to the level of the women."[19] Wagner, it is implied, has succumbed to the adoring women by transforming music into mere spectacle, theater, delusion:

> I have explained where Wagner belongs—*not* in the history of music. What does he signify nevertheless in that history? *The emergence of the actor in music.* . . . One can grasp it with one's very hands: great success, success with the masses no longer sides with those who are authentic—

one has to be an actor to achieve that. Victor Hugo and Richard Wagner—they signify the same thing: in declining cultures, wherever the
decision comes to rest with the masses, authenticity becomes superflu-
ous, disadvantageous, a liability. Only the actor still arouses *great* enthusiasm.[20]

And then Wagner, the theater, the mass, woman—all become a web
of signification outside of, and in opposition to, true art: "No one
brings along the finest senses of his art to the theater, least of all the
artist who works for the theater—solitude is lacking; whatever is perfect suffers no witnesses. In the theater one becomes people, herd,
female, pharisee, voting cattle, patron, idiot—*Wagnerian*."[21] What
Nietzsche articulates here is of course not an attack on the drama or
the tragedy, which to him remain some of the highest manifestations
of culture. When Nietzsche calls theater a "revolt of the masses,"[22] he
anticipates what the situationists would later elaborate as the society
of the spectacle, and what Baudrillard chastises as the simulacrum.
At the same time, it is no coincidence that the philosopher blames
theatricality for the decline of culture. After all, the theater in bourgeois society was one of the few spaces which allowed women a prime
place in the arts, precisely because acting was seen as imitative
and reproductive, rather than original and productive. Thus, in
Nietzsche's attack on what he perceives as Wagner's feminization of
music, his "infinite melody"—"one walks into the sea, gradually loses
one's secure footing, and finally surrenders oneself to the elements
without reservation"[23]—an extremely perceptive critique of the
mechanisms of bourgeois culture goes hand in hand with an exhibition
of that culture's sexist biases and prejudices.


## III.

The fact that the identification of woman with mass has major political implications is easily recognized. Thus Mallarmé's quip about
*"reportage universel"* (i.e., mass culture), with its not so subtle allusion
to *"suffrage universel,"* is more than just a clever pun. The problem
goes far beyond questions of art and literature. In the late nineteenth
century, a specific traditional male image of woman served as a re-
ceptacle for all kinds of projections, displaced fears, and anxieties
(both personal and political), which were brought about by modernization and the new social conflicts, as well as by specific historical
events such as the 1848 revolution, the 1870 Commune, and the rise
of reactionary mass movements which, as in Austria, threatened the
liberal order.[24] An examination of the magazines and the newspapers
of the period will show that the proletarian and petit-bourgeois masses

were persistently described in terms of a feminine threat. Images of
the raging mob as hysterical, of the engulfing floods of revolt and
revolution, of the swamp of big city life, of the spreading ooze of
massification, of the figure of the red whore at the barricades—all of
these pervade the writing of the mainstream media, as well as that of
right-wing ideologues of the late nineteenth and early twentieth centuries whose social psychology Klaus Theweleit has perceptively analyzed in his study *Male Phantasies*.[25] The fear of the masses in this age
of declining liberalism is always also a fear of woman, a fear of nature
out of control, a fear of the unconscious, of sexuality, of the loss of
identity and stable ego boundaries in the mass.

This kind of thinking is exemplified by Gustave Le Bon's enormously influential *The Crowd* (*La Psychologie des foules*, 1895), which as
Freud observed in his own *Mass Psychology and Ego Analysis* (1921)
merely summarizes arguments pervasive in Europe at the time. In Le
Bon's study, the male fear of woman and the bourgeois fear of the
masses become indistinguishable: "Crowds are everywhere distinguished by feminine characteristics."[26] And: "The simplicity and exaggeration of the sentiments of crowds have for a result that a throng
knows neither doubt nor uncertainty. Like women, it goes at once to
extremes. . . . A commencement of antipathy or disapprobation,
which in the case of an isolated individual would not gain strength,
becomes at once furious hatred in the case of an individual in a
crowd."[27] And then he summarizes his fears with a reference to that
icon which perhaps more than any other in the nineteenth century—
more even than the Judiths and Salomés so often portrayed on sym-
bolist canvases—stood for the feminine threat to civilization: "Crowds
are somewhat like the sphinx of ancient fable: it is necessary to arrive
at a solution of the problems offered by their psychology or to resign
ourselves to being devoured by them."[28] Male fears of an engulfing
femininity are here projected onto the metropolitan masses, who did
indeed represent a threat to the rational bourgeois order. The haunt-
ing specter of a loss of power combines with the fear of losing one's
fortified and stable ego boundaries, which represent the *sine qua non*
of male psychology in that bourgeois order. We may want to relate
Le Bon's social psychology of the masses back to modernism's own
fears of being sphinxed. Thus the nightmare of being devoured by
mass culture through co-optation, commodification, and the "wrong"
kind of success is the constant fear of the modernist artist, who tries
to stake out his territory by fortifying the boundaries between genuine
art and inauthentic mass culture. Again, the problem is not the desire
to differentiate between forms of high art and depraved forms of
mass culture and its co-optations. The problem is rather the persistent
gendering as feminine of that which is devalued.

## IV.

Seen in relation to this kind of paranoid view of mass culture and the masses, the modernist aesthetic itself—at least in one of its basic registers—begins to look more and more like a reaction formation, rather than like the heroic feat steeled in the fires of the modern experience. At the risk of oversimplifying, I would suggest that one can identify something like a core of the modernist aesthetic which has held sway over many decades, which manifests itself (with variations due to respective media) in literature, music, architecture, and the visual arts, and which has had an enormous impact on the history of criticism and cultural ideology. If we were to construct an ideal type notion of what the modernist art work has become as a result of successive canonizations—and I will exclude here the poststructuralist archeology of modernism which has shifted the grounds of the debate—it would probably look somewhat like this:

—The work is autonomous and totally separate from the realms of mass culture and everyday life.
—It is self-referential, self-conscious, frequently ironic, ambiguous, and rigorously experimental.
—It is the expression of a purely individual consciousness rather than of a Zeitgeist or a collective state of mind.
—Its experimental nature makes it analogous to science, and like science it produces and carries knowledge.
—Modernist literature, since Flaubert, is a persistent exploration of and encounter with language. Modernist painting, since Manet, is an equally persistent elaboration of the medium itself: the flatness of the canvas, the structuring of notation, paint and brushwork, the problem of the frame.
—The major premise of the modernist art work is the rejection of all classical systems of representation, the effacement of "content," the erasure of subjectivity and authorial voice, the repudiation of likeness and verisimilitude, and the exorcism of any demand for realism of whatever kind.
—Only by fortifying its boundaries, by maintaining its purity and autonomy, and by avoiding any contamination with mass culture and with the signifying systems of everyday life can the art work maintain its adversary stance: adversary to the bourgeois culture of everyday life as well as adversary to mass culture and entertainment which are seen as the primary forms of bourgeois cultural articulation.

One of the first examples of this aesthetic would be Flaubert's famous "impassibilité" and his desire to write "a book about nothing, a book without external attachments which would hold together by itself through the internal force of its style." Flaubert can be said to ground modernism in literature, both for its champions (from Nietzsche to

Roland Barthes) and for its detractors (such as Georg Lukács). Other historical forms of this modernist aesthetic would be the clinical, dissecting gaze of the naturalist;[29] the doctrine of art for art's sake in its various classicist or romantic guises since the late nineteenth century; the insistence on the art-life dichotomy so frequently found at the turn of the century, with its inscription of art on the side of death and masculinity and its evaluation of life as inferior and feminine; and finally, the absolutist claims of abstraction, from Kandinsky to the New York School.

But it was only in the 1940s and 1950s that the modernism gospel and the concomitant condemnation of kitsch became something like the equivalent of the one-party state in the realm of aesthetics. And it is still an open question to what extent current poststructuralist notions of language and writing and of sexuality and the unconscious are a postmodern departure toward entirely new cultural horizons; or whether, despite their powerful critique of older notions of modernism, they do not rather represent another mutation of modernism itself.

My point here is not to reduce the complex history of modernism to an abstraction. Obviously, the various layers and components of the ideal modernist work would have to be read in and through specific works in specific historical and cultural constellations. The notion of autonomy, for instance, has quite different historical determinations for Kant, who first articulated it in his *Kritik der Urteilskraft*, than for Flaubert in the 1850s, for Adorno during World War II, or again for Frank Stella today. My point is rather that the champions of modernism themselves were the ones who made that complex history into a schematic paradigm, the main purpose of which often seemed to be the justification of current aesthetic practice, rather than the richest possible reading of the past in relation to the present.

My point is also not to say that there is only one, male, sexual politics to modernism, against which women would have to find their own voices, their own language, their own feminine aesthetic. What I am saying is that the powerful masculinist mystique which is explicit in modernists such as Marinetti, Jünger, Benn, Wyndham Lewis, Céline, et al. (not to speak of Marx, Nietzsche, and Freud), and implicit in many others, has to be somehow related to the persistent gendering of mass culture as feminine and inferior—even if, as a result, the heroism of the moderns won't look quite as heroic any more. The autonomy of the modernist art work, after all, is always the result of a resistance, an abstention, and a suppression—resistance to the seductive lure of mass culture, abstention from the pleasure of trying to please a larger audience, suppression of everything that might be threatening to the rigorous demands of being modern and at the edge

of time. There seem to be fairly obvious homologies between this
modernist insistence on purity and autonomy in art, Freud's privileging of the ego over the id and his insistence on stable, if flexible,
ego boundaries, and Marx's privileging of production over consumption. The lure of mass culture, after all, has traditionally been described as the threat of losing oneself in dreams and delusions and
of merely consuming rather than producing.[30] Thus, despite its un-
deniable adversary stance toward bourgeois society, the modernist
aesthetic and its rigorous work ethic as described here seem in some
fundamental way to be located also on the side of that society's reality
principle, rather than on that of the pleasure principle. It is to this
fact that we owe some of the greatest works of modernism, but the
greatness of these works cannot be separated from the often one-
dimensional gender inscriptions inherent in their very constitution as
autonomous masterworks of modernity.

V.

The deeper problem at stake here pertains to the relationship of
modernism to the matrix of modernization which gave birth to it and
nurtured it through its various stages. In less suggestive terms, the
question is why, despite the obvious heterogeneity of the modernist
project, a certain universalizing account of the modern has been able
to hold sway for so long in literary and art criticism, and why even
today it is far from having been decisively displaced from its position
of hegemony in cultural institutions. What has to be put in question
is the presumably adversary relationship of the modernist aesthetic
to the myth and ideology of modernization and progress, which it
ostensibly rejects in its fixation upon the eternal and timeless power
of the poetic word. From the vantage point of our postmodern age,
which has begun in a variety of discourses to question seriously the
belief in unhampered progress and in the blessings of modernity, it
becomes clear how modernism, even in its most adversary, anti-bour-
geois manifestations, is deeply implicated in the processes and pres-
sures of the same mundane modernization it so ostensibly repudiates.
It is especially in light of the ecological and environmental critique of
industrial and postindustrial capitalism, and of the different yet concomitant feminist critique of bourgeois patriarchy, that the subter-
ranean collusion of modernism with the myth of modernization
becomes visible.

I want to show this briefly for two of the most influential and by
now classical accounts of the historical trajectory of modernism—the
accounts of Clement Greenberg in painting and of Theodor W.
Adorno in music and literature. For both critics, mass culture remains

the other of modernism, the specter that haunts it, the threat against which high art has to shore up its terrain. And even though mass culture is no longer imagined as primarily feminine, both critics remain under the sway of the old paradigm in their conceptualization of modernism.

Indeed, both Greenberg and Adorno are often taken to be the last ditch defenders of the purity of the modernist aesthetic, and they have become known since the late 1930s as uncompromising enemies of modern mass culture. (Mass culture had by then of course become an effective tool of totalitarian domination in a number of countries, which all banished modernism as degenerate or decadent.) While there are major differences between the two men, both in temperament and in the scope of their analyses, they both share a notion of the inevitability of the evolution of modern art. To put it bluntly, they believe in progress—if not in society, then certainly in art. The metaphors of linear evolution and of a teleology of art are conspicuous in their work. I quote Greenberg: "It has been in search of the absolute that the avant-garde has arrived at 'abstract' or 'nonobjective' art—and poetry, too."[31] It is well known how Greenberg constructs the story of modernist painting as a single-minded trajectory, from the first French modernist avant-garde of the 1860s to the New York School of abstract expressionism—his moment of truth.

Similarly, Adorno sees a historical logic at work in the move from late romantic music to Wagner and ultimately to Schönberg and the second school of Vienna, which represent *his* moment of truth. To be sure, both critics acknowledge retarding elements in these trajectories—Stravinsky in Adorno's account, surrealism in Greenberg's—but the logic of history, or rather the logic of aesthetic evolution, prevails, giving a certain rigidity to Greenberg's and Adorno's theorizing. Obstacles and detours, it seems, only highlight the dramatic and inevitable path of modernism toward its telos, whether this telos is described as triumph as in Greenberg, or as pure negativity as in Adorno. In the work of both critics, the theory of modernism appears as a theory of modernization displaced to the aesthetic realm; this is precisely its historical strength, and what makes it different from the mere academic formalism of which it is so often accused. Adorno and Greenberg further share a notion of decline that they see as following on the climax of development in high modernism. Adorno wrote about "Das Altern der Neuen Musik," and Greenberg unleashed his wrath on the reappearance of representation in painting since the advent of Pop Art.

At the same time, both Adorno and Greenberg were quite aware of the costs of modernization, and they both understood that it was the ever-increasing pace of commodification and colonization of cultural space which actually propelled modernism forward—or rather, pushed it toward the outer margins of the cultural terrain. Adorno especially never lost sight of the fact that, ever since their simultaneous emergence in the mid-nineteenth century, modernism and mass culture have been engaged in a compulsive *pas de deux*. To him, autonomy was a relational phenomenon, not a mechanism to justify formalist amnesia. His analysis of the transition in music from Wagner to Schönberg makes it clear that Adorno never saw modernism as anything other than a reaction formation to mass culture and commodification, a reaction formation which operated on the level of form and artistic material. The same awareness that mass culture, on some basic level, determined the shape and course of modernism is pervasive in Clement Greenberg's essays of the late 1930s. To a large extent, it is by the distance we have traveled from this "great divide" between mass culture and modernism that we can measure our own cultural postmodernity. And yet, I still know of no better aphorism about the imaginary adversaries, modernism and mass culture, than that which Adorno articulated in a letter to Walter Benjamin: "Both [modernist art and mass culture] bear the scars of capitalism, both contain elements of change. Both are torn halves of freedom to which, however, they do not add up."[32]

But the discussion cannot end here. The postmodern crisis of high modernism and its classical accounts has to be seen as a crisis both of capitalist modernization itself and of the deeply patriarchal structures that support it. The traditional dichotomy, in which mass culture appears as monolithic, engulfing, totalitarian, and on the side of regression and the feminine ("Totalitarianism appeals to the desire to return to the womb," said T. S. Eliot[33]) and modernism appears as progressive, dynamic, and indicative of male superiority in culture, has been challenged empirically and theoretically in a variety of ways in the past twenty years or so. New versions of the history of modern culture, the nature of language, and artistic autonomy have been elaborated, and new theoretical questions have been brought to bear on mass culture and modernism; most of us would probably share the sense that the ideology of modernism, as I have sketched it here, is a thing of the past, even if it still occupies major bastions in cultural institutions such as the museum or the academy. The attacks on high modernism, waged in the name of the postmodern since the late 1950s, have left their mark on our culture, and we are still trying to figure out the gains and the losses which this shift has brought about.

VI.

What then of the relationship of postmodernism to mass culture, and what of its gender inscriptions? What of postmodernism's relationship to the myth of modernization? After all, if the masculinist inscriptions in the modernist aesthetic are somehow subliminally linked to the history of modernization, with its insistence on instrumental rationality, teleological progress, fortified ego boundaries, discipline, and self-control; if, furthermore, both modernism and modernization are ever more emphatically subjected to critique in the name of the postmodern—then we must ask to what extent postmodernism offers possibilities for genuine cultural change, or to what extent the postmodern raiders of a lost past produce only simulacra, a fast-image culture that makes the latest thrust of modernization more palatable by covering up its economic and social dislocations. I think that postmodernism does both, but I will focus here only on some of the signs of promising cultural change.

A few somewhat tentative reflections will have to suffice, as the amorphous and politically volatile nature of postmodernism makes the phenomenon itself remarkably elusive, and the definition of its boundaries exceedingly difficult, if not *per se* impossible. Furthermore, one critic's postmodernism is another critic's modernism (or variant thereof), while certain vigorously new forms of contemporary culture (such as the emergence into a broader public's view of distinct minority cultures and of a wide variety of feminist work in literature and the arts) have so far rarely been discussed *as* postmodern, even though these phenomena have manifestly affected both the culture at large and the ways in which we approach the politics of the aesthetic today. In some sense it is the very existence of these phenomena which challenges the traditional belief in the necessary advances of modernism and the avant-garde. If postmodernism is to be more than just another revolt of the modern against itself, then it would certainly have to be defined in terms of this challenge to the constitutive forward thrust of avant-gardism.

I do not intend here to add yet another definition of what the postmodern *really* is, but it seems clear to me that both mass culture and women's (feminist) art are emphatically implicated in any attempt to map the specificity of contemporary culture and thus to gauge this culture's distance from high modernism. Whether one uses the term "postmodernism" or not, there cannot be any question about the fact that the position of women in contemporary culture and society, and their effect on that culture, is fundamentally different from what it used to be in the period of high modernism and the historical avant-garde. It also seems clear that the uses high art makes of certain forms of mass culture (and vice versa) have increasingly blurred the boundaries between the two; where modernism's great wall once kept the barbarians out and safeguarded the culture within, there is now only slippery ground which may prove fertile for some and treacherous for others.

At stake in this debate about the postmodern is the great divide between modern art and mass culture, which the art movements of the 1960s intentionally began to dismantle in their practical critique of the high modernist canon, and which the cultural neo-conservatives are trying to re-erect today.[34] One of the few widely agreed upon features of postmodernism is its attempt to negotiate forms of high art with certain forms and genres of mass culture and the culture of everyday life.[35] I suspect that it is probably no coincidence that such merger attempts occurred more or less simultaneously with the emergence of feminism and women as major forces in the arts, and with the concomitant reevaluation of formerly devalued forms and genres of cultural expression (e.g., the decorative arts, autobiographic texts, letters, etc.). However, the original impetus to merge high art and popular culture—for example, in Pop Art in the early 1960s— did not yet have anything to do with the later feminist critique of modernism. It was, rather, indebted to the historical avant-garde— art movements such as Dada, constructivism, and surrealism—which had aimed, unsuccessfully, at freeing art from its aestheticist ghetto and reintegrating art and life.[36] Indeed, the early American post-modernists' attempts to open up the realm of high art to the imagery of everyday life and American mass culture are in some ways reminiscent of the historical avant-garde's attempt to work in the interstices of high art and mass culture. In retrospect, it thus seems quite significant that major artists of the 1920s used precisely the then widespread "Americanism" (associated with jazz, sports, cars, technology, movies, and photography) in order to overcome bourgeois aestheticism and its separateness from "life." Brecht is the paradigmatic example here, and he was in turn strongly influenced by the postrevolutionary Russian avant-garde and its daydream of creating a revolutionary avant-garde culture for the masses. It seems that the European Americanism of the 1920s then returned to America in the 1960s, fueling the fight of the early postmodernists against the high-culture doctrines of Anglo-American modernism. The difference is that the historical avant-garde—even where it rejected Leninist vanguard politics as oppressive to the artist—always negotiated its political *Selbstverständnis* in relation to the revolutionary claims for a new society which would be the *sine qua non* of the new art. Between 1916—the "outbreak" of Dada in Zurich—and 1933/34—the liquidation of the historical avant-garde by German fascism and Stalinism—many major artists took the claim inherent in the avant-garde's name very seriously: namely, to lead the whole of society toward new horizons of culture, and to create an avant-garde art for the masses. This ethos of a symbiosis between revolutionary art and revolutionary politics certainly vanished after World War II, not just because of Mc-

Carthyism, but even more because of what Stalin's henchmen had done to the left aesthetic avant-garde of the 1920s. Yet the attempt by the American postmodernists of the 1960s to renegotiate the relationship between high art and mass culture gained its own political momentum in the context of the emerging new social movements of those years—among which feminism has perhaps had the most lasting effects on our culture, as it cuts across class, race, and gender.

In relation to gender and sexuality, though, the historical avant-garde was by and large as patriarchal, misogynist, and masculinist as the major trends of modernism. One needs only to look at the metaphors in Marinetti's "Futurist Manifesto," or to read Marie Luise Fleisser's trenchant description of her relationship to Bert Brecht in a prose text entitled "Avant-garde"—in which the gullible, literarily ambitious young woman from the Bavarian province becomes a guinea pig in the machinations of the notorious metropolitan author. Or, again, one may think of how the Russian avant-garde fetishized production, machines, and science, and of how the writings and paintings of the French surrealists treated women primarily as objects of male phantasy and desire.

There is not much evidence that things were very different with the American postmodernists of the late 1950s and early 1960s. However, the avant-garde's attack on the autonomy aesthetic, its politically motivated critique of the highness of high art, and its urge to validate other, formerly neglected or ostracized forms of cultural expression created an aesthetic climate in which the political aesthetic of feminism could thrive and develop its critique of patriarchal gazing and penmanship. The aesthetic transgressions of the happenings, actions, and performances of the 1960s were clearly inspired by Dada, Informel, and action painting, and with few exceptions—the work of Valie Export, Charlotte Moorman and Carolee Schneemann—these forms did not transport feminist sensibilities or experiences. But it seems historically significant that women artists increasingly used these forms in order to give voice to their experiences.[37] The road from the avant-garde's experiments to contemporary women's art seems to have been shorter, less tortuous, and ultimately more productive than the less frequently traveled road from high modernism. Looking at the contemporary art scene, one may well want to ask the hypothetical question whether performance and "body art" would have remained so dominant during the 1970s had it not been for the vitality of feminism in the arts and the ways in which women artists articulated experiences of the body and of performance in gender-specific terms. I only mention the work of Yvonne Rainer and Laurie Anderson. Similarly, in literature the reemergence of the concern with perception and identification, with sensual experience and subjectivity in relation to gender and sexuality would hardly have gained the foreground in aesthetic debates (against even the powerful poststructuralist argument about the death of the subject and the Derridean expropriation of the feminine), had it not been for the social and political presence of a women's movement, and women's insistence that male notions of perception and subjectivity (or the lack thereof) did not really apply to them. Thus the turn toward a "new subjectivity" in the German prose of the 1970s was initiated not just by Peter Schneider's *Lenz* (1973), as is so often claimed, but even more so by Karin Struck's *Klassenliebe* (also 1973) and, in retrospect, by Ingeborg Bachmann's *Malina* (1971).

However one answers the question of the extent to which women's art and literature have affected the course of postmodernism, it seems clear that feminism's radical questioning of patriarchal structures in society and in the various discourses of art, literature, science, and philosophy must be one of the measures by which we gauge the specificity of contemporary culture, as well as its distance from modernism and its mystique of mass culture as feminine. Mass culture and the masses as feminine threat—such notions belong to another age, Jean Baudrillard's recent ascription of femininity to the masses notwithstanding. Of course, Baudrillard gives the old dichotomy a new twist by applauding the femininity of the masses rather than denigrating it; but his move may be no more than yet another Nietzschean simulacrum.[38] After the feminist critique of the multi-layered sexism in television, Hollywood, advertising, rock 'n' roll, etc., the lure of the old rhetoric simply does not work any longer. The claim that the threats (or, for that matter, the benefits) of mass culture are somehow "feminine" has finally lost its persuasive power. If anything, a kind of reverse statement would make more sense: certain forms of mass culture, with their obsession with gendered violence, are more of a threat to women than to men. After all, it has always been men rather than women who have had real control over the productions of mass culture.

In conclusion, then, it seems clear that the gendering of mass culture as feminine and inferior had its primary historical place in the late nineteenth century, even though the underlying dichotomy did not lose its power until quite recently. It also seems evident that the decline of this pattern of thought coincides historically with the decline of modernism itself. But I would submit that it is primarily the visible and public presence of women artists in *high* art, as well as the emergence of new kinds of women performers and producers in mass culture, which make the old gendering device obsolete. The universalizing ascription of femininity to mass culture always depended on the very real exclusion of women from high culture and its institutions. Such exclusions are, hopefully forever, a thing of the past. Thus, the old rhetoric has lost its persuasive power because the realities have changed.

## NOTES

1. Gustave Flaubert, *Madame Bovary*, trans. Merloyd Lawrence (Boston: Houghton Mifflin, 1969), p. 29.

2. Ibid., p. 30.

3. Cf. Gertrud Koch, "Zwitter-Schwestern: Weiblichkeitswahn und Frauenhass—Jean-Paul Sartres Thesen von der androgynen Kunst," in *Sartres Flaubert lesen: Essays zu Der Idiot der Familie*, ed. Traugott König (Rowohlt: Reinbek, 1980), pp. 44–59.

4. Christa Wolf, *Cassandra: A Novel and Four Essays* (New York: Farrar, Straus, Giroux, 1984), p. 300.

5. Ibid., p. 301.

6. Ibid., p. 300.

7. Stuart Hall, paper given at the Conference on Mass Culture at the Center for Twentieth Century Studies, Spring 1984.

8. Theodor W. Adorno, "Culture Industry Reconsidered," *New German Critique* 6 (Fall 1975): 12.

9. Max Horkheimer and Theodor W. Adorno, *Dialectic of Enlightenment* (New York: Continuum, 1982), p. 141.

10. Max Horkheimer and Theodor W. Adorno, "Das Schema der Massenkultur," in Adorno, *Gesammelte Schriften* 3 (Frankfurt am Main: Suhrkamp, 1981), p. 305.

11. Siegfried Kracauer, "The Mass Ornament," *New German Critique* 5 (Spring 1975):67–76.

12. Sandra M. Gilbert and Susan Gubar, "Sexual Linguistics: Gender, Language, Sexuality," *New Literary History* 16, no. 3 (Spring 1985):516.

13. For an excellent study of male images of femininity since the eighteenth century, see Silvia Bovenschen, *Die imaginierte Weiblichkeit* (Frankfurt am Main: Suhrkamp, 1979).

14. Teresa de Lauretis, "The Violence of Rhetoric: Considerations on Representation and Gender," *Semiotica* (Spring 1985), special issue on the Rhetoric of Violence.

15. Edmond and Jules de Goncourt, *Germinie Lacerteux*, trans. Leonard Tancock (Harmondsworth: Penguin, 1984), p. 15.

16. *Die Gesellschaft* 1, no. 1 (January 1885).

17. Cf. Cäcilia Rentmeister, "Berufsverbot für Musen," *Ästhetik und Kommunikation* 25 (September 1976): 92–113.

18. Cf. for instance the essays by Carol Duncan and Norma Broude in *Feminism and Art History*, ed. Norma Broude and Mary D. Garrard (New York: Harper & Row, 1982) or the documentation of relevant quotes by Valerie Jaudon and Joyce Kozloff, " 'Art Hysterical Notions' of Progress and Culture," *Heresies* 1, no. 4 (Winter 1978): 38–42.

19. Friedrich Nietzsche, *The Case of Wagner*, in *The Birth of Tragedy and the Case of Wagner*, trans. Walter Kaufmann (New York: Random House, 1967), p. 161.

20. Ibid., p. 179.

21. Friedrich Nietzsche, *Nietzsche Contra Wagner*, in *The Portable Nietzsche*, ed. and trans. Walter Kaufmann (Harmondsworth and New York: Penguin, 1976), p. 665.

22. Nietzsche, *The Case of Wagner*, p. 183.

23. Nietzsche, *Nietzsche Contra Wagner*, p. 666.

24. For a recent discussion of semantic shifts in the political and sociological discourse of masses, elites, and leaders from the late nineteenth century to fascism, see Helmuth Berking, "Mythos und Politik: Zur historischen Semantik des Massenbegriffs," *Ästhetik und Kommunikation* 56 (November 1984):35–42.

25. An English translation of the two-volume work will soon be published by the University of Minnesota Press.

26. Gustave Le Bon, *The Crowd* (Harmondsworth and New York: Penguin, 1981), p. 39.

27. Ibid., p. 50.

28. Ibid., p. 102.

29. Naturalism is not always included in the history of modernism because of its close relationship to realistic description, but it clearly belongs to this context, as Georg Lukács never ceased to point out.

30. On the relationship of the production/consumption paradigm to the mass culture debate, see Tania Modleski, "Femininity as Mas(s)querade: A Feminist Approach to Mass Culture," forthcoming in *High Theory, Low Culture*, ed. Colin McCabe (Manchester: The University of Manchester Press, 1986).

31. Clement Greenberg, "Avant-Garde and Kitsch," in *Art and Culture: Critical Essays* (Boston: Beacon Press, 1961), p. 5.

32. Letter of March 18, 1936, in Walter Benjamin, *Gesammelte Schriften* 1, no. 3 (Frankfurt am Main: Suhrkamp, 1974), p. 1003.

33. T. S. Eliot, *Notes Towards the Definition of Culture*, published with *The Idea of a Christian Society* as *Christianity and Culture* (New York: Harcourt, Brace, 1968), p. 142.

34. For a discussion of the neo-conservatives' hostility toward postmodernism, see my essay "Mapping the Postmodern," *New German Critique* 33 (Fall 1984): 5–52, especially 28–36.

35. While critics seem to agree on this point in theory, there is a dearth of specific readings of texts or art works in which such a merger has been attempted. Much more concrete analysis has to be done to assess the results of this new constellation. There is no doubt in my mind that there are as many failures as there are successful attempts by artists, and sometimes success and failure reside side by side in the work of one artist.

36. On this distinction between late nineteenth century modernism and the historical avant-garde, see Peter Bürger, *Theory of the Avant-Garde* (Minneapolis: University of Minnesota Press, 1984).

37. Cf. Gislind Nabakowski, Helke Sander, and Peter Gorsen, *Frauen in der Kunst* (Frankfurt am Main: Suhrkamp, 1980), especially the contributions by Valie Export and Gislind Nabakowski in volume 1.

38. I owe this critical reference to Baudrillard to Tania Modleski's essay "Femininity as Mas(s)querade."

# CONTRIBUTORS

RICK ALTMAN is associate professor of film, French, and comparative literature at the University of Iowa. His article on sound in the cinema, "Moving Lips: Cinema as Ventriloquism," appeared in *Yale French Studies* (1980), and his book on the American film musical is being published by Indiana University Press.

JEAN FRANCO is professor of Spanish at Columbia University, and is the author of *An Introduction to Spanish-American Literature* (1969) and *César Vallejo: The Dialectics of Poetry and Silence* (1976). A founding editor of *Tabloid: A Review of Mass Culture and Everyday Life*, she is currently at work on a book entitled *Plotting Women*, a study of women and culture in Mexico.

BERNARD GENDRON, associate professor of philosophy at the University of Wisconsin-Milwaukee, has published *Technology and the Human Condition* (1977) and articles in *National Forum, Philosophy Forum* and *Journal of Philosophy*. He is currently writing a book on rock 'n' roll.

STEPHEN HEATH is fellow and lecturer at Jesus College, Cambridge. His books include *The Nouveau Roman: A Study in the Practice of Writing* (1972), *Vértige du déplacement* (1974), *Questions of Cinema* (1981), and *The Sexual Fix* (1982). He also translated Roland Barthes' *Image-Music-Text* (1977).

ANDREAS HUYSSEN is professor of German at Columbia University, and is the author of *Drama des Sturm und Drang* (1981) and *After the Great Divide*, a book on modernism, mass culture, and postmodernism being published by Indiana University Press. He is also an editor of, and frequent contributor to, *New German Critique*.

PATRICIA MELLENCAMP is associate professor of film in the Art History Department at the University of Wisconsin-Milwaukee. She has edited *Cinema and Language* (1983) with Stephen Heath, and *Re-Vision: Essays in Feminist Film Criticism* (1984) with Mary Ann Doane and Linda Williams.

TANIA MODLESKI is associate professor of film in the English Department at the University of Wisconsin-Milwaukee. She is the author of *Loving with a Vengeance: Mass-Produced Fantasies for Women* (1982), and is at work on a book-length essay on feminist criticism, focusing on the works of Alfred Hitchcock.

MARGARET MORSE teaches at the University of San Francisco and is the author of several articles on mass culture, including "Sport and Television: Replay and Display" in *Regarding Television* (1983) and "Talk, Talk, Talk: The Space of Discourse in Television News, Sportcasts, Talk Shows and Advertising" in *Screen* (1985).

DANA POLAN is associate professor of film in the English Department at the University of Pittsburgh, and is the author of *The Politics of Film and the Avant-Garde* (1984) and *Power and Paranoia: History, Narrative and the American Cinema, 1940–1950* (1986). He has also translated *Kafka* by Gilles Deleuze and Félix Guattari.

KAJA SILVERMAN, associate professor of film and women's studies at Simon Fraser University, British Columbia, is the author of *The Subject of Semiotics* (1983) and of the forthcoming *The Acoustic Mirror: The Female Voice in Cinema.*

GILLIAN SKIRROW teaches film at the University of Strathclyde, Glasgow, Scotland and is the co-author, with Stephen Heath, of "Television, a World in Action," which appeared in *Screen* (1977).

RAYMOND WILLIAMS is fellow of Jesus College and university reader in poetry and drama at Cambridge University. He is the author of many books on literature, drama, and the media, including *Culture and Society* (1958), *The Country and the City* (1973), and *Television: Technology and Cultural Form* (1975).

JUDITH WILLIAMSON teaches cultural studies and history of art and design at Middlesex Polytechnic in London. Also a filmmaker (*A Sign is a Fine Investment*, 1983), she is the author of *Decoding Advertisements* (1978) and a book on gender, representation, and politics, *Consuming Passions.*

### Theories of Contemporary Culture